SUICIDE:
Assessment
and Intervention

SUICIDE:
Assessment
and Intervention

Corrine Loing Hatton, R.N., M.N.
Assistant Clinical Professor
University of California, Los Angeles
Los Angeles, California

Sharon McBride Valente, R.N., M.N.
Instructor
Mount Saint Mary's College, Doheny Campus
Los Angeles, California

Alice Rink, R.N., M.N.
Instructor
Mount Saint Mary's College, Doheny Campus
Los Angeles, California

Foreword by
Edwin S. Shneidman, Ph.D.
Professor of Thanatology
Director, Laboratory for the Study of
Life-Threatening Behavior
University of California, Los Angeles
Los Angeles, California

APPLETON-CENTURY-CROFTS / New York

Library of Congress Cataloging in Publication Data

Main Entry under title:

Suicide.

　　Includes index.
　　1. Suicide.　2. Suicide--Prevention.
I. Hatton, Corrine Loing,]935-
II. Valente, Sharon McBride, 1945-
III. Rink, Alice, 1940-
RC569.S934　　　　616.8'5844　　　　77-2354
ISBN 0-8385-8697-X

Copyright © 1977 by APPLETON-CENTURY-CROFTS
A Publishing Division of Prentice-Hall, Inc.

77 78 79 80 81/10 9 8 7 6 5 4 3 2 1

Prentice-Hall International, Inc., London
Prentice-Hall of Australia, Pty. Ltd., Sydney
Prentice-Hall of India Private Limited, New Delhi
Prentice-Hall of Japan, Inc., Tokyo
Prentice-Hall of Southeast Asia (Pte.) Ltd., Singapore
Whitehall Books Ltd., Wellington, New Zealand

PRINTED IN THE UNITED STATES OF AMERICA

Cover design: Johanna Cooper

Contributors

NANCY H. ALLEN, M.P.H.
Health Education Specialist, Laboratory for the Study of Life-Threatening Behavior, Neuropsychiatric Institute, UCLA, Los Angeles, California

ELSIE R. CHRISTIAN, M.S.W.
Psychiatric Social Worker, Los Angeles, California

BARBARA BELL FOGLIA, R.N., M.N.
Clinical Specialist, Mental Health, Los Angeles, California

JANET S. GREEN
Statistical Researcher, Los Angeles Suicide Prevention Center, Los Angeles, California

SAM M. HEILIG, M.S.W.
Executive Director, Los Angeles Suicide Prevention Center, Los Angeles, California

NAOMI JAMES, Ph.D.
Staff Psychologist, Thalians, Los Angeles, California

DONNA ZIEBARTH JUNGHARDT, R.N., B.S.
Mental Health-Public Health Nurse, San Bernardino County Department of Public Health, San Bernardino, California

ROBERT E. LITMAN, M.D.
Co-Director and Chief Psychiatrist, Los Angeles Suicide Prevention Center; Professor of Psychiatry, UCLA, Los Angeles, California

MICHAEL L. PECK, Ph.D.
Director of Youth Services, Los Angeles Suicide Prevention Center; Diplomate in Clinical Psychology; Associate Clinical Professor of Psychiatry (Psychology), USC School of Medicine, Los Angeles, California

PAUL W. PRETZEL, Th.D.
Private Practice, Arcadia, California

CARL I. WOLD, Ph.D.
Director of Clinical Services, Los Angeles Suicide Prevention Center;
Associate Clinical Professor of Psychiatry (Psychology), USC School of
Medicine, Los Angeles, California

Why This Book?

The seeds for this book were planted about three years ago when the Hatton portion of this troika was the supervisor of graduate student nurse trainees at the Los Angeles Suicide Prevention Center and the Valente and Rink portions were graduate students. It seemed that we had an abundance of books, articles, and references to carry around and read from, but we lacked a definitive book about suicidology, covering prevention and treatment concisely, inclusively, and in a practical manner.

The idea germinated and continued to grow as we began conducting community-based workshops, seminars, and classes on suicide and suicide prevention to students, trainees, and caregivers of all disciplines. We were constantly being asked by these participants for a single source to use as a guide in their learning and practice. They were distressed by trying to glean and integrate this knowledge from such a widespread variety of references.

As each of us continued our individual clinical work and teaching we began to see an urgent need for a book that would combine theory and practice into a meaningful whole with a logical sequence from assessment to intervention. We were impressed with the vast, widely disseminated collection of articles, books, and other publications and materials on all aspects of suicide that had been offered in the past 20 years. Basically, we grew up professionally with Farberow and Shneidman's *Cry for Help* (1961), and one of us had her early professional training about the time those same authors were roaming around the basement at a Veteran's Administration hospital collecting data for their first book, *Clues to Suicide* (1957). However, despite all this background and information, we were not satisfied at that time that we were meeting the learning needs of our students and trainees.

Therefore, we began gathering our ideas and knowledge in this format.

Generally, we hope this book will be beneficial to caregivers (nurses, physicians, social workers, psychologists, teachers, clergy, police, and counselors) everywhere. And we are particularly hopeful that it be useful for teaching students, trainees, and would-be caregivers. It is a book designed for those in training, be they at a community-based treatment center, in a classroom, or in an academic setting.

Acknowledgments

We are greatly indebted to the staff at the Los Angeles Suicide Prevention Center for their knowledge, counsel, direction, and devotion.

To those who have assisted us in reviewing and preparing the manuscript—Mary Brown, Brenda Ingebretson, Barbara Foglia, Sue and Paul Knoll, Carl Wold, Mickey Heilig, and Jane Lavery—we offer our thanks and appreciation. All their help and comments were exceedingly useful.

And lastly and chiefly, to our dearest friends and family, Mario Valente, and Colin, David, and Andrew Hatton, we owe them our utmost thanks for their support, understanding, and patience.

Contents

Foreword

Happily, the day is over when one can register surprise at the appearance of a substantial book on suicidology. The legitimacy of that field seems to be firmly established; the novelty factor has long since worn off, and the word "neologism" to describe suicidology would now be pointless. In a new volume one now looks for quality of writing, range of coverage, depth and applicability of contents— the qualities one looks for in a book in an established field.

What is the most important book to a practicing physician? Gray's *Anatomy*? One can hardly practice medicine from that book, propaeduetic as it is. *Principles of Medicine*? Indispensible, but really not sufficient to conduct an active practice. I would suggest that the most important book would be the *Physicians' Desk Reference.* The point of my citing these references is to say that in *this* present volume, we have a book which aspires to be the Suicidology Desk Reference—an indispensible manual for *practitioners* in suicide prevention.

What is impressive about this volume is its practicality. It is written by practitioners, addressed to caregivers, and presented in an understandable language. All of us have read reviews that commend a volume by saying that it ought to be on everyone's shelf; this book belongs on every suicidologist's *desk*.

It is only fair to place this book in the context of other books in this field. I can think of another book, *The Psychology of Suicide*, that has much to offer, but it does not have the bite of immediacy that is so prominent in this current volume. I would also think of two other recent books, albeit more theoretical and furnishing a heuristic background for a suicidologist—Seymour Perlin's *A Handbook for the Study of Suicide* and my own edited volume, *Suicidology: Contemporary Developments*—but, again, neither is the kind of desk reference that this new work represents. This present volume stands alone in the way that it advertently addresses the day-to-day practical issues of a person working in a suicide prevention setting.

In the main, this book accomplishes what it sets out to do. It is practical, down-to-earth, timely, sensible, and humane. Working suicidologists, professionals, and volunteers should welcome it and keep it on their desks.

UCLA   Edwin S. Shneidman
July 1976

Introduction

This work deals predominantly with two areas of suicide. The first is risk detection, ie, the concern and prediction that someone may be contemplating suicide in the near or distant future. The second concerns the actions that can be taken by caregivers. It is our belief, based on clinical experience, that for most people who are contemplating suicide, the wish to die is counterbalanced by a wish to live. And persons in caregiving situations can often be the force or influence that tips this balance and leads the suicidal person to contemplate a solution other than death. We have found that suicidal persons are usually grateful for another chance at life and a new opportunity to deal with problems that they had previously found too hard to face.

The first chapter gives a brief history and background of suicidology written by Nancy Allen, who was the president of the American Association of Suicidology in 1975–76. This introduction will offer a perspective of the breadth and depth of this new field of inquiry.

The theoretical framework offered in Chapter 2 identifies and explains what a suicidal position can mean to the victim and to the caregiver. Naomi James' ideas on psychologic states experienced by suicidal persons developed while she was coordinating a training program on suicide and suicide prevention. The areas of concern or conflict for the caregiver are usually discussed in training or educational settings but rarely identified in the literature.

The third chapter outlines the process of assessment for suicidal risk detection, identifies the characteristics of low-, moderate-, and high-lethality ratings, and pinpoints the differences that assist a caregiver in making a distinction between an emergency risk rating and a long-term risk rating.

Because of the variety of possible interventions, depending on settings, individuals, facilities, economics, and so on, in Chapter 4 we give an overview of general principles of intervention and then identify in outline form what is to be expected from a variety of services. Once a *thorough* assessment has been made, so that the client has a clear perception of the problem and is in a position to entertain alternatives to suicide, we believe that the client can often identify the interventions that seem appropriate at that time.

All too often the significant others (or as some theoreticians say, survivor-victims) are ignored or forgotten, especially following a completed suicide. In Chapter 5, Barbara Bell Foglia reviews the literature on this topic, while Donna Ziebarth Junghardt discusses her role as a caregiver to the survivors of the tragedy of suicide.

In Chapter 6, there is an attempt to identify the difficulties in interpreting statistics and a discussion of the meaning of statistics in assessment and intervention. Jan Green discusses some of her findings in Los Angeles County over the past five to seven years. Elsie Christian follows this with a study of suicide in the Black population and the differences and impact on statistics, assessment, and intervention. This is a portion of a larger study undertaken by Ms. Christian while she was a graduate student.

Chapter 7 is an attempt to identify and discuss some special need areas in suicide assessment and intervention. Even though very little information is available about children and suicide, we have included a brief statement in reference to this area of concern. It is our hope that this will generate further study and research. One area of special need, as we see it, is adolescent suicide; Michael Peck discusses the reasons that adolescent suicide is of particular concern in today's society. Another area chosen for special emphasis is that concerned with the chronically suicidal person. The sad reality is that little help seems to be available for this group. As Carl Wold and Robert Litman state in their section in Chapter 7, "Although crisis intervention offers some support to the chronically suicidal person, this is not enough to effect change. Research data show that we do not yet have a successful treatment plan which significantly alters personality patterns of the chronically suicidal person." Finally, we have included some suggestions about how to manage an emergency situation when someone has attempted suicide.

The aim of the clinical case studies presented in Chapter 8 is twofold: to present examples that are readily accessible to assessment and intervention, and also to present situations where the issues and answers were not easily discernible for one reason or another. We further believe that a beginner in suicidology learns a great deal from clinical presentations, and it is our wish that this group of examples will identify the multitude of complexities in this work of suicide assessment and intervention.

Paul Pretzel and Sam. M. Heilig make personal statements about suicide prevention in Chapter 9. These statements come at a time in our social history when issues concerning the personal choice of living or dying, the dignity of life, and the humanness of existence are publicly discussed.

SUICIDE:
Assessment
and Intervention

CHAPTER 1
History and Background of Suicidology

Nancy Allen

Looking at the past can help us understand the present. An historical perspective of the ideas and individuals that shaped the beginnings of suicidology can be useful to caregivers not only in their everyday work, but in their approach to plans for the future.

The first act of suicide probably occurred before the beginning of written records. In order to explore the history of suicide with any understanding, one must have some conception of the prevailing taboos and attitudes toward this behavioral phenomenon. Historically, society's attitudes toward suicide and the suicidal act reveal a wide range between a rational one of acceptance, an irrational one of superstition, and a hostile one of punishment. Suicide is now regarded as an act whose empirical and theoretical dimensions can be investigated scientifically.

It might seem reasonable to start our exploration with a definition of the word "suicide," but the word and its definition did not appear until centuries after the first recordings of the act and references to it. Scientific research and theory of a sociologic, psychologic, and statistical nature began to appear in the literature toward the end of the nineteenth century. These writings provided the systematic foundations of twentieth century suicidology and contributed to the development of a philosophy of suicide prevention.

1

HISTORICAL HIGHLIGHTS

The first known document dealing with suicide is an Egyptian record known by several titles—"The Dispute of a Man with His Soul," "The Dialogue of a Misanthrope with His Soul," or "The Suicide." This document has been dated by historians as having been inscribed before the Eleventh Egyptian Dynasty, or some time between 2000 and 1900 years B.C. (Williams, 1962). Although a literary work of high merit, it has perplexed scholars for 75 years and has been interpreted in a variety of ways. Because of the damaged state of the papyrus, the beginning of the text is lacking and nothing is known of the setting of the work. This loss is compounded by several small gaps in the manuscript, by a number of scribal errors, and by the use of rare or unknown words (Williams, 1962). Choron (1972) describes a man tired of life because of a series of misfortunes and contemplating suicide. He wants to convince his soul to accompany him into death. The soul hesitates because it is afraid that in committing suicide, the man will be deprived of a proper funeral and thus forfeit the soul's chances of a blissful afterlife. Some Egyptologists look at this document in a different light, claiming that suicide does not figure in the text at all and that the work is concerned with two different concepts of death: (1) man looking forward to a blessed immortality and (2) his *bai*,* irreligiously insisting on a total denial of immortality (Williams, 1962).

Ellis (1961) describes some early groups like the ancient Gauls and the Germanic tribes as having no fear of suicide. It was the conviction of the tribal warrior that a violent death was the key of Valhalla; thus, being killed in battle or taking one's own life ensured happiness in the next world.

In early Hebrew history suicide refers to an escape from the consequences of political or military defeat (Rosen, 1975). This was exemplified as early as 876 B.C. by Ahitophel, who supported Absalom in his ill-fated revolt against David. "He saddled his ass and went home to his own city and he set his house in order and hanged himself."

Another early historical Hebrew recording of suicide is engraved in the fortress of Masada where, in 73 A.D., 964 Jews chose mass suicide in preference to capture and enslavement by the Romans.

Ancient Greek legends and the writings of Homer, who died be-

---

*The word *soul* was not known when this dialogue was written; *bai* was considered a state that man could reach after death, a manifestation of someone who has become a god.

fore 700 B.C., depict suicide as good and admirable. The earliest suicide mentioned in Greek literature is that of Jocasta, mother of Oedipus, who hanged herself upon discovering that she had been living with her son, the murderer of her husband. Later the Greeks treated suicide as a political offense against the state on the ground that the community had been deprived of a useful member. Several early Greek philosophers opposed suicide: Pythagoras (582–507 B.C.), a mathematician, argued that since humans were the slaves and soldiers of God, they had no right to leave the world without His permission (Choron, 1963).

Socrates (469–399 B.C.) supported Pythagoras' views but felt that in some circumstances it would be permissible and even necessary for a man to end his own life (Plato). Socrates' philosophy was internalized when the Athenian court found him guilty of a variety of state offenses and ordered him to drink the immortalized cup of hemlock. Even though escape was possible, Socrates chose to die as directed by the authorities. Plato (428–347 B.C.) supported the general philosophy against the suicidal act, with the following exceptions: suicide ordered by state and extreme cases of poverty, sorrow, or disgrace.

Aristotle (384–322 B.C.) supported the Pythagorean philosophy of suicide as a cowardly act and an offense against the state. Yet after the death of Alexander, Aristotle was forced to flee Athens when he was accused, like Socrates, of impiety. At Chalcisin in 322 B.C. he committed suicide (Spelios, 1967). There appears to be some disagreement regarding the death of Aristotle—the *Encyclopaedia Britannica* refers to the cause of his death as stomach illness. Some Greeks feel that the deaths of Aristotle and Socrates should be considered homicides because the suicide of each was forced by the state.

The philosophy that man's conscience and not the government should rule his life and death arose as older schools of thought weakened. Attitudes toward suicide among the Greeks and Romans varied widely in the course of time: between condemnation and admiration; between strong disapproval and approval as a perfect way of gaining freedom from suffering. Epicureanism and Stoicism especially had a strong influence on the Greco-Roman world. Both Stoics and Epicureans considered suicide a natural solution to many intolerable life situations. Eventually, suicide became so common in the Roman Empire that the act was consummated with great ease. Suicides induced by grief, loss of honor, desire to save another, sickness, or great pain were exempt from punishment, but suicide committed for no apparent reason was punishable.

A well-known historical example of sacrificial suicide is Antinoüs, a constant companion of the Emperor Hadrian (76–138 A.D.). In 130 A.D. Antinoüs fell into the Nile River and drowned. It was widely believed that he had cast himself into the river as a sacrifice in order to prolong Hadrian's life. The youth was honored as a heroic suicide by his Emperor, and statues of Antinoüs became a common sight. One of the most famous of these statues is located at the Museum of Delphi.

It was not uncommon for Romans accused of crimes against the state to commit suicide and thus maintain their honor, rather than await formal execution. Since the state confiscated the property of all those executed for a crime, the act of suicide provided for the survivors of the deceased.

With the decline of the Roman Empire, attitudes toward suicide changed (Stengel, 1964). Neither the Old nor the New Testament prohibits suicide, nor is it condoned by either. There are six instances of suicide reported in the Hebrew Bible and one in the New Testament. Jewish law, expressed in the Talmud, states that a suicide shall not be honored with a eulogy of public mourning; but suicide is defined loosely so that if there is doubt, the benefit may be given the deceased.

The Oriental religions were significantly more tolerant toward suicidal death than were Christianity or Judaism. Buddhists and Hindus taught a philosophy based on transmigration of the soul and the unimportance of this life, one which logically leads to an acceptance of self-destruction.

The earliest Christians were morbidly obsessed with self-destruction and committed suicide in large numbers for religious reasons. For several centuries the Church regarded self-sacrifice and martyrdom with approval and as a measure of human worth. As the Christian word spread, it increasingly denounced other religions, but the Church did not turn against all suicide until the first quarter of the fifth century, when St. Augustine (354–430 A.D.) spoke out against the taking of one's own life. In his *City of God* Augustine discusses suicide at great length. He terms it a "detestable and damnable wickedness," concluding that "it is homicide, a violation of the commandment *Thou shalt not kill* and thus never justifiable." St. Augustine further postulated a divine prohibition against suicide, although he did not specify that it should be punishable. He rationalized that suicides occurring before his new theologic theory had been divinely inspired to kill themselves.

The earliest recorded general condemnation of suicide took place in 533 A.D. at the second Council of Orleans. In 563 A.D. at the Council of Braga, suicide was condemned by the Church. Funeral rites were to be refused those who committed suicide. In the succeeding centuries there was little official action that added to the denial of funeral rites until late in the thirteenth century, when the Synod of Nimes extended the religious penality on the completed suicide by refusing burial in consecrated ground. This policy of denying the suicide religious funeral rites and burial in holy ground was subsequently incorporated into civil law throughout Europe. In fact, during the Middle Ages, not only were indignities inflicted upon the corpse of a suicide, but the heirs suffered material loss through confiscation of the suicide's goods and land, to say nothing of the mental anguish occasioned by their loved one's mode of death; resulting in their poverty and their ostracism from society.

St. Thomas Aquinas (1225–1274) expounded St. Augustine's view by characterizing suicide as an unnatural act toward oneself, detrimental to the community, an act that usurps God's will in the circumstances (the where, when, and how) of a person's death.

During the Middle Ages the frequency of suicide decreased significantly. Reasons given for this are the influence of Church laws and the comparatively stable society in which people lived. Other possible reasons worth considering are that before these times many suicide victims may have chosen more equivocal methods of self-destruction, such as an "accident" that would not be detected as a suicide by the authorities. Also, techniques of record-keeping and the investigation of deaths were unsophisticated in medieval times.

The Christian suicide ethic remained essentially unchanged from the sixth to the sixteenth century. Suicide fell under the control of the ecclesiastical laws, having been condemned by the Common Law of the Church and having become a part of English law in 1673. Attempted suicide was first recognized as a crime in 1854. Change had come with the Reformation and the rediscovery of Classical learning. Philosophers deliberated on the significance of self-destruction and their writings both influenced and reflected the attitudes toward suicide of that time.

Sir Thomas More (1478–1535) suggested in his *Utopia* an unprejudiced approach to suicide. This is one of the first signs of a shift in social attitudes.

John Donne (1573–1631), the English poet, launched the first full-scale attack on the attitude of the Church. In *Biathanatos*, published by his son in 1644, he states that "self-homicide is not so naturally sin that it may never be otherwise." This work reflected Donne's denial that suicide is invariably sinful and it made a plea for the reader's charity and understanding.

David Hume (1711–1776), English philosopher–essayist of the Enlightenment Period, noted in his essay on suicide that the Bible does not prohibit suicide. He interpreted the Commandment *Thou Shalt Not Kill* to forbid only the killing of others. Hume felt that man has a right to dispose of his own life, although he viewed suicidal people as somewhat deranged mentally, otherwise they would not violate the instinct for self-preservation.

Immanuel Kant (1724–1804), German philosopher, denied the right to suicide. In his *Metaphysics of Ethics* he regards the taking of one's own life as an offense against the universal law of nature. Kant had a lasting regard for religion and found also that suicide was inconsistent with reason.

The seventeenth century theologians conceded that under some circumstances suicide was not a sin. By the eighteenth century popular opinion was gradually turning against the barbaric indignities inflicted on the bodies of persons who committed suicide. Punitive laws remained on the books but the social customs gradually changed. The public opinion expressed on self-destruction in Europe and North America has been as ambivalent and divided as that of ancient Greece and Rome. Dishonoring the body of a suicide never became an American custom, although suicide was an illegal act. There was one exception of short duration—in Massachusetts, a dishonorable, profane burial was practiced on suicides (ie, hanging the body in the street, driving stakes through the dead body, etc).

French intellectuals like Montaigne, Voltaire, Rousseau, and Diderot encouraged humane treatment of the suicide and swept away all sanctions against the body and the property of suicides. Jean Pierre Falret (1794–1870), a student of Pinel and Esquirol, published *De L'Hypocondrie et du Suicide* in 1822 (Fuller, 1973). This scholarly work delved deep into the causes of suicide. Falret reported the kind of people who become suicidal and described their treatment, foreshadowing subsequent developments in research and theory.

Other great philosophers explored the meaning of suicide: Arthur Schopenhauer (1788–1860), German philosopher, although agreeing with the penalties visited on suicide, wrote that suicide was a futile and foolish act. Friedrich Wilhelm Nietzsche (1844–1900), German poet, musician, essayist, classical philologist, and philosopher, supported the case for suicide. In *The Twilight of the Idols*, he affirmed that "one should die proudly when it is no longer possible to live proudly."

John Stuart Mill (1806–1873) and Herbert Spencer (1820–1903), nineteenth century philosophers representing the utilitarian viewpoint, believed the appropriate criterion of morality to be the greatest happiness for the greatest number of people. They declared that if a man believed his suicide would increase the happiness of others, this would give him the right to end his life.

William James (1842–1910), noted by many as the most popular philosopher America has produced, was a great supporter of Mill. He regarded religious faith as the most powerful safeguard against suicide, but considered the ultimate fate of human life on earth a matter for pragmatic consideration. He believed that by exercising our power of choice we can help make the world a better place.

Some current religious views are still reflective of early thinking. For example, in 1966 suicide became a criminal offense in Israel. When suicide is verified, the Orthodox Jew is refused religious burial rites. Islamic law also forbids suicide. The act is viewed by Islam as a form of murder, and since murder is most evil, it is "logical" that suicide too must be forbidden. The performer of this criminal act is not free from the curse of God. Obviously the crime cannot be punished on earth, but Paradise will be denied the malefactor. Catholic opposition to suicide remains an unbroken tradition, based on the principle that "life belongs to God and only God may terminate it." However, when a Catholic does commit suicide, funeral rites are often conducted on the assumption that the victim was not in possession of his or her faculties at the time, hence not responsible for the act.

Going back in time, in the early nineteenth century, attitudes toward suicide were revealing a less moral or theologic bias and by the middle of the nineteenth century opinions with noticeable social and medical overtones were being heard. Medical writers began to have an influence on public opinion about suicide, giving rise to the popular feeling that no decent or respectable person ever takes his life. Medical workers were at that time seeking the psychologic causes of suicide and they came to the conclusion that the person who took his life was insane. This viewpoint intensified existing prejudice against suicide by casting aspersions on the sanity of the entire family. Thus, suicide stigmatized an entire family and its descendants. These prevailing attitudes caused families to avoid any talk of suicide in order to protect the family reputation. Suicide had over the years changed

status from a sin to a disgrace and, as a topic of discussion, a taboo—
an attitude still quite prevalent today.

DEFINITION OF SUICIDE

In the past, numerous definitions of suicide have been proposed.
According to the *Oxford English Dictionary*, the word was first used by
Walter Charleton in 1651, when he said, "to vindicate one's self
from . . . inevitable calamity, by sui-cide is not a crime." Alvarez
(1972) pointed out that the word was actually used earlier by Sir
Thomas Browne in his *Religio Medici*, written in 1635 and published in
1642. Browne poses the following question: "Herein are they not extreme that can allow a man to be his own assassin and so highly extoll
the end, by suicide, of Cato." Douglas (1968), Durkheim (1897), and
many other sociologists and psychologists who have attempted carefully to define suicide have assumed that the investigator should ar-
bitrarily define his concept to fit his scientific methods and his
theoretical purposes, but without deviating too far from common usage. Durkheim further assumed that the most common definition of
suicide was that of death caused by an action initiated by a person
with the intention of causing his own death.

The term "suicide" as used by coroners in the certification of
death is a medicolegal term which takes into consideration the intention of the deceased and the role he or she played in bringing about
death. Suicide defined from the point of view of the coroner or the
vital statistician is simply one of the four modes of death: natural, accidental, homicidal, and suicidal, plus the revised* category of "undetermined," used when death is too equivocal to permit an accurate
determination of mode.

Shneidman (1971) noted that in 1621, when Robert Burton published his *Anatomy of Melancholy*, the word suicide according to the
Oxford English Dictionary, had not yet been invented. The words Burton used to convey the concept of suicide were "made away with
themselves," "violence unto himself," and "hanged themselves."
Shneidman defines suicide as "the human act of self-inflicted, self-
intended cessation." In 1929, the term "suicidologie" was used in a
text by a Dutch professor, W. A. Bonger. Suicidology in the meaning
we recognize today—the scientific study of suicidal phenomena—
was first mentioned in 1964 by Shneidman, in a review of Dublin's

---

*"Eight Revision of the *International Classification of Diseases*" Monthly Vital Statistics
Report, National Center for Health Statistics, DHEW 17, 8, October 1968.

book, *Suicide: A Sociological and Statistical Study* (1963), referring to Dublin as the "grand old man of suicidology." The word was again used by Shneidman in 1967 to describe a training program, "Fellowship in Suicidology," and in 1968 to label a new national professional organization the American Association of Suicidology.

For purposes of this discussion, the definition of suicide accepted here is that given in Webster's *Third New International Dictionary*: "the act or an instance of taking one's own life voluntarily and intentionally."

THEORY AND RESEARCH

The earliest scientific study of suicide was reported by the French alienist Esquirol in *Mental Maladies: A Treatise on Insanity*, published in 1838. The section on suicide contained not only case studies, but statistical tables. Two years later the *Anatomy of Suicide* was published. In this book Dr. Forbes Winston noted statistical data on suicide. So by the turn of the nineteenth century, the approach to an understanding of suicide had changed from a religious, moral, and philosophical approach to one psychologic, statistical, and sociologic. The research and interpretation of suicidal phenomena made their greatest advance in the twentieth century. Although the contributions of these last three disciplines will be treated separately in this discussion, it should be borne in mind that progress was made concurrently in more than one discipline and sometimes multidisciplinarily.

Sociologic Contributions

Emile Durkheim (1858–1917). French sociologist, established a model for sociologic investigations of suicide. In 1897 he published *Le Suicide*, a work reprinted in the United States in 1951. Durkheim's work has had a profound effect on research throughout the world and even today is frequently used as a reference. This author was the first to theorize about the causes of suicide. He considered extreme loneliness a major cause. He believed that the more isolated a man is, the greater the danger that he will kill himself. Durkheim described three basic types of suicide, each resulting from man's relationship to his society:

1. *Altruistic suicide* is recognized by some societies as the honorable

way out of an unfortunate situation—for example, the traditional Japanese hara-kiri or the act of the Hindu widow who cremates herself on the funeral pyre of her husband.

2. *Egoistic suicide* is that of the person who has too few ties with his community, in consequence suffering from the loneliness and isolation observed by Durkheim.

3. *Anomic suicide* occurs when the familiar relationship between an individual and society ends or changes abruptly, as with the loss of a loved one, the loss of a job, or the discovery of a major health problem.

The two last-named categories are found most often in the Western world.

Andrew Henry and James Short, Jr. (1954) researched the economic, sociologic, and psychologic aspects of aggression. In their book *Suicide and Homicide*, they propose an inverse relationship between suicide and homicide where social and psychologic factors determine this choice—that is, as suicide rates increase, homicide rates decrease. Common factors associated with suicide (and homicide) are:

1. Aggression which is often a consequence of frustration
2. Business cycles which produce changes in the hierarchical ranking of persons and groups
3. Frustrations which are generated by interference with the stable maintenance of a position of steadily increasing status

Henry and Short also noted that suicide occurs more often among high-status achievers, and homicides more often among lower socioeconomic populations.

Jack Gibbs and Walter Martin (1964), in their sociologic observations on self-destruction, proposed that the greater the status integration—that is, the greater the stability and durability of a population's social relations—the lower the suicide rate of that population.

Jack Douglas in 1967 wrote that "the most significant contribution of the works by sociologists on suicide has been the sociological perspective itself: the insistence on seeing suicidal actions as in some way the result of social factors." He characterized suicidal actions as meaningful, thus implying that something is fundamentally wrong with the social situation in which they take place.

Psychologic Contributions

Sigmund Freud (1856–1939) was responsible for detailing the psychologic theory of self-destruction. In his opinion suicide is essentially a basic concept of the human mind and everyone is in some measure vulnerable to suicide. Freud considered suicide an intra-psychic phenomenon originating primarily within the unconscious. The pressure impelling a person toward death could increase, depending on life events, and, under conditions of enormous stress, a person could be expected to regress to more primitive ego states. Freud felt that life and death forces are in constant conflict within the individual. He conceptualized that persons identify ambivalently with their own internalized love objects. When a person is frustrated, the aggressive side of his or her conflicting emotions becomes inner-directed. Suicide in this context may be viewed as a form of murder, with the suicide victim unconsciously wanting the other entity of a dyad dead. Litman (1968) traced Freud's writings on suicide from 1881 to 1939 and described Freud's explanations of suicide not only as theoretical and philosophical in essence but also based on psychoanalytic experiences.

In 1937, Alfred Adler (1870–1957) described the suicidal individual as an inferiority-ridden person who hurts others by injuring the self. The self-destructive person thinks too little of others and too much of himself or herself so that he or she cannot relate satisfactorily to others (Farberow–Shneidman, 1961).

Gregory Zilboorg (1891–1959) viewed suicide as a way of thwarting outside sources which are making life impossible. According to Shneidman, Zilboorg found that "every suicidal case contained strong unconscious hostility combined with an unusual lack of capacity to love others. He [Zilboorg] maintained that the role of the broken home in suicidal proneness demonstrated that suicide has intra-psychic and external etiological elements" (Shneidman, 1973). In his study of institutionalized suicides, Zilboorg concluded that these suicides suffered from depressive psychosis, compulsive neurosis, and schizophrenia.

Carl Jung (1875–1961) defined suicide as a way of escaping from current intolerable conditions and an effort to attain rebirth (Farberow–Shneidman, 1961).

Karl Menninger, in his book *Man Against Himself* (1938), describes suicide as the winning of the death instinct over the life instinct—under conditions of stress and conflict. He perceives three main components of suicide: the wish to kill, the wish to be killed, and the wish to die. Menninger further identifies three categories of the suicidal impulse: *chronic suicide*, as seen in addiction to martyrdom and psychosis; *focal suicide*, as seen in self-multilation, multiple accidents, and impotence; and *organic suicide*, where the death wish comes from a physical illness such as some chronic or terminal disease.

Menninger mentions the taboo against suicide when he says: "So great is the taboo on suicide that some people will not say the word, some newspapers will not print accounts of it and even scientists have avoided it as a subject of research." He further emphasizes the point that suicide must not be ignored if prevention is to take place.

The taboos against suicide have been slowly disappearing and research on the phenomenon has increased manyfold. Today, psychologic and sociologic theories of causation are blending. Self-destructive behavior is not only examined in terms of a person's relation to current events in society, but also in terms of the surrounding psychologic pressures on that person and his or her ability or inability to resolve life's problems. We now know that individuals kill themselves for a variety of psychologic reasons—not only out of hate and a desire for revenge, but also because of loneliness, isolation, shame, fear, guilt and/or loss of self-image. It is important to remember that there is no single factor in causation.

Contributions of Statistics

The taboos against suicide have made it difficult to collect accurate statistics on suicide and suicidal attempts. Suicide deaths may go unreported as such because of the stigma attached to them, because of guilt feelings of the survivors, or because of the extreme sensitivity of feeling associated with the taking of one's life. External forces influencing these statistics originate in the attitudes of family, church, and insurance companies. The taboo also affects coroners, medical examiners, and physicians, who may at times be inclined to list a more socially acceptable mode of death on the death certificate.

Shneidman (1973) points out that

. . . the demographic uses of statistics on suicide perhaps were given their greatest impetus by John Graunt and Johann Peter Süssmilch. Graunt was a London tradesman who in 1662 published a small book of observations on London bills of mortality. He separated various lists of information contained in these rolls of names of the dead into separate categories and organized the information systematically, finally constructing mortality tables—the first attempt to organize data in that manner.

In 1741, Süssmilch, a Prussian clergyman, began keeping vital statistics by analyzing vital data from church records. In 1825, J. L. Casper, a Prussian physician, was the first to use statistics as the prin-

cipal tool of research on suicide (Rosen, 1975).* When Brière de Boismont published *Du Suicide et de la Folie Suicide* in 1856, he used available statistics and enumerated the causes of suicide as alcoholism,
illness, family troubles, poverty, love problems, and problems of
society.

Douglas in 1968 noted that there had been many discussions in
the literature of the inadequacies of official statistics before Durkheim.
For example, De Gurry, in his report published in 1835, *Statistique
Morale de la France*, disputed the statistical finding that suicides were
increasing rapidly throughout Europe early in the nineteenth century. Douglas pointed out further that Esquirol in 1838, Briére de
Boismont in 1856, Legoyt in 1881, and Strahan in 1893 expressed the
opinion that the official statistics grossly underreflected the actual
number of suicides. In fact, until the turn of the century, most scientists were highly critical of the official statistics on suicide.

Suicide statistics come from individual certifications of deaths.
The completion and filing of the death certificate is the responsibility
of the county coroner or the medical examiner. Procedures for certification vary among communities, states and nations. In some cases
certifications are made by the family physician only. Statistical errors
occur for reasons such as inadvertent mistakes in diagnosis (calling an
equivocal death an accident; reporting the cause of death as undetermined rather than taking the time for a thorough investigation) and
deliberate or unconscious suppression of the mode of death because
of the prevailing taboos.

Dublin (1963) points out that research omits from consideration
statistical data earlier than 1900 because of their inaccuracy.
Eighteenth and nineteenth century statistics on suicide were considered "moral" statistics by researchers. Since the turn of the century
we do know that the death rate from suicide has changed from year to
year. Comparisons of different age groups, the sexes, racial groups,
methods or weapons used, and setting (urban versus rural) of
suicides have been made for the past 75 years. It has also been possible to make correlations between suicide death rates and economic
conditions. For example, the rate of suicide in the United States at the
beginning of the century was 10.2 per 100,000 population; by 1915 the
rate had increased to 16.2, or by 60 percent. A change occurred with
America's entry into World War I, when the suicide rate fell, and it
continued to fall through the war period and immediately afterward,

*The word *statistic* is derived from the Latin word *status* meaning state in the political
sense. Statistics, therefore, was originally a form of "political arithmetic," later called
vital statistics.

reaching 10.2 by 1920. In 1921 the national rate again increased, to 12.4, and climbed steadily upward thereafter reaching its maximum of 17.4 in 1932 (the Depression). The rate dropped slowly from that point, reaching a new low during World War II.

The statistical method has been the chief tool at our disposal for these analyses (source: the National Center for Health Statistics). When looking at suicide statistics, however, one must be careful not to jump to unfounded conclusions. One must recognize that the development of statistical data throughout the United States and the world and the changes that have taken place in the procedures for certification of death during this period limit the comparability of data gathered.

National death statistics were first collected by the Bureau of the Census of the Federal Government. The first "unified" death reports for the states encompassed the years 1900 to 1904. Not until the 1950s did the government transfer the collection of national mortality figures to the Public Health Service.

The official statistics on causes of death in the United States are based upon medical certifications made out by the physician in attendance, or in medicolegal cases by the coroner or the medical examiner; these are the key persons to meaningful reporting of statistics on suicide. The medical certifications are classified for statistical purposes in the terminology and the categories of the *International Classification of Diseases* in accordance with international rules first set forth in August 1900 at an international conference in Paris, where 26 countries participated in the selection of causes of death for primary mortality tabulations. This classification scheme and the rules supporting it are currently maintained by the World Health Organization and are revised approximately every decade. Today's statistics reflect the eighth revision (1968) of the *International Classification of Diseases,* which provided for a new classification or mode of death under "undetermined circumstances," the classification used when a death investigation fails to uncover sufficient evidence to certify a violent death as an accident, a suicide, or a homicide, the circumstances usually being equivocal.

Coroners generally consider their primary responsibility in a death investigation that of ruling out homicide. The thoroughness with which a coroner investigates a case depends on several factors. In the case of an equivocal death, many coroners extend their inquiry beyond the immediate family to significant others in the deceased's life. The immediate environment is searched for signs of self-destruction—for example, empty prescription bottles, guns, powder burns, or a suicide note (found in 15 to 25 percent of suicide cases).

There are times when a coroner will yield to outside pressures from the victim's family, from an insurance company, or because of the illegality of taking one's own life in some states. This is most commonly seen in cases where the circumstances of death are equivocal.

Suicide deaths are still underreported and statistics vary from county to county, state to state, and nation to nation. The reported rate for the United States has ranged between 10.0 and 12.6 per 100,000 population during the past decade. Recent national death statistics have shown an increase in the suicide rate. Some suicidologists have related this increase to the accompanying national economic instability and depressed social conditions. The actual number of suicides recorded as occurring in the United States during 1975 is 26,960 (National Center for Health Statistics). Suicidologists feel, however, that because of the underreporting of the cause of death from suicide, the number may be closer to 50,000.

A statistic more startling is that of the 5 million persons in the United States who have at one time or other attempted to end their lives. A recent trend currently being statistically demonstrated in the nation is an increase in suicide among adolescents, minority groups, and women.

The most recent international death rates from suicide (1969) show the United States ranking eighteenth among the 43 nations reporting with a rate of 11.1 per 100,000 population. The highest suicide rate, of 43.6 per 100,000 population, is seen in West Berlin (which reports statistics as a separate country), followed by Hungary, with a rate of 33.1 per 100,000.

Methods of taking one's life vary, but the three leading methods are (1) firearms and explosives, (2) poisons and gases, and (3) hanging and strangulation. These have been the primary methods of committing suicide in this country since the beginning of the century. Their relative importance varies from state to state. For example, in California the leading method is poisons and gases, whereas in the states of Montana and Wyoming guns far outrank any other method. Dublin (1963) noted a continuous overall increase in the use of firearms: from 1901 to 1905, nearly one in four, or 24.4 percent of suicide deaths were attributed to firearms; and in the period 1955 to 1959, nearly half, or 47.1 percent of suicide deaths were attributed to firearms.

SUICIDE PREVENTION

Choron (1968) points out what is probably the first recorded instance of suicide prevention, that reported by Plutarch (46–119 A.D.), who notes an ordinance of the magistrates of Miletus, which was intended to put an end to a sudden epidemic of suicides among the young women of that Greek city.

In the United States, suicide prevention was slow in the beginning. This sluggishness reflected to a great extent the negative attitudes of the population toward suicides as well as toward those attempting suicide. Social and legal measures against suicide have gradually been turning away from making charges of guilt and enforcing punishment toward measures protecting suicidal persons and helping the families of suicides. At the national and international level the mental health movement has been equally as negative in the attitudes of its members and as gradual in developing a program of prevention.

The first United States service for the suicidal was started in 1905 (Table 1). First known as "The Parish of All Strangers," its name changed in 1906 to "The National Save-A-Life League." This outreach service began its operations when its founder, Harry M. Warren (a New York City Central Park Baptist minister), talked to a 20-year-old girl after she had been hospitalized for taking an overdose of poison. Before she died she told Dr. Warren, "Maybe if I had talked to someone like you I wouldn't have done it." Her death led Rev. Warren to place an ad in New York newspapers asking any suicidal person to call him first before making an attempt to commit suicide.

The shift from the view of suicide as an ugly, tabooed secret to a respectable subject of research began in the late 1950s. In 1958 the Los Angeles Suicide Prevention Center (LASPC) was opened by two psychologists, Edwin S. Shneidman and Norman L. Farberow, funded by a grant from the National Institute of Mental Health. The LASPC became a leader in providing services, training personnel, conducting research, and developing a theoretical framework for suicide prevention that served as a model for other centers springing up across the country.

A review of the literature reveals a definite change in the way investigators have viewed and are now viewing the phenomenon of suicide. The history of changes in the approach to suicide reflect both the changes within each discipline involved in study and prevention and the growing emphasis on a multidisciplinary approach to prevention so well demonstrated by the Los Angeles Center. Staff and associates at the Los Angeles Suicide Prevention Center represent the disciplines of psychology, psychiatry, nursing, social work, theology, sociology, anthropology, forensic medicine, philosophy, and education.

TABLE 1. Milestones in Suicide Prevention: A Chronology

Year	Facility	Founder
1905	The Parish of All Strangers (in 1906 named the National Save-A-Life League), New York, N.Y.	Rev. Harry M. Warren
1906	The London Anti-Suicide Department, London, England	The Salvation Army
1933	The Suicide Flotilla (a squadron of suicide prevention boats that patrolled the Danube River to rescue potential suicides), Budapest, Hungary	No known founder
1947	The Society for the Care of People Tired of Life, Vienna, Austria	Dr. Erwin Ringel
1953	The Samaritans, London, England	Rev. Chad Varah
1958	The Los Angeles Suicide Prevention Center, Los Angeles, Calif.	Dr. E.S. Shneidman and Dr. N.L. Farberow
1961	The International Association for Suicide Prevention (headquarters in Vienna, Austria)	Dr. Erwin Ringel
1966	Center for the Study of Suicide Prevention of the National Institute of Mental Health	NIMH, US Department of Health, Education and Welfare
1968	The American Association of Suicidology, formed after the first national conference on suicidology	Dr. Edwin S. Shneidman

Volunteers in prevention work were used as early as 1905, and the Los Angeles Center began using the volunteer worker in 1964, when professional staff could not handle the volume of incoming telephone calls for help. In most of the 166 suicide prevention centers in the United States today, volunteers are the backbone of the Center. They are dedicated individuals, carefully selected and well trained.

A chronologic listing of the significant events regarding suicide prevention activities is given in Table 1.

Starting in the 1960s, the National Mental Health Association played a significant role in assisting and promoting the development of suicide prevention centers. The suicide prevention center is a specially designed facility that provides an important public and mental health service within the community. The main goal is to save lives.

Most of the research on suicide has been done in the twentieth century. Without these studies and their findings, the suicide prevention movement would not have been possible. The prevailing actions and attitudes of society are reflected in an acceleration of suicide intervention activities by many of the health disciplines and tempered by the realization that while every citizen has the right to take his own life, we all have a greater responsibility to make our society a place of dignity and worth where everyone will want to live.

The past 25 years have seen a proliferation of activities in the field of suicidology. Studies are now available on attitudes toward suicide and suicidal attempts; completed suicides and the methods used; adolescent suicide and suicide in older citizens; survivors of suicide and "postvention"*; suicide prevention centers, and other aspects of suicide and suicidology.

REFERENCES

Allen NH: Suicide in California 1960–1970. Sacramento, State of Calif, 1973

Alvarez A: The Savage God: A Study of Suicide. New York, Random House, 1972

Aristotle: Nicomachean Ethics. In Great Books of the Western World, Vol 9. Chicago, Encyclopaedia Britannica, 1952, p 339

Bindman AJ, Speigel AD (eds): Perspectives in Community Mental Health. Chicago, Aldine, 1969

Choron J: Death and Western Thought. New York, Collier, 1963, p 32

————: Notes on Suicide Prevention in Antiquity. Bull Suicidol. Washington, DC, Natl Clgh M H Information, DHEW, July 1968, p 46

————: Suicide, New York, Scribner, 1972, p 12

Douglas J: The Social Meaning of Suicide. Princeton, NJ, Princeton Univ Press, 1967

————: Suicide—Social Aspects. In International Encyclopedia of Social Sciences. New York, Crowell-Collier, 1968, p 375

Dublin L: Suicide: A Sociological and Statistical Study. New York, Ronald Press, 1963.

————: Suicide: An Overview of a Health and Social Problem. Bull Suicidol. Washington, DC, Natl Clgh M H Information; DHEW, Dec 1967, p 25

Durkheim E: Suicide (1897). Spaulding JA, Simpson G (trans). Glencoe, Ill, Free Press, 1951

Ellis ER, Allen GN: Traitor Within—Our Suicide Problem. New York, Doubleday, 1961

Epicurus: Letter to Menoccus. Quoted in Fedden HR: Suicide: A Social and Historical Study. New York, B Blom, 1972, p 70

Farberow NL: Suicide. New Jersey, General Learning Press, 1974, p 30

————, ES Shneidman (eds): The Cry for Help. New York, McGraw-Hill, 1961

Fuller M: Suicide past and present: a note on Jean Pierre Falret. Life Threat Behav 3:58, 1973

---

*Shneidman's word denoting those activities following the death of a significant other (by suicide) that serve to assist the survivors in coping with their emotional and psychologic responses to the loss.

Gibbs JP, Martin WT: Status Integration and Suicide. Eugene, Ore, Univ of Oregon Books, 1964

Henry AF, Short JF: Suicide and Homicide. Glencoe, Ill, Free Press, 1954

Kant I: Metaphysics of Ethics. Semple JW (trans): 3rd ed. Edinburgh, T & T Clark, 1871, p 239

Litman RE: Sigmund Freud on Suicide. Bull Suicidol Washington, DC, Natl Clgh M H Information, DHEW, July 1968, p 11–23

Menninger K: Man Against Himself. New York, Harcourt, Brace, World, 1933

National Center for Health Statistics: Health Resources Statistics; Suicide Prevention Centers. Washington, DC, DHEW, 1975, p 25

————: Suicide in the United States 1950–1964. Washington, DC, DHEW, Series 20, No 5, 1967

Plato: On Laws. In Great Books of the Western World, Vol 70. Chicago, Encyclopaedia Britannica, 1952, p 753

————: Phaedo. In Great Books of the Western World, Vol 70 Chicago, Encyclopaedia Britannica, 1952, p 233

Rosen G: History. In Perlin S (ed): A Handbook for the Study of Suicide. London, Oxford University Press, 1975

Saint Augustine: City of God. New York, Dutton, 1947

Shneidman ES: Suicide. In Farberow NL (ed): Taboo Topics. New York, Atherton, 1963, pp 33–43

————: Suicide and suicidology: a brief etymological note. Life Threat Behav 1:260, 1971

————: Suicide. In Encyclopaedia Britannica, Vol 210. Chicago, Benton, 1973, pp 383–86

————, Farberow NL, Litman RE: The Psychology of Suicide. New York, Science House, 1970, p 37

Spelios T: Pictorial History of Greece. New York, Crown, 1967, p 633

Stengel E: Suicide and Attempted Suicide. Baltimore, Penguin, 1964

Williams RJ: Reflections on the Lebensmüde. J Egypt Archaeol (London, Egypt Exploration Soc) 48: 1962

Wright WK: A History of Modern Philosophy. New York, Macmillan, 1941, p 633

CHAPTER 2
Theoretical Framework

It is not our intent to present numerous theoretical or philosophical positions that explain the "why" of suicidal behavior. Rather, our purpose is to identify terms, clarify misconceptions, and offer what we believe to be the experience that suicidal persons go through.

SUICIDE AS A CRISIS

Corrine Loing Hatton
Sharon McBride Valente
Alice Rink

There is a close relationship between suicide theory and crisis theory. The risk of suicide is always assessed in any kind of crisis clinic or other caregiving facility and is an essential part of crisis intervention. Similarly, suicidal thoughts, threats or attempts are viewed as expressions of a crisis situation in an individual's life and perhaps that of the family as well.

In the absence of a lengthy discourse on crisis intervention theory, the reader is invited to read two inclusive and dynamic works (Aguilera and Messick, 1974; Jacobson, 1974) for an in-depth study of this relevant field of inquiry and clinical treatment. For greater clarity, however, a few definitions will be enumerated here that are used interchangeably between the fields of crisis intervention and suicidology. These are useful and practical terms that seem to have gained validity through common use by the two professional specialties.

Hazard—An event in the life of an individual which may pose an actual or potential threat to that person's otherwise steady state of functioning. This hazard may be viewed as an external event happening to someone and will constitute a threat, depending on the meaning it has for the individual and how equipped that individual is to handle it. A hazard can be maturational (occurring anywhere along the developmental sequence from infancy and early childhood through adolescence, into adulthood and old age); or situational (loss of a loved one through separation, death, or divorce; physical illness; role change, or in fact any stressful event that constitutes a threat to the individual).

Crisis—The internal emotional disruption (often referred to as symptoms) that occurs due to the threat from the external event. These symptoms may be of a somatic nature (eg, stomach upset, headache, backache, fatigue, loss of appetite) or of a psychologic nature (eg, anxiety, fear, anger, loneliness, depression). The degree of disorganization demonstrated will probably be proportional to the individual's ability to adapt to the feelings prompted by the crisis.

Coping Devices—The way an individual habitually deals with the various stressful situations encountered within the self and in the outer world. Coping is generally viewed as maladaptive when it is destructive to the person and/or significant others around that person—for example, homicide, suicide, alcoholism, or drug addiction. It is adaptive when it is constructive to the person and/or significant others—for example, talking to others, reading, sports activities, job interests.

Significant Others—Person(s) in an individual's world who are necessary to the psychic functioning of that individual. Such person(s) could be anyone who is needed for support, reassurance, or surcease, and whose relationship to the subject varies across a broad spectrum of social importance all the way from a marital partner to the local bartender or a neighbor.

PSYCHOLOGIC STATES EXPERIENCED BY SUICIDAL PERSONS

Naomi James

Innumerable books and articles have been written about suicidal behavior and countless studies have examined the epidemiology of suicide, the cultural aspects of suicidal behavior, and the psychologic characteristics of suicidal persons. But when the caregiver comes face to face with a suicidal client, all that concentrated wisdom pales before this person's experience of the suicidal state and all that has gone into it—the client's life, family, work, and the pain of failure or loss, or the sheer complexity of circumstance.

Because the caregiver comes from a background that differs educationally, psychologically, and experientially, recasting suicidal behavior so that the *how* or *for what purpose* are sought out rather than the *why* will enable the caregiver to enter the very personal experience of the suicidal client at the point where change, if any, can begin.

When we speak of a person's characteristics, we infer something permanent; when we talk of a person's experience, we infer process. Process implies movement, change, the flow of experience—it is never static. The caregiver who is able to think in these terms may be helped in working with suicidal persons. Changing the way someone *is* may be a big order, but helping someone expand the flow of experience so that their manner of living is altered, would certainly seem to be within our reach.

Considering suicide specifically, it is the manner in which a client communicates suicidal feelings and intentions to others that provides clues to the quality and direction of his or her experience. Most suicidal persons report feelings of depression, ambivalence, loneliness, isolation, hopelessness, and helplessness. Many suicidal persons also display manipulative behavior, or they may tend to view their situation with tunnel vision as will be discussed later. That these behaviors and feelings occur among suicidal persons has been well established by scientific research and clinical experience. What the caregiver must bear in mind, however, is that these phenomena may occur in multiple combinations and in varying degree. In order to assist the suicidal individual, these feelings and behaviors must be understood by the caregiver within the specific context of that person's experience.

Experience of Depression

Depression has been defined as a complex feeling, ranging from unhappiness to deep dejection and hopelessness, often accompanied by more or less absurd feelings of guilt, failure, and worthlessness, as well as self-destructive tendencies. Usually, the physical concomitants of depression are disturbances in sleeping pattern and appetite and a general slowing-down of many physiologic processes (Watslawick, 1967).

What is the difference, then, between the experience of depression and that of sadness or grief? This definition of depression contains several key words which also seem to characterize sadness or grief in one respect or another. A person who feels sad does not necessarily feel worthless or guilty. Grief does not bring with it feelings of failure or even necessarily a negative orientation to the future. But when a person is depressed, the view beyond the depression is often obscured. To be sure, it is sometimes difficult to separate these various feelings into well-defined entities, but it is important to bear in mind that they are not identical states.

There is by no means concurrence on the etiology of depression. Briefly, the models which have been most often used as referents should be identified.

A biologic basis for depression has been assigned by some investigators, who view depression as resulting from hormonal changes such as those brought about by postpartum, premenstrual, or involutional periods; from metabolic dysfunction; or from changes in the functioning of the central nervous system. A genetic predisposition to depression has also been considered by some theorists as a possible cause.

The view of depression which has been most often considered is that advanced by Freud (1917), in which intrapsychic conflict leads to a turning of aggressive impulses against the self. Other psychoanalytic explanations have been offered by Bowlby (1973), who suggests that depression accompanies the experience of loss and separation, and by Spitz (1946), who noted that deprivation of human contact in infancy and childhood can lead to severe depression and ultimately to death.

Seligman (1974) suggested that depression is a form of learned helplessness. This state results from the inability to escape painful stimuli, so that only withdrawal and helplessness follow any stressful event. Lewinsohn (1974) has reported that behavior identified as depressed follows the loss of positive reinforcers in the life of the subject.

Beck's formulations (1970) are based on a cognitive approach which ties depression to a negative self-image or negative self-esteem and a pessimistic view of the world and the future.

Certainly these views of depression hardly provide a complete description. Moreover, many of the theoretical formulations of depression have changed through the years. From the author's point of view ascertaining the etiology of depression is less important than understanding its effect on the individual and its function as communication. Depression is an extremely painful state. It is so painful for many persons that it is described as a physical symptom. But depression serves several purposes and thus can be viewed from an operational standpoint. It raises the threshold of pain for incoming stimuli, thereby reducing or blunting further painful experiences.

Most important, since it is so often apparent to others, depression can be viewed as communication of a self-inflicted state of deprivation. Thus, at the same time that depression serves to protect the subject from more pain than that already being felt, it has an outward movement as communication to the environment which can be viewed as an attempt of sorts to effect change.

To the observer it may appear that depression is a moving away, a withdrawal, a giving up, or a surrender. This may also describe the client's subjective experience of depression. On the other hand, depression considered as communication and as a defense can be viewed as active rather than passive in nature—it is an active withdrawal; it is a potent statement that says "I will not involve myself," and it is a powerful plea to others to "Do something," "Take care of me," or simply, "Treat me as a person who is immobilized and depressed." If we understand that there is no such thing as non-behavior, then we can realize that the manifestations of depression must be seen not as they appear—that is, as a lack of communication—but rather as a very powerful display of an internal condition.

Often, when we encounter a client who is depressed and isolated, withdrawing from significant others or avoiding intellectual or business pursuits, we are inclined to the opinion that the solution of the problem must involve more social contacts and activities. What we may fail to recognize is that these behaviors, because they are subtly different at various times for each person, must be responded to only after the function of the particular symptom is clearly understood. Caregivers would do well to search out the minute but significant individual differences in depression that may offer the key to the function it performs for that person. To attempt to dispel depression by replacing it with activity invalidates its function as a medium of communication. Helping a client first to understand the function of this emotional state and subsequently moving toward the incorporation of some new or resumed activity will usually produce more gratifying results. In general, caregivers would do well also to avoid any theoretical orientation which tends to pigeonhole the client or limit the range of the caregiver's response.

Frequently, the lifting of a serious depression ushers in another danger period, since the release of energy resulting from a decrease in symptoms may be utilized to act out further self-destructive impulses. The caregiver must be particularly sensitive to this transition of the client from immobilization to movement. It is at this time, however, that there is also great potential for therapeutic change.

Experience of Hopelessness and Helplessness

Depression has several traveling companions which often accompany it in varying degrees. Feelings of hopelessness and
helplessness are usually also evident. These are perhaps the feelings
most accessible to the consciousness of the client and are more easily
pointed out when a client first comes for help. Hopelessness has been
found to be a more accurate indicator of the seriousness of the suicidal
state than depression (Kovacs et al, 1975; Minkoff et al, 1973; Beck
and Beck, 1972). In fact, the caregiver may use the client's ability or
inability to project into the future and make plans as a gauge of the
seriousness of suicidal intent. Feelings of hopelessness may be more
clearly expressed by the client than feelings of depression. Such
communications take the form of remarks like "Nothing feels good to
me any more and probably never will," "Things will never work out,"
"I can't see that things will ever be any different."

Helplessness is an expression of the client's experience of impotence. One hears helplessness expressed as "I can't do anything about
it," "No matter what I do, it will never change," "I can't solve this
problem by myself." It may appear to the caregiver that the client is
resigned to a helpless state especially if the client should say, "Don't
bother—you probably can't do anything for me, either." Recognition
of this as a covert request for help enables the caregiver to bring this
fact to the awareness of the client. More than likely it is an indication
that the client has difficulty asking for anything directly. It may be a
typical manner of interacting with most other persons in the client's
life.

Other covert queries about the caregiver's ability or desire to help
must not go unanswered. The expression of helplessness may take
myriad forms, depending upon the personality of the client. The
caregiver must cope not only with the direct messages but also with
the unstated, implied requests so often typical of the suicidal person
who, for one reason or another, finds it painful to ask openly for assistance. If the caregiver is able to clarify in the mind of the suicidal
client the nature of the latter communications and the concerns that
underlie them, it may be possible to initiate a relationship where
therapeutic movement can take place.

Experience of Isolation and Withdrawal

Behavioral clues and verbal and nonverbal communications help
the caregiver understand and deal with the suicidal client. Many be-

havioral manifestations of suicidal feelings are easily identified. Others, which may emanate from the same feelings, may be misinterpreted or overlooked. Consider the behavior of isolation or withdrawal. When people isolate themselves from human contact or seclude themselves in their rooms, we hypothesize that they are depressed. But, when depression, feelings of isolation, and a need to withdraw are masked by behaviors which can be interpreted as incompatible with depression, we may be misled in our diagnosis (Lesse, 1974). Superficially these behaviors may appear to be just the opposite of those expressing withdrawal and isolation.

For instance, one might mask or hide a depression by making the rounds of cocktail parties and social events at which large numbers of persons are present. One who feels the need to withdraw need not retreat into the isolation of an unoccupied room but has only to become unavailable to human contact even though surrounded by others. Here, social activity is a mask for retreat inward. An astute observer should look for two clues: first, subtle signs of depression that belie an authenic connection with others—going through the motions mechanically, so to speak; second, the subtle communicational indications of depression which may be actual attempts on the part of the suicidal person (albeit not necessarily conscious) to let others know of his/her suffering.

Often such suicidal persons will come for help in the guise of seeking assistance for another problem (ie, physical symptoms which may be difficult to pinpoint), or for another person ("I know somebody who has this problem"). The caregiver may be able to determine the presence and severity of depression and hopelessness by exploring the range of daily activities with the client. Questions like "How do you feel while you are having dinner with your friends" or observations like "Even though you are involved in a lot of activities, you seem to feel cut off from others," help the caregiver assess the significance the behavioral channels through which the depression is expressed.

Experience of Hostility and Depression

Although depression has been defined as "anger turned inward," and high levels of hostility have been found by some investigators in suicide attempters (Weissman et al, 1973), these authors point out that there is little evidence of a causal relationship. Rather, depression and hostility appear to be independent states which may exist concurrently. Therefore, assigning a causal relationship between them when attempting to help a suicidal person hinders the course of therapy. Until such a relationship has been clearly demonstrated and documented, the caregiver will do more harm than good by operating on assumptions.

Suicidal clients who are at the same time hostile and angry will, of course, be encountered by all caregivers during the course of their counseling experience. Anger, like any other behavior, can be seen as a communication which must be heeded by the caregiver. In most instances it can also be seen as a representative sample of the client's usual manner of relating with others. As such, the caregiver's role involves dealing both with the anger and with the distance it interposes between them as seriously as he deals with the suicidal behavior itself.

Experience of Ambivalence

There is documented clinical evidence that persons with suicidal problems express a great deal of ambivalence. Ambivalence can be seen as a desire to reach mutually exclusive goals. That is to say, either the person is equally drawn to two conflicting goals or he both wants and does not want something at the same time.

All persons feel ambivalent from time to time. The intensity of the ambivalence ranges across a broad segment of human conflict. At one extreme a person's ambivalence may be associated with extreme indecisiveness and total inability to make decisions or resolve problems (eg, I love my spouse but I hate my spouse; or I want to get married but I don't want to get married); at the normal end of the spectrum is the fleeting conflict (I want to go to this movie and that concert on the same and only evening I can go out).

Ambivalence is difficult to understand much of the time, yet it may be the crucial factor in a diminution of the suicidal state and a return to more productive behavior. Since ambivalence has two poles, the caregiver may utilize this structural feature in working with the suicidal client, strengthening the attraction of that pole of the ambivalence which will draw the client away from the suicidal state, this is, of course, the desired direction of the intervention.

Again, the focus is on the communicational function of this state.

Depending upon the individual and the conditions, ambivalence is either simple or difficult to identify and to mobilize. Ambivalence as expressed by the individual would appear to be consonant with his usual style of interacting with others.

Ambivalence is perhaps best considered along a continuum which runs parallel to that describing chronically suicidal states and suicidal crises in a stable personality. Let us call the ambivalence of a person in the suicidal crisis, whose life style may be described as generally stable,* *content ambivalence.*† That is to say, at one end of the continuum, ambivalence surrounds the issue of life or death, here and now, and may not of itself be a feature of the client's usual style of functioning. When the positive pole of the ambivalence can be well mobilized in a client who is generally stable, that client stands a good chance of making a recovery to a state of equilibrium within a short period of time, perhaps no longer than two months.

Ambivalence in a person who is not necessarily stable or who manifests a chronically suicidal life style is more difficult to identify and to mobilize. It is not unlikely that this life style is in itself ambivalent in its very structure. Let us call this *process ambivalence*, which is located at the other end of the continuum. The caregiver should realize that mobilizing the positive forces in process ambivalence is not as clearly charted a task as mobilizing the positive forces in content ambivalence. Not only is the chronically suicidal, chronically ambivalent person unable to decide whether or not to take his life, but in all probability he is ambivalent about almost any choices facing him. This includes ambivalence in deciding whether or not to enter a relationship with the caregiver.

As the midpoint of the continuum between content and process is approached, the identification of ambivalence becomes very confusing. Mixed ambivalence presents more of a problem than either that of pure content or pure process in that it is much more difficult for the caregiver to identify specific factors which might be utilized in turning the course of the suicidal state toward the desired resolution. Neither is it clear that the suicidal person should or should not be referred for ongoing long-term therapy in order to resolve the conflicts.

The purpose of viewing ambivalence along a continuum such as that described here is that it underscores the danger of viewing am-

---

*A stable life style is characterized by satisfying interpersonal relationships, work history, intimate relationships, and sexual adjustment.

†This formulation of ambivalence was devised by the author.

bivalence simplistically as a single phenomenon to be eliminated or ignored rather than utilized in the therapeutic regimen.

Experience of Tunnel Vision

In the face of crisis, depressed and suicidal persons are frequently unable to see choices or alternatives that might ameliorate their situation. A kind of tunnel vision prevents the client from pursuing the course which will lead out of this desperate state. Tunnel vision. as the term suggests, covers a narrow field of perception such that only one alternative appears to be available in coping with the problem situation. By clarifying the hazard for the client and by facilitating the expression of negative feelings, the caregiver strives to open up the perceptual field of the client so that one or more choices will be revealed as viable alternatives to the impasse. Feelings of helplessness or hopelessness often spring from this inability to perceive choices in one's frame of reference.

Tunnel vision is not necessarily limited to the suicidal client. Pressures stemming from a highly charged situation may communicate themselves to the intervenor, engendering a parallel process within the caregiver. As a result of this insidious "infection," the caregiver as well as the client may view the hazard and the crisis in a manner which precludes the perception of choices. The caregiver gets caught up in the hopelessness and helplessness expressed by the client. This may be due to the caregiver's own unresolved feelings or conflicts, which interfere with a clear evaluation of the client's problems. Needless to say, in order to do effective counseling, caregivers must have a clear picture of their own emotional functioning.

Finally, tunnel vision on the part of a caregiver may be the result of philosophical inflexibility. The caregiver who has assumed a stance where all suicidal behavior and all suicidal persons can only be viewed in simplistic fashion is likely to apply the same resources, techniques, and solutions over and over again to all suicidal clients and all their problems. From such a stance the caregiver does not perceive and utilize alternatives any more than does the client. One need not point out how potentially disastrous the outcome when the caregiver is not flexible enough to assess the situation and to allow interaction with the client to follow a natural course based on the client's needs. Because each human being is unique, it follows that the interaction between any given client and any caregiver will take a highly individual course. When the caregiver recognizes the uniqueness of both the client and the situation, it is infinitely more likely that a whole range of possible intervention will be considered.

Alcoholism

The alcoholic as a client presents a particularly complex problem. First, we must assess our own attitudes about alcoholism. It is not uncommon that a counselor finds alcoholic behavior repugnant. Such an attitude interferes with therapy, since treatment in a situation of this sort tends to be punitive and guilt instilling. The counselor who recognizes the existence of personal bias must, when presented with an alcoholic as a client, seek immediate consultation in order to make a clear decision about the effect of the bias on the therapeutic relationship and whether to continue work with this client.

Aside from any preconceived prejudice toward alcoholics, the loneliness, isolation, and dependency reported by the alcoholic in the course of therapy may be overwhelming to the caregiver. Soon after our first contact we are often able to discern the hopelessness which hides behind the massive denial system of the "happy drunk." As the alcoholic's defenses begin to crumble under stress, we are struck by the tremendous needs which the alcoholic is often unable to verbalize. On the other hand, should the alcoholic begin to stabilize, we can rest assured that the denial system will shortly begin to operate once again unless adequate support from Alcoholics Anonymous or some other kind of rehabilitative counseling is provided. It is only a matter of time before events that led to this most recent suicidal crisis repeat themselves.

The use of alcohol by a person not habituated to it usually indicates that the individual is attempting to dull intensely felt pain. Such persons may be seen as high-emergency risks because their judgment has been radically impaired, and the usual barriers to impulsive acting out of conflicts have been lowered. The overall picture for such drinkers has a more favorable prognosis than that of chronic drinkers, although the immediate risk is extremely high.

Small wonder, however, that a caregiver may feel unequal to the task. Alcoholics are often so needy that it seems as though they will consume the counselor along with whatever provisions he can offer in meeting these needs. Great benefit may be derived in this situation from an endeavor to "get behind" the alcoholism so that some understanding of the underlying problems and conflicts can be achieved. Myriad life problems, among them job instability, stormy interpersonal relationships, sexual maladjustment, and disruption of intimate relationships, frequently accompany alcoholism. Whether we consider alcoholism as cause or effect, we are impressed by the fragility of the alcoholic's personality and the tenuousness of the counselor-client alliance.

Difficulty in establishing rapport with an alcoholic in a therapeutic situation is but another facet of the multisided difficulty experienced by the alcoholic in establishing any adult relationship. The alcohol abuser seeks the nurturance of a maternal relationship. Attempts to engage the caregiver in this type of interaction will typify most of the client's efforts to influence the therapeutic relationship.

The Need to Manipulate

It is not unusual in the experience of those counseling suicidal clients to hear from others (sometimes even those in the mental health professions) that suicide threats and behaviors should be ignored because they are "merely manipulations." Webster's *Third New International Dictionary* defines the term as "handling skillfully. . . ." How the word came to have a pejorative connotation is not certain. In a broad sense, however, all persons manipulate, if we are willing to consider manipulation as examining and utilizing the most likely means of getting what we want from our environment.

Between two persons, an interaction can be viewed as an ongoing attempt to define and redefine the nature of the relationship so that needs are met while the individual identity of the parties is maintained. This, in effect, is a form of manipulation and should not be considered pathologic. Such behavior becomes pathologic, just as does any other behavior, in relation to the extent and purpose to which it is employed. Within the context of suicide, the caregiver must bear in mind that manipulation may only be the last resort of the client in a series of efforts to affect the environment. It becomes necessary, then, for the caregiver to look beyond the simple fact of manipulation toward an understanding that the client is struggling to control the circumstances which affect his or her life. If the caregiver is able to view the latter's manipulations in this context, then anxiety and impatience with the client can be put aside. Sometimes such manipulation may be tolerated in order to set in motion a series of therapeutic interactions. By countenancing the client's manipulation the caregiver may be able to convey to the client the caregiver's realization that there are concerns prompting these client's attempts to control the relationship. By such means caregivers let it be known that they have sensed a covert message behind this type of behavior.

Unheeded, pathologic manipulative behavior may become dangerous. For example, when the caregiver is aware that a suicidal behavior is being employed by the client to bring about a desired response or to influence the response of significant others; it would be wise to let the client know at once that this kind of behavior is not necessary to elicit a concerned response. If manipulative behavior is not interrupted by such a clear message, the client may increase the frequency or lethality of such self-destructive behavior. For if the first communication of suicidal intent goes unrecognized, misinterpreted, or unheeded, the client may feel compelled to make a low-intensity suicide attempt to reinforce the communication that was apparently unclear. If the succeeding attempt is not heeded, it may then be necessary to increase the frequency or intensity of still more attempts. Unless the caregiver intervenes in this manipulatory spiral, the client may go on to complete the act.

The Inner versus the Outer World

Is suicidal behavior prompted by an internal or an external stimulus? The dialogue concerning etiology and motivation has been in progress for many years. Does causation make a difference in the treatment of a suicidal client? As yet we really don't know. One thing is certain—the caregiver must deal both with the feeling state of the client and with the client's way of being in the world. It does little good if the client has insights into his or her internal conflicts but is unable to apply them to interactions of daily living.

Conversely, dealing only with the interactional aspects of suicidal behavior may rob a client of the experience of examining the inner world. After all, everyone exists to some extent in both worlds. The whole person must come to grips both with unconscious conflicts on the one hand and the inescapable need to get along with people on the other. Optimally, we are integrated in both spheres so that we reflect how we experience ourselves by the way in which we relate to others. Depending on the client, the caregiver may wish to focus on either intrapsychic phenomena or interpersonal relationships, but effective therapy usually takes both into consideration.

The Caregiver's Task

The psychologic events mentioned throughout this chapter reflect states of being and relating to the world experienced by suicidal persons which are directed toward satisfying needs, alleviating pain, and, ultimately, changing the course of events. Some persons seem to be blessed, in that they live out their lives with a minimum of painful events and an abundance of rewarding experiences. Others, perhaps less endowed with emotional stability, or perhaps having suffered greater trauma and stress, seem unprepared to withstand unsettling occurrences. It is among the latter that we see a final relinquishment of freedom and responsibility. Whether precipitously or haltingly, these persons are propelled into physical illness, madness, or suicide. Yet, even those of us who have escaped a personal experience with desperation of this magnitude do not go unscathed for we belong to the family of man. Those of us in a position to heed the "cry for help" have both a responsibility and a unique opportunity to share with those in pain the potentially healing experience of the search for meaning, for beauty, and for love.

AREAS OF CONCERN OR CONFLICT
FOR THE CAREGIVER

Corrine Loing Hatton
Sharon McBride Valente
Alice Rink

Just as there are areas of concern or conflict experienced by suicidal persons, there are other areas of concern or conflict experienced by the caregiver. The caregiver, like the client, is a human being with a set of values, principles, and behaviors inherent or learned in coping with the surrounding world. Often the caregiver will attempt to repress these feelings and behaviors in an effort to maintain objectivity in approaching a client. Somehow, "being objective" has frequently been misinterpreted to mean the negation of feeling levels inside oneself. Rather than impair this state of feeling in the caregiver, we might attempt to identify and assess the concern or conflict that could arise in the therapeutic transaction and then deal with it as it appears and reappears.

Rather than become a passive recipient of the suicidal client's confidences, the caregiver becomes an active, sharing individual who, *possessing self-awareness,* can make a more accurate and caring assessment leading toward an appropriate intervention. Attempts should be made by the caregiver to foster the client's self-awareness as well, and to deal effectively with the feelings of concern or conflict that are experienced by the latter.

Nine Critical Areas for Every Caregiver

There are nine areas of concern or conflict that are of interest to caregivers in their work with potentially suicidal individuals. A seasoned caregiver has at some point looked at and dealt with problems in these areas, and feels quite comfortable in handling them. To the beginning caregiver, these areas are as meaningful to discuss and evaluate as are the techniques of assessment and intervention. It is important for all caregivers, whether seasoned or beginners, to bear in mind that these areas of concern or conflict need constant attention and evaluation. As caregivers, we grow, change, and shift with the ebb and flow of our internal processes, which should be attended to as diligently as we attend to the processes of the client.

The areas of concern or conflict presented here are not discussed in any hierarchical or chronologic order, nor are they mutually exclusive in the individual's processes.

Building Trust and Rapport.   One of the caregiver's first concerns in undertaking a therapeutic relationship with the client is whether the client is telling the truth and whether the client's story accurately reflects the realities. The caregiver should bear in mind that the client's story must be accepted as truthful and accurate in the absence of data to the contrary. Most people will tell you honestly whether or not they are suicidal. The caregiver should form a mental hypothesis and ask questions the answers to which will verify or rule out this hypothesis. For example, Mrs. X says, "If it weren't for my children, things would be different." You, as a caregiver, hypothesize that she means she'd kill herself if it weren't for her children. You then ask, "Are you saying that if it weren't for your children, you'd kill yourself?" She answers, "Yes."

The client will probably place as much trust in the caregiver as the latter places in the client. Generally, rapport and trust must be established quickly and often success is only a reflection of the comfort of the caregiver in this phase of the relationship.

Feelings of Professional Inadequacy.   The caregiver may feel insufficiently equipped intellectually to handle the problem—feel that he or she doesn't "know enough" about suicide, hasn't mastered the necessary skills to assess the situation correctly and intervene successfully. Certainly some theoretical background and knowledge about suicide and some repertoire of techniques and skills are essential to the caregiver in making a useful assessment and intervention. However, even the experts feel anxiety on occasion. Pleading lack of knowledge is an ineffectual maneuver in handling such anxiety, so often generated in the caregiver who attempts to help a suicidal client. The best maneuver in restoring self-confidence, if this is possible, may be to consult with another professional. Or it may be necessary to persist through the experience of anxiety while recognizing that the client is more anxious than you are.

Fear of Responsibility for Decisions. The vulnerability of the caregiver is brought to the surface by concerns like the responsibility for making some kind of decision in the assessment. What might be the consequences of that decision? Will it prove to be right or wrong? What happens if it turns out to be a mistake?

Feeling the weight of such responsibility can be so threatening to the caregiver that it impedes the process of care. Usually, experience over time and consultation with co-workers will alleviate these feelings of vulnerability. Sharing them with others is perhaps the surest way of gaining confidence in decision making.

Suicidal Feelings in the Caregiver. The caregiver may feel threatened by the suicidal client, whose plight evokes responsive doubts. "I've felt this miserable in the past," reflects the caregiver. "Was I suicidal? I feel terrible right now, myself. Will I become suicidal? Would I be able to cope with a similar situation?"

Even agreeing with the long-held theory that we all share suicidal feelings with other human beings, the caregiver can find them conflicting and threatening. Working closely with suicidal persons often reactivates old fears or activates repressed ones. It becomes essential to gain a clear and comfortable understanding of one's own feelings and seek professional counseling, if necessary, in order to do so.

Resentment of the Client. The caregiver may be very disturbed by personal feelings toward a certain client. "This client is making me mad. I can't handle all this misery and I'm bored listening to it. I ought to be ashamed of myself. . . I should be feeling differently."

For numerous reasons, the caregiver may become annoyed, appropriately or inappropriately, and bored or indifferent toward a client. Usually, merely acknowledging the existence of such feelings makes it possible to find out what causes them or at what points they are likely to surface. Learning to handle such feelings makes a useful addition to the skills of the caregiver in becoming a more efficient, more effective intervenor.

Subjective Comparisons.   The web of conflict in which the caregiver can become enoangled by making comparisons with the client can bog down the therapeutic regimen. "What kind of person would do that to a child (husband or friend)?" "If I had all that time (talent or money), I wouldn't want to kill myself." Or just "What a stupid way to handle such a situation. . . I wouldn't have done it that way!"

Making value judgments based on what the caregiver would do in a similar situation usually results in unwise, unclear assessments and interventions. Different people react to the world around them with different coping strategies. It is essential to understand the world from the client's frame of reference and not one's own, even though this can be exceedingly painful on occasion and at times frightening.

Listening Difficulties.   "How can I listen to this drivel when I have problems of my own? This person isn't worth listening to. I'm here to get a job done, not to listen to how awful somebody feels."

The ability to listen is the first skill needed in order to become any kind of caregiver. In intervention this is not just a matter of hearing, but rather of attending with all five senses to the client. Often significant statements, garbled messages, sounds or even smells are ignored by the caregiver because of lack of time, effort, or attention. A suicidal message may be sent out when and where it is least expected. Learning to listen empathetically and to focus on what is concerning the client can bring out something for a client that may be useful and meaningful to his progress.

Confidentiality and Protection. Legal concerns are often in conflict with the client's message, and the caregiver may well ask, "My client wants to tell me something in confidence, but if it should result in a death could I be held liable? What kind of protection do I have? Doesn't this client have a right to expect that what he (or she) is revealing to me will be held in confidence? And how about other people's rights, including mine?"

It is imperative to know the law, the agency, and the rights of the client in any given situation. All rights and protections applicable should be clearly understood by both the client and the caregiver. Fears of unwarranted and unnecessary disclosure can be allayed, but the web of secrecy must be cast aside, especially where it could provide cover for an actual suicide or homicide.

Sociocultural Stereotyping.   Sociocultural statistics and research results may unwittingly be used to reinforce stereotypes held by the

TABLE 2. Common Misconceptions about Suicide

False	True
1. People who talk about suicide rarely commit suicide.	1. People who commit suicide have given some clue or warning of intent. Suicide threats and attempts must be taken seriously.
2. The tendency toward suicide is inherited and passed on from one generation to another.	2. Suicide does not "run in families." It has no characteristic genetic quality.
3. The suicidal person wants to die and feels there is no turning back.	3. Suicidal persons most often reveal ambivalence about living versus dying and frequently call for help immediately following the suicide attempt.
4. Everyone who commits suicide is depressed.	4. Although depression is often associated with suicidal feelings, not all people who kill themselves are obviously depressed: Some are anxious, agitated, psychotic, organically impaired, or wish to escape their life situation.
5. There is very little correlation between alcoholism and suicide.	5. Alcoholism and suicide often go hand in hand; that is, a person who commits suicide is often also an alcoholic.
6. A person who commits suicide is mentally ill.	6. Although persons who commit suicide were often distraught, upset, or depressed, many of them would not have been medically diagnosed as mentally ill.
7. A suicide attempt means that the attempter will always entertain thoughts of suicide.	7. Often, a suicide attempt is made during a particularly stressful period. If the remainder of that period can be appropriately managed, then the attempter can go on with life.
8. If you ask a client directly "Do you feel like killing yourself?" this will lead him to make a suicide attempt.	8. Asking a client directly about suicidal intent will often minimize the anxiety surrounding the feeling and act as a deterrent to the suicidal behavior.
9. Suicide is more common among the lower socioeconomic groups than elsewhere in our society.	9. Suicide crosses all socioeconomic groups and no one group is more susceptible than another.
10. Suicidal persons rarely seek medical help.	10. In retrospective studies of committed suicide, more than half had sought medical help within the 6 months preceding the suicide.

These misconceptions are based in part on Shneidman ES, Farberow N: Some Facts About Suicide, PHS Publ No 852, Washington, DC: US Government Printing Office, 1961.

caregiver. For example, "The literature says young females rarely kill themselves. All women are alike. Therefore, this is a low-risk situation." Or, "Statistics show that young Blacks are a high suicidal risk. All Blacks are alike. Therefore, this is obviously a high-risk situation." Table 2 lists a number of common misconceptions about suicide which can also complicate the caregiver's task.

Although it may be useful to cite statistics, it can be dangerous to use them simplistically. Room must always be reserved for the client who does not at this time of crisis fit into the statistics. The bias based on color, creed, sex, or other sociocultural characteristic can block successful assessment and intervention. Probably no one client fits into the exact niche constructed by the statistics for a person of his or her sociocultural characteristics, and this is doubly true of clients suspected of suicidal behavior. Sociocultural studies and statistics should certainly not be ignored, but rather used as adjuncts in making a clear assessment of a particular situation and an individual.

REFERENCES

Aquilera DC, Messick JM: Crisis Intervention: Theory and Methodology. Missouri, Mosby, 1974

Beck AT: The core problem in depression: the cognitive triad. Science and Psychoanalysis 17:47, 1970

Bowlby J: Separation. New York, Basic Books, 1973

Freud S: Mourning and melancholia (1917). In Jones E (ed): The Collected Papers of Sigmund Freud. New York, Basic Books. 1959

Jacobson GF: Programs and techniques of crisis intervention. In Arieti S (ed): American Handbook of Psychiatry, 2nd ed, Vol 2, 1974, pp 810—25

Kovacs M, Beck A, Weissman MW: Hopelessness: an indicator of suicidal risk. Suicide 5:98, 1975

Lesse S (ed): Masked Depression. New York, Jason Aronson, 1974

Lewinsohn PM: A behavioral approach to depression. In Friedman RJ, Katz MM (eds): The Psychology of Depression: Contemporary Theory and Research. Washington, DC, Winston, 1974

Minkhoff K, Bergman E, Beck A, Beck R: Hopelessness, depression, and attempted suicide. Am J Psychiatry 130:455, 1973

Seligman MEP: Depression and learned helplessness. In Friedman RJ, Katz MM (eds): The Psychology of Depression: Contemporary Theory and Research. Washington, DC, Winston, 1974

Spitz RA: Anaclitic depression. Psychoanal Study Child 2:313, 1946

Watslawick P, Beavin JH, Jackson D: Pragmatics of Human Communication: A Study of Interactional Patterns, Pathologies, and Paradoxes. New York, Norton, 1967

Weissman M, Fox K, Kerman G: Hostility and depression associated with suicide attempts. Am J Psychiatry 130:450, 1973

CHAPTER 3
Assessment of Suicidal Risk

Corrine Loing Hatton
Sharon McBride Valente
Alice Rink

A thorough and accurate assessment of the problem forms the foundation of any caregiving relationship. Unfortunately, caregivers often skimp on the assessment process in their own need to "do something" for the client at once. Although proficiency in assessment techniques requires practice on the part of the caregiver, the basics, presented here in detail, can be studied. Case histories, also presented here, can help the caregiver integrate what has been learned into actual practice.

The identification of a suicidal risk is called assessment. By assessing critical elements in the suicidal person's communication with the caregiver, the latter can make a reasonable prediction of risk on a low to high continuum of suicide potential. The position of the risk on the continuum will then determine when and what kind of intervention is considered necessary.

Assessment of suicidal risk is generally of concern to the caregivers and clients (patients, callers, consultees) of suicide prevention centers, crisis centers, hot lines, hospital emergency rooms, and any private or public walk-in or referral service of a mental health center. Assessment techniques could also be considered useful on a hospital unit with reference to a patient who becomes suicidal in the course of treatment for another condition. They could also be useful to nonprofessionals in the ordinary course of daily living. In the context of

39

human relationships everywhere, some person or other may present a picture of behavior that could be viewed as suicidal.

RESEARCHING THE DATA BASE FOR ASSESSMENT

Determining the seriousness of the risk is one of the major objectives in suicide prevention and is also a major problem area fraught with conflict. The problem is perhaps best stated in the form of a question: Can scientific research and investigation be conducted to yield a data base for assessment that will make possible accurate and valid predictions of an individual's suicide potential?

Obviously, this question cannot be exhaustively and conclusively answered here. However, it seems useful to discuss some of the salient concerns of the caregiver about assessment if for no other reason than that caregivers must always be concerned with the unique, particular, individual case. At the same time, they should have some historical perspective indicating where the field of inquiry has come from, where it is, and where it is going. Perhaps, too, more caregivers may in this way become instrumental in further refinement of assessment techniques and procedures. Several questions, then, may be proposed for answer within the scope of this discussion* and in answer to the first question:

1. Can useful definitions of risk be formulated and valid prediction scales be devised?
2. Are demographic data and clinical characteristics valid components in the prediction of suicide risk? If so, what is the relative importance of each factor?
3. Is it possible to base a valid procedure for the assessment of risk on the demographic characteristics of a large population or should we be searching for specific signs and symptoms of the individual within a designated group and setting?
4. Are any of the prediction procedures in current use measurably preventing suicides in the United States?

Neuringer's book (1974) is based on his examination of the re-

---

*The authors owe much of the remainder of this discussion to Charles Neuringer's opening chapter, "Problems of Assessing Suicidal Risk," in *Psychological Assessment of Suicide Risk* (1974). Beck, Resnik, and Lettieri, *The Prediction of Suicide* (1974), and Brown and Sheran, "Suicide Prediction: A Review" in *Life Threatening Behavior* (1972), have also been invaluable in the development of the historical perspective, as well as the discussion of current issues. In fact, any student or caregiver who wishes to get further into this subject should consider these selections mandatory reading.

search that had already been done in assessing suicidal risk, and his attempt to evaluate this research for the methodology used and the results obtained:

> In this volume is to be found a history of attempts to validly predict self-incurred premature death. It is a story full of blind alleys, false starts, brilliant ideas, major and minor triumphs, and the dawning of a new way of thinking about suicide.

This author voices his belief that research should supply the data base for making an eventual decision in suicide assessment and that we should continue to pursue refinements and extensions to assessment procedures and techniques (Neuringer, 1974).

Extensive research studies have been undertaken in the construction of scales, models, and theoretical frameworks for assessment.* Important and relevant as these studies are, there remains the question whether they constitute sophisticated research. In any case, these same studies have prompted further efforts to arrive at clearer research design and methodology for future research. It is from this base of knowledge, unscientific though it may be, that the assessment process in current use originated.

An academic argument seems to be in progress as to which data base is the more valid, demographic data or clinical considerations. Some writers see inadequacies and weaknesses in the use of demographic data for prediction purposes (Diggory, in Beck et al, 1974). Others see value in using both kinds of data (Lester et al, in Beck et al, 1974; Tuckman and Youngman, 1968).

Another question which has attracted discussion in the field is whether any of these methods of prediction are measurably preventing suicide in the United States. Some theorists maintain that despite new preventive activity suicide is not being prevented, according to evidence presented by suicide rates (Maris, 1969). This is disheartening news to the caregivers who spend hours on hotlines or in mental health centers dealing with myriad numbers of people and suicidal problems. They feel that their work is justified by their own results and will cite from personal experience individual examples of persons saved from the threshold of suicide by having called a center or having been seen in a clinic.

One interesting study affords an explanation for this difference of opinion, "the findings of which suggest that the suicide prevention center attracts, as self-callers, a predominance of chronically psychiat-

*See Beck et al, 1974; Buglass and Horton, 1974; Griest et al, 1973; Morse, 1973; Brown and Sheran, 1972; and Tuckman and Youngman, 1968, to mention a few.

rically ill people, with a minority of the acutely ill (who seem to present more serious suicidal risk)" (Murphy et al, 1969). Numerous points could be made on both sides of this argument, but the need remains rather to gain some sensible data base for assessing suicidal risk.

A more useful position for caregivers would be similar to that taken by Litman et al:

> No one knows at present to what extent suicides are being prevented in the United States—mental health workers believe that their therapeutic endeavors are not wasted, but must recognize that they are only beginning to build the conceptual and methodological tools needed to establish which interventions are effective and which are not. [*Litman et al, in Beck et al, 1974*]

Despite the fact, then, that a data base for the assessment of suicidal risk has not been scientifically established, caregivers find themselves in a position where they need to assess suicidal risk, and they need the tools that so far have been of help to them.

DEMOGRAPHIC DATA

Demographic data (Table 3) are gathered in an effort to identify an individual by certain vital statistics and sociocultural characteristics and place all these facts in perspective with the clinical characteristics of that person. Taken alone, neither kind of data has significance in assessment of suicidal risk, but taken in combination, the information they provide may add greatly to the value of the assessment.

Identity of the Client

Some hotlines and other telephone crisis services do not attempt to obtain the name of the caller—some in fact specifically request that the caller remain anonymous. Similarly, the caller often wishes anonymity for one reason or another. If a client insists on remaining anonymous, his wish is respected. In the event of a high-lethality assessment, however, it may be useful or even necessary to obtain the client's name so that appropriate intervention procedures can be instituted without delay. Usually, following the establishment of trust, the client is willing to identify himself or herself, although if not, an expressed insistence on anonymity is still respected by the caregiver.

Where a client is seen in a clinic or other health facility, identifica-

TABLE 3. Components of the Assessment Process

I. DEMOGRAPHIC DATA

Name
Age
Sex
Race
Education
Religion
Living arrangements

II. CLINICAL CHARACTERISTICS

Hazard
Crisis
Coping strategies (devices)
Significant others
Resources (social, personal)
Past suicide attempts
Past psychiatric history
Current psychiatric or medical history
Life style
Plan
  Method
  Availability
  Specificity
  Lethality

III. HIGH-RISK FACTORS

Multiple high-lethality suicide attempts.
Alcohol abuse
Isolation and withdrawal
Disoriented and disorganized behavior
Hostility

IV. RISK-RATING CATEGORIES

Low, moderate, high
Emergency risk
Long-term risk

tion by name is not a matter for discussion, as there are almost invariably admission forms to be filled out, which eliminates this as a future problem.

Race, Sex, and Age

Those persons at greatest risk of suicide as measured by their age and sex are males over the age of 35. There are more accomplished suicides for men between 35 and 50 than in any other age bracket, although there is also a high incidence of suicide among men over 65, especially those who feel isolated, alienated, and/or deprived physically or mentally.

It is a fact that more women than men attempt suicide, but there are more accomplished suicides in the male population. In past years young girls between the ages of 17 and 20 were generally not considered at high risk, because there were few attempts or accomplished suicides. However, this is no longer true. Recent statistics indicate that girls in that age bracket are attempting suicide in greater numbers. Although not necessarily successful in their attempts, they are depressed, withdrawn, and confused.

There are ethnic variables in the suicide rate when it comes to race and suicide. The long-held erroneous sterotypes about race and the part it did or did not play in suicide risk have been shattered (fortunately) in recent years. Ethnic groups like Blacks, Asians, Mexican-Americans, and Indians have their own special problems and risks besides those that afflict the mass of the white population.

What is needed to make more accurate assessments is additional studies and the assembly of descriptive data on individuals from various ethnic groups. Only when all these ethnic groups have been covered will there be any comparative evidence to make valid conclusions possible. The caregiver should not ignore the racial background of an individual yet he must not stereotype the person by his race to the point of rendering him a nonperson. It poses a formidable task for the caregiver but an exceedingly necessary and humane one.

Education and Religion

There are no statistical or clinical data that identify religion or education as a major variable in the suicide potential of the individual. Attempted and/or accomplished suicides cross all religious denominations and educational levels. It is possible, of course, that more accurate pinpointing of the effects of these variables may produce other results. However at the present time there is little difference, if any, in suicide risk on the basis of educational level or religious preference.

Living Arrangements

The old category marital status is now "living arrangements," because the old phrase no longer accurately describes the current picture of society. The questions that need to be answered by the data gathered are:

Who is (are) the person(s) the client is living with in the same dwelling at the present time?
What is the quality and what is the quantity of their relationship(s)?
Is the client satisfied?
Are these arrangements economically, emotionally, and socially adequate for the client at the present time?

Obviously, the greater the satisfaction of the client, the lower the risk of suicide.

CLINICAL CHARACTERISTICS

The Hazard

When making the assessment, the caregiver must also make a careful attempt to ascertain what has happened in the client's world within the past 24 hours or perhaps as far back as the past two or three weeks. Usually, the hazard for which the client is seeking help has occurred some time within the past three weeks, and it is up to the caregiver to make a very careful attempt to pinpoint the event. Questions to be asked the client are:

Why did you come or call today?
What has happened recently in your life that is different?
When did it happen?

Look for any recent behavioral changes! The hazard could be a maturational or situational crisis, as noted previously in another context.
Any recent event which is perceived by the client as a threat or a potential threat to the self could be hazardous. Anniversary dates of the death of a significant other can be particularly stressful for some people. Another threat could be that of arrest and/or prosecution. The most frequent threat that proves clinically to be hazardous is the loss or potential loss of a significant relationship through death or other separation. Such an event can precipitate an exceedingly stressful period that is further aggravated if there are sequential losses leaving very little time for recovery in between. A job promotion is sometimes viewed as a catastrophic loss in that one is separating from a known

and moving to an unknown position where the stresses may be greater and support systems less available than before.

It is not only important and necessary to identify the recent event
precipitating a suicidal attempt but to ascertain the *meaning* of that
event to the individual. Events have various qualitative meanings to
various people. Going after a clear description of the event will enable
the caregiver to gain a picture of its meaning within the client's frame
of reference. What does it mean to a person who is now miserable and
suffering at this time? In fact, how realistic a perception does the
client have of the event? Does his perception seem accurate, distorted, or confused? Is he too upset just now to get a clear picture of
the situation? Is it seen by the client as something that will continue to
have negative impact in years to come? The answers to these questions will be useful when it comes to helping the client cope with the
situation.

The Crisis

The crisis, as noted before is what the suicidal person is experiencing internally. The caregiver must find out how serious the
crisis is—that is, how bad the feeling is inside. Are somatic or
psychologic symptoms mild, moderate, or severe? Are there eating,
sleeping, or work disturbances? Is the ability to maintain normal daily
activities unimpaired? How severe is the client's anxiety, agitation, or
panic? Is anxiety so great such that the client "has to take" several
drinks (or pills) during the day or before retirement at night? Getting
a clear idea of the *severity* of the symptoms is as important as identifying them. Obviously, we worry more about someone who is not
going to work, who is not eating well, who has lost weight, and who
is not able to carry on the daily routine than about one who has no
such altered living patterns.

The major clue to suicide potential is the severity of the client's
depression. Is the depression severe enough to kill the self or someone else? Is the accompanying sadness and anger directed at the self
or someone else? Can this sadness and rage be channeled appropriately in such a way that it is not destructive to self or others?

Generally, if a client is asked about his suicidal thoughts or behavior by the caretaker, the latter can accept the response given as
true unless or until valid data indicating otherwise become available.
When a client is suicidal, he usually reveals this (unless, of course, the
caregiver somehow communicates the message that such a response
would not be acceptable). Often a client will mention that he has been

thinking about suicide but wouldn't carry out his thoughts because of family, religion, or cowardice. Cowardice may or may not be a deterrent, depending on other aspects of the assessment.

Coping Strategies and Devices

How people customarily manage their world and their problems is usually instrumental in determining the way they are going to manage the current impasse. It is thus important to find out whether a suicidal client has suffered some kind of situational or maturational hazard in the past and in consequence gone into some kind of crisis. How did he cope with this crisis? How did he manage the situation? Have methods of coping formerly used been tried in the current situation? If so, and they have proved ineffective, why are they not working now?

What is the level of the client's impulse control? Among the foremost inappropriate coping strategies to verify or rule out is a client's habitual recourse to excessive drinking to solve emotional problems, a dependency on therapeutic drugs or misuse of drugs, or a past history of violent acting out against someone else or the self. Obviously, these are coping devices which can be exceedingly destructive, although their verification or exclusion will provide useful information to the caregiver when helping the client find new and appropriate coping strategies.

There are an enormous number and variety of coping strategies that people employ. These may include gainful employment, care of children and family, talking with friends, sports activities, hobbies, and the quietude of reading or listening to music.

The caregiver should also find out what the client feels would reduce his or her feelings of stress. In the client's personal opinion, what could be done to relieve the situation? In this way the caregiver involves the client by asking him or her to do some problem solving and then the caregiver assists in this endeavor.

Significant Others

As defined earlier, significant others are people in a person's world necessary for that person's psychic functioning. The caregiver should identify those whom the client normally relies on when in distress. In this situation, the significant other need not be someone who lives with the client. It could be a neighbor, friend, teacher, minister, relative, or colleague. It may be necessary for the caregiver to be the one who contacts the significant other or to recommend that the client rely on this person during a stressful period.

It is also useful for the caretaker to find out what the client believes would be the reaction of significant others to the current situation. And to ascertain whether or not the client's perception is valid and real. Finally, it may be necessary to obtain information about the client from the significant others so that the assessment can proceed.

Social and Personal Resources

A person's resources are those social and personal factors available to him or her that facilitate functioning in the environment. Social factors are (1) basic necessities for daily living—housing, food, and clothing; (2) transportation or other necessary conveyances; and (3) health care facilities. Personal factors are (1) money, (2) time, (3) physical and mental abilities, (4) job and/or hobbies, (5) significant others.

The more resources available to a client, the more likely that the crisis can be coped with. This will in turn lower the suicide risk. It is therefore necessary for the caregiver to assess all the resources available and even to assist the client to regain access to some assets which seem to have been exhausted.

Past Suicide Attempts

It is the general belief, based on clinical data, that a suicide attempt in the past increases the current risk of suicide. Whether this is so, however, would depend on the seriousness of the prior attempt, the mode used, and the availability of meaningful help to the client following the prior attempt. If the client has used suicidal gestures or attempts in the past to cope with stress, this would increase his current risk potential. Naturally, the more frequent his past suicide attempts, the higher the current risk.

History of Psychiatric Problems

One of the possibilities significant to the assessment is whether the client has been previously hospitalized for any kind of psychiatric problem (including a suicide attempt) and if so what was the *meaning* of that hospitalization. At one time, anyone with a history of psychiatric hospitalization for a suicide attempt or in fact any emotional problem would automatically be assessed as a higher suicidal risk at a subsequent period of stress than one with no such history. However, recent research and clinical experience have shown that this is not necessarily true. It is of greater diagnostic significance to check out the *meaning* of prior hospitalizations or treatments to that individual's mental health. If it turns out that help was given to solve problems and that subsequently the client felt relief, then the likelihood is that this person could again use hospitalization or treatment as a coping device. Viewed in this light, a history of hospitalization or treatment successfully utilized as a coping device decreases the current suicide risk.

Another experience of the client which the caregiver should confirm or exclude is that of past psychiatric intervention in his behalf or any kind of previous contact or counseling with a helping agency. When the client replies, "Yes, I've made three previous suicide attempts and each time the help I got wasn't any good and I thought it was all worthless," then the likelihood is that encouraging the client to seek the same kind of help will not be very beneficial in the current situation. On the contrary, such a suggestion may increase the client's annoyance or feelings of despair and in this way increase the risk of suicide. In a situation of this kind, perhaps the caregiver and the client can arrive together at some other kind of acceptable intervention.

Of course, some people may be quite unstable, with chronic, long-standing problems but without a history of psychiatric care. For one reason or another, such a client may not have been referred for help, may not have asked for help, or may have been referred for help but refused the referral. Therefore, the absence of psychiatric care from a client's history does not necessarily indicate stability.

Current Psychiatric or Medical Status

Whether the client is or is not currently receiving some form of counseling, psychiatric treatment, or hospitalization will probably affect the level of risk. For example, a client may be in therapy with a counselor but feels annoyed or in some way threatened and is looking to another caregiver for surcease or reduction of stress. Even though extremely agitated, such a client may be calmed by an empathetic response from the caregiver that feeling this way is acceptable. And equally likely, the client may only need the assurance that a call to his or her therapist would be acceptable to the therapist and helpful to the client.

There are times when a person can become more depressed and even suicidal in the context of ongoing therapy. Such a client may not feel comfortable about calling the regular therapist at 3 o'clock in the morning and therefore may resort to a hotline service in an effort to relieve mounting anxiety. It is thus critical for the caregiver to ascertain whether the client is currently undergoing some form of counseling. If the client is in ongoing counseling, the client is usually referred back to that therapist after suicidal risk is assessed.

Does the client have an acute or chronic physical illness? Is there a lengthy medical history for a physiologic problem? If so, how is this affecting the client's life? How has the client coped with it in the past and what if anything is impeding the coping process now? The answers to all these questions have a strong bearing on the caregiver's assessment of risk. Obviously, a physical illness may reduce one's ability to cope with additional stress or it may actually be the precipitating factor in the current crisis. For example, a person may be living with problems and stresses that are manageable, but the addition of a physical illness to this load may push the level of stress beyond the capacity to cope.

Has the client consulted a physician for any reason at all in the past six months? There are clinical and statistical data which indicate that a majority of committed suicides have consulted a physician within six months of the act. Some people will present themselves to a physician for any number of somatic complaints, from sleeplessness to backache. They may ask explicitly for medication for "nervousness" but could in reality be asking for emotional help or hoping to clear up or alleviate an underlying depression in this way. Often the physician has not the time, the desire, or the knowledge to assess the stress factor that is engendering suicidal feelings that call for referral to another caregiver. The authors consider that this is one of the great statistical tragedies, that so many people have "cried out" for help in one way or another and have received so little help in response to their cries. These cries may be muffled, distorted or confused, yet it is the responsibility of all medical professionals to recognize the cry for help and either attend to it or see that someone else does.

Life Style

A person's life style may be defined as the quality and maintenance over a period of time of that person's job, interpersonal relationships, and coping strategies. If a person feels fulfilled and satisfied in the job, has established and is maintaining interpersonal relationships that are emotionally, sexually, and intellectually satisfying, and manages personal conflicts and problems in a fairly constructive way, one could say that this person has a stable life style. On the other hand, if a person has had a number or variety of ungratifying jobs, has poor personal and interpersonal rapport, has no close friends or relatives or breaks off relationships frequently, copes with problems and conflicts in destructive ways like drinking or using drugs to excess, making suicide attempts or becoming physically or verbally abusive to self or others, one could say that this person has an unstable life style.

For example, Mr. A, age 48, has a sporadic work record, has made multiple geographic moves, has had three divorces, is estranged from his three children, has few friends, has made two suicide attempts, and drinks to excess. One could reasonably say that he has an unstable life style. But if Mr. A has a relatively stable and satisfying work record and, although divorced, has gratifying relationship with a woman he has been living with for several years, keeps in close contact with two of his three children, has several friends and associates, enjoys a hobby, and has employed constructive means in handling his problems, one could say that he has a stable life style.

Caution is always called for when evaluating the life style of another person. People can be relatively stable in one or two aspects of living and at the same time unstable in other aspects. This does not necessarily constitute an unstable life style. One has to assess the "gestalt" or totality of activities and functions that make up a person's life. There are also people who function fairly well for comparatively long periods of time, who under certain kinds of stress may break down. However, with some help such persons can regain stability and maintain it until the next stress period. In other words, some people who are vulnerable during stressful periods do not have an unstable life style.

A person's life style has been one of the most recent illuminating assessment characteristics to receive attention in suicidology during the past five or six years. Currently it is thought that an individual in a state of crisis who is having difficulty in coping will come out functioning well following this crisis if his general life style is stable. However, someone who has demonstrated a chronically unstable life style may not be able to handle even minor crises, and this places such persons in a vulnerable position for coping with more stressful situations.

The Suicidal Plan

The suicidal plan can be defined as those suicidal ideations or conceptualizations of suicide and the ways and means of suicide that can lead a person to the final act of taking his or her life. This plan can be vague or clear, general or specific, and reflect on a practical level the intensity of the client's distress. To make an accurate assessment of the significance of the suicidal plan, the caregiver must be specific, succinct, and clear in questioning the client and must not become frightened at the content of the plan. There are four criteria to measure in assessing the seriousness of a suicidal plan: method, availability, specificity, and lethality.

Method.   Has the client specified a method of choice (pills, slashing the wrists, shooting, hanging, other)?

Availability.   Is the method of choice available to the attempter? Is access to the method easy or difficult? If the method is not readily available, could access be obtained within a brief period of time? When a client says, "I'd jump off a bridge or a tall building," but the tallest building in town is only two stories and there are no bridges in town or leading into town, the method is not available unless the client leaves town and has the wherewithal to get to a suitable building or bridge.

Specificity.   How specific is the suicidal plan? If the method is concrete and detailed, with access to it right at hand, the suicide risk obviously increases. But if the method is unclear or only fleetingly considered, with no reference to practical details or access, this would decrease the likelihood of suicide for the time being. In illustration, Mrs. W may say, "I'll wait until my husband goes to sleep tonight around 11:00 P.M.—then I'll go into the garage, get into the car, turn on the motor, and kill myself with carbon monoxide poison." In this statement of the plan, the method, the availability, the time and the place are all specified, and the more specific the plan, the higher the risk; the less specific the plan, the lower the risk.

Lethality.   How lethal is the method? The most lethal method of suicide in our culture is shooting. The second most lethal method is hanging. Probably the least lethal is slashing one's wrists. When the person has a detailed plan of suicide involving the use of a gun, the current risk is high in the assessment. If the specific plan involves an overdose of aspirin or slashing one's wrists, the attempt will probably not succeed, but will likely produce illness. Although many drugs are lethal, their use as the method often allows time for rescue before the dosage has been completely absorbed, as opposed to a gunshot wound or hanging, which takes effect almost immediately.

One assessment is not enough. It is exceedingly important to assess and reassess as needed all four criteria of the suicidal plan. In this way the caregiver can determine what kind of intervention may be called for. This will in turn determine whether the client needs support today or tomorrow. In turn, these will determine whether or not emergency measures must be taken at once, and the answers to these questions will determine whether additional help must be secured immediately.

It does not matter where the caregiver interviews the client—in a clinic, a general hospital, an emergency room, at a distance through a telephone answering service, or even indirectly by talking to a friend or neighbor. The caregiver must get a clear picture of the suicidal plan before an accurate assessment will be possible.

Actually, most will tell you what their suicide plan is. As has been mentioned, the client shows great ambivalence between wanting to live and wanting to die but usually will tell you the plan. *Of course, the very fact that the client has contacted you is an indication that some part of him or her wants to be helped.* Under normal conditions, a caregiver should be able to obtain from a client the full details of the plan once rapport is established.

HIGH-RISK FACTORS

Some clinical characteristics or behaviors place an individual in a category of higher risk than those already discussed in this presentation. Some of these high-risk factors are discussed elsewhere in text. However, in these writers' opinion, these factors should all be grouped under a special category of high risk for special consideration. It is probably safe to say that if a psychological autopsy were performed on every suicide committed, one of these five factors would be identified as predominating and relevant to the situation. Individuals demonstrating any one of these factors as a prominent presenting symptom will have greater difficulty in coping with their problems and their environment than others not so handicapped. These high-risk factors could be viewed as the very means by which some persons cope with their world, albeit destructive and certainly not conducive to the solution of life problems, the resolution of conflict, or the weathering of a suicidal crisis.

Multiple High-Lethality Suicide Attempts

If a person who is being interviewed gives a history of multiple high-lethality suicide attempts of the method chosen—by shooting, hanging, potent drug overdose or poisoning, or involvement in numerous reckless driving charges and many automobile accidents, with sustained injuries—you would rate this person as a higher risk than the usual client. The probability is that one of these attempts will be successful. Furthermore, no matter what the current hazard and crisis, no matter what the current coping devices employed, and no matter what the sex and current age of the caller, these multiple, high-lethality suicide attempts must place the attempter in the highest category of risk.

Alcohol Abuse

Alcohol abuse is defined as the consumption of alcohol such that it is destructive to the drinker's physical and psychic functioning. The research data collected at the LASPC indicate that the committed suicide is rare in which alcohol abuse was *not* a symptom. Alcoholism figures prominently in the behaviors of the chronically suicidal person, as discussed in Chapter 7.

Isolation/Withdrawal

Some people are painfully alone and isolated. Whether by design or accident (usually by design), there are some people who have no family, no friends or associates, and have withdrawn from social situations. They tell us they are "terribly, terribly alone" and see no point in going on with the business of living. Some of these individuals may have alienated their last support system. Or perhaps they feel that no one cares because they have been alienated by others for one reason or another. In any case, the isolation of such a client is total, making itself felt as a pervasive, gnawing presence. Knowing this, the caretaker must adjust the risk of suicide upward, because there is *no one* and nothing to which the client can turn for surcease or help. Of course, many such persons seem to create their own aloneness—that is, they are in contact with others and may even live in the same household with friends or relatives, yet still feel isolated and detached.

Disorientation/Disorganization

There is the suicidal individual who at the time of crisis is not viewing the world in a realistic, clearly perceived way. The thought processes seem to be disorganized, fragmented, or distorted, with little orientation to reality. You as the caregiver may be making this determination or be receiving this information from family members or friends so that you will be in a position to make some kind of assessment. This pattern of disorientation and disorganization may have been caused by psychologic stress, physical illness, alcohol abuse, drug reaction, or mental disturbance. When a person is expressing suicidal thoughts or making suicidal threats or attempts and is in a conspicuously confused state of mind, there is always a heightened concern that suicide is imminent. When a person is in a state of mind to reason effectively or to control his behavior, the risk of his suicide is greater than that of someone who is still able to view the situation from a realistic vantage point.

Hostility

In most instances where a client may be displaying rampant hostility toward the self or others, this hostility is usually of a long-standing nature and, like a festering wound, only keeps getting more painful. This raging hostility may not look realistic or useful to the caregiver; however, to the client it may seem completely realistic while serving a functional or psychic need. The danger here is that this hostility, due to its severity, may erupt or be provoked into action by an otherwise benign incident. Regardless of its origin or its function, however, this rampant hostility must be considered as more dangerous than not, and may actually make it impossible for the caregiver to help the client.

RISK-RATING CATEGORIES

The rating categories for suicide risk are low, moderate, and high, which may be marked off on a hypothetical scale from 1 to 9. Thus, a low category of risk would be at 1 to 3 on the scale; moderate, 4 to 6; high, 7 to 9. The question is, what data are needed and what characteristics or behaviors would one identify for a client upon which to base an assessment of the risk potential? Table 4 itemizes the characteristics and behaviors of a suicidal client which, evaluated for intensity as low, moderate, or high, can help the caregiver make a determination of risk. These parameters are based on findings and conclusions from theoretical research and clinical work. They are not mutually exclusive, nor are they hierarchical in sequence. *And all need not necessarily be present in the rating of any one individual.*

TABLE 4. Assessing the Degree of Suicidal Risk

BEHAVIOR OR SYMPTOM	INTENSITY OF RISK		
	Low	Moderate	High
Anxiety	Mild	Moderate	High, or panic state
Depression	Mild	Moderate	Severe
Isolation/ withdrawal	Vague feelings of depression, no withdrawal	Some feelings of helplessness, hopelessness and withdrawal	Hopeless, helpless, withdrawn, and self-deprecating
Daily functioning	Fairly good in most activities	Moderately good in some activities	Not good in any activities
Resources	Several	Some	Few or none
Coping strategies / devices being utilized	Generally constructive	Some that are constructive	Predominantly destructive
Significant others	Several who are available	Few or only one available	Only one, or none available
Psychiatric help in past	None, or positive attitude toward	Yes, and moderately satisfied with	Negative view of help received
Life style	Stable	Moderately stable or unstable	Unstable
Alcohol/drug use	Infrequently to excess	Frequently to excess	Continual abuse
Previous suicide attempts	None, or of low lethality	None to one or more of moderate lethality	None to multiple attempts of high lethality
Disorientation/ disorganization	None	Some	Marked
Hostility	Little or none	Some	Marked
Suicidal plan	Vague, fleeting thoughts but no plan	Frequent thoughts, occasional ideas about a plan	Frequent or constant thought with a specific plan

There are times when the caregiver may have an "intuitive feeling" about a client being rated and estimate the risk as higher than the observed characteristics and behaviors warrant. This is not to be dismissed lightly as a subjective error, since the caregiver may be attending to certain nonverbal cues or some feeling tone which suggests that the cry for help has been muffled by some interference as yet unidentified, which is actually stifling a piercing scream. Generally, such intuitive feelings later turn out to have accurately appraised the risk. People who are in pain, agony, and confusion may not come across as either structured or clear while narrating their story. Thus it becomes all the more important for the caregiver to acquire basic knowledge about how to communicate in a therapeutic way and develop interviewing skills. People are often fearful of seeking help, or they feel threatened or consider themselves failures and are reluctant to reveal their real concerns. It is therefore imperative for the interviewer to be responsive not only to the content of what is being said but also to the process of how it is being said. The person seeking help may be attempting to send a message that must get through the noise and distractions of the visual and verbal world. It is difficult to say, "I feel hated, unloved, a failure," as the client sits before the caregiver who perhaps looks smartly dressed, composed, and seemingly in control of the situation.

Emergency versus Long-term Risk Rating

Another major matter to be determined besides the emergency risk rating is the long-term risk rating. It is only in recent years, based on data from recent research, that the necessity for rating these two discrete risks has become clear. It is of value to know the difference between these two ratings and the determining factors for discriminating between them. Briefly, an emergency risk rating may be defined as the potential of the person for killing himself or herself within the next 24 hours; the long-term risk rating may be defined as the likelihood that a person will kill himself or herself within the next two years.

How does one arrive at such determinations? Generally speaking, the three most significant assessment factors that identify for the caregiver the difference between these two ratings are (1) the coping strategies, (2) the life style, and (3) the suicidal feelings of the client. Although all assessment factors are important, these three are the most significant. The examples which follow illustrate how these critical factors determine the ratings:

Case 1: Mr. Smith

Mr. Smith is a 45-year-old Caucasian whose wife of 20 years recently told him she wanted a separation, with an eventual divorce.

This came as a tremendous shock to Mr. Smith, even though he realized that the past two or three years had not been particularly satisfying for either of them. But for Mrs. Smith to take such a sudden stand seemed particularly cruel to him. He believes that it is the recent women's liberation movement that prompted his wife to make such a dramatic move. This marriage had been generally quite satisfying. The three children have now grown up and only one remains in the home. Mrs. Smith, also age 45, has not been employed outside the home since the children were born but before that had been a secretary. She is now telling Mr. Smith that he is not meeting her sexual and social needs and she wants to give up some of her mothering and wifely chores and go back to work.

Mr. Smith is exceedingly upset and depressed about this situation. He has not been functioning well at his job, is having trouble sleeping, and is spending some time at the local bar, where he is drinking in excess of his normal consumption. He feels very suicidal at this time—he wants to take a gun and go out in a field and shoot himself. Guns are available, as hunting and sharpshooting are two of his hobbies. Some specific suicide plan is forming in his mind, and such ideas pervade his thinking every day.

Mr. Smith is also very angry. He feels his wife has let him down, as they had been talking about their life together "after the children move away." She had been as eager as he to spend more time at their hobbies of bridge, boating, and fishing. He is angry at her for disrupting these plans. He is also angry at himself for being a failure in his wife's eyes, and finding himself in such a position at his age. He cannot imagine himself living like a bachelor again, trying to meet and date other women, or living without the social and emotional support of his wife. He is anxious and depressed, cries frequently, and definitely wants to kill himself.

In further questioning Mr. Smith, it develops that he has made no previous suicide attempts and has no psychiatric history. He has had a stable job as an engineer in the same company for the past 15 years, has good relationships with his children, and has numerous friends and hobbies. From all these, he gains a great deal of emotional and intellectual gratification. Both parents died within the past 5 to 10 years, and although he was sad about losing each one, he managed to cope with these losses quite well. Mr. Smith has never previously lost a long-term relationship with a woman and had not dated many women prior to marriage. He has never been an alcohol abuser nor has he ever used drugs. Generally, as far as can be ascertained Mr. Smith has functioned quite well in his life and has worked out a fairly stable life style. However, at this time he feels very suicidal and angry, at a total loss, and can't bear to think of the future.

You perhaps would rate this man on an emergency risk scale as high. He feels suicidal and a highly lethal method is available to him. However, as a long-term risk you may rate him low because of his stable life style and the coping strategies available to him. He has hobbies to occupy his time, friends and family for emotional support, and the demonstrated ability to invest self in other people.

The likelihood is that this man, if he receives some help within the next 24 hours, will be able to reconstitute himself. If he gets this emergency help, he should be able to manage his life quite well based on his survival of previous experiences of loss. However, if he is not given effective emergency help and his situation continues to deteriorate, the likelihood of his killing himself in the long run increases.

Case 2: Mr. Jones

Let's take the reverse situation of Mr. Jones. Mr. Jones is also 45 years old and is currently experiencing a breakup of his marriage of 10 years. This is Mr. Jones' third marriage, the previous two having ended in divorce. In each case, the woman told him he was not satisfying her. His relationship with his children, all three from his two previous marriages, is not close, and although a son lives in the area, Mr. Jones rarely sees him.

Mr. Jone's job is currently in jeopardy. As an engineer he has been laid off frequently and he is again threatened with the loss of his job, which makes him feel nervous and unhappy. At the age of 45 he fears he may not readily find another position.

The Jones marriage has always been strained and marked by recurring arguments. Mrs. Jones resents the fact that Mr. Jones stops regularly at a bar after work and quite frequently drinks to excess. They have few friends and hobbies and mostly watch television or read for entertainment. On the other hand, Mr. Jones is angry at his wife for letting him down. He feels he's made the major effort "to make this marriage work."

Nevertheless, Mr. Jones chastises himself a great deal, is self-effacing and self-deprecating. He believes he has made a mess of his life in general. He seems to be negative about himself, his life, and those around him. Following the breakups of his previous marriages, he made suicide attempts, using pills, and in each case was treated for the overdose, although he did not receive any therapeutic intervention.

Currently Mr. Jones is angry and moderately upset. He feels "let down" and has vague feelings that he is "going nowhere." The mere thought of trying to invest himself in another relationship leaves him exhausted. He has infrequent, fleeting thoughts of suicide using a gun, but does not own one and has never used a gun except during military service. He doesn't feel suicidal at this time.

With this kind of information, you would probably rate Mr. Jones as a low emergency risk. Although he does have fleeting thoughts of suicide, he does not feel suicidal for any length of time and has no means readily available and no real plan. However, because of his relatively unstable life style with its superficial relationships and frequent job layoffs, taken together with his suicide attempt following both previous marital losses and his few constructive coping strategies, you would probably rate Mr. Jones higher on a long-term scale of risk than on the emergency scale. The likelihood is that with the breakup of another relationship and the possible loss of his job straining his few resources and worsening his chronic feelings of failure, Mr. Jones might very likely kill himself some time within the next two years.

Although at the present time the concern for Mr. Jones's life is not acute, the necessity of helping him find other support systems *is* acute. For if some regimen of continuing care is not instituted fairly soon, or if he is not willing to become involved in one, the likelihood is great that he will commit suicide some time within the next two years.

Emergency and long-term risks don't always differ markedly of course. The emergency risk rating *and* the long-term risk rating might be of the same intensity—they might both be moderate, both high, or both low. The chief factors determining category of risk are life style, previous and current coping strategies, and suicidal thoughts (intent and specificity of plan).

The chief value of making these two kinds of risks rating is that it clarifies the type of intervention called for. Even though a client may not be an emergency risk, we as caregivers are concerned with hearing and attending to the cry for help. At the least, we will be in a position to identify for the client what may become the problems and concerns in the future.

For a variety of reasons, it is easier to institute emergency care for a suicidal client than it is to initiate a regimen of continuing care.

Often facilities are not available for long-term ongoing treatment, or we as professionals have not been successful in convincing such clients of their need for help, nor are they ready and willingly to make that kind of commitment.

REFERENCES

Beck AT, Resnik HLP, Lettieri DJ (eds): The Prediction of Suicide. Bowie, Md, Charles Press, 1974

Brown T, Sheran TJ: Suicide prediction: a review. Life Threat Behav 2:67, 1972

Buglass D, Horton J: A scale for predicting subsequent suicidal behavior. Brit J Psychiatry 124:573, June 1974

Diggory JC: Predicting suicide: will-o-the-wisp or reasonable challenge? In Beck AT, Resnik HLP, Lettieri DJ (eds): The Prediction of Suicide. Bowie, Md, Charles Press, 1974, pp 59–70

Griest JH, Gustafson DH, Strauss FF, et al: A computer interview for suicide-risk prediction. Am J Psychiatry, 1973, p 1327

Lester D: Demographic versus clinical prediction of suicidal behaviors: a look at some issues. In Beck AT, Resnik HLP, Lettieri DJ (eds): The Prediction of Suicide. Bowie, Md, Charles Press, 1974, pp 71–84

Litman RE, Farberow NL, Wold CI, Brown TI: Prediction models of suicidal behavior. In Beck AT, Resnik HLP, Lettieri DJ (eds):The Prediction of Suicide. Bowie, Md, Charles Press, 1974, pp 141–59

Maris RE: Social Forces in Urban Suicide. Homewood, Ill, Dorsey Press, 1969

Morse S: The after-pleasure of suicide. Brit J Med Psychol 46:227, 1973

Murphy GE: The clinical identification of suicidal risk. In Beck AT, Resnik HLP, Lettieri DJ (eds): The Prediction of Suicide. Bowie, Md, Charles Press, 1974, pp 109–18

Murphy GE, Wetzel RD, Swallow CS, McClure JN: Who calls the suicide prevention center: a study of 55 persons calling on their own behalf. Am J Psychiatry 126:314, September 1976

Neuringer C (ed): Psychological Assessment of Suicidal Risk. Springfield, Ill, Thomas, 1974

Rosen A: Detection of suicidal patients: an example of some limitations in the prediction of infrequent events. J Consult Psychol 18:397, 1954

Tuckman J, Youngman WF: A scale for assessing suicide risk or attempted suicides. J Clin Psychol 24:17, 1968

CHAPTER 4
Intervention

Corrine Loing Hatton
Sharon McBride Valente
Alice Rink

The difficulty of education is to put theory into practice.

SCOPE OF THE PROCESS

After the initial assessment which gives everyone a clear perspective of both the situation and the alternatives possible, the client may respond more or less as follows: "You are all the same—all talk and no go. I came here because I wanted you to make me feel better. All I ever get is talk, talk, talk. . . . When are you going to do something to make me feel better? I am going to leave here after all this talk, and I feel just as scared—I feel just as bad. . . I want to die. . . I'm going home to those pills. What are you doing to make me happy?"

Occasionally the assessment process itself has provided enough relief and perspective for the client to plot a course actively away from suicide. Ordinarily, however, the beginning caregiver struggles with the following questions.

When is intervention indicated?

Intervention is indicated immediately upon the first suspicion of suicidal ideation or upon discovery of any suicidal clue. The clue itself may seem no more than a vague and elusive message. Caregivers must try to overcome barriers of culture and custom, which can interfere with the proper response to these indirect messages because of the caretaker's need to respect the client's privacy or protect the latter from embarrassment.

Where does intervention begin and end?

Following assessment, intervention begins in the most private location immediately available, where client, family, and caregiver can meet. Sometimes the telephone or the client's home is as practical a milieu for communication as the caregiver's office. If the client's lethality of intent is low, immediate intervention may only consist of scheduling another appointment and obtaining the client's verbal contract to avoid suicidal actions or situations until the appointment.

Crisis intervention continues until the suicidal crisis is resolved. If the client is to be referred for further therapy because the suicidal crisis has been resolved without resolution of deeper underlying problems, intervention continues until the client's referral has been completed.

Who intervenes?

It is essential that the person who perceives a suicidal clue in the interview or suspects suicidal intent respond to the client with concern. If the client is suicidal, then the listener needs to connect the client with help or elect to become the primary caregiver. It is important that caregivers see themselves as part of a network of community services available to the client. Since it is often the case that the client needs services not provided by the caregiver, it will be useful to explore the resources the caregiver can call upon from such agencies as community mental health centers, hotlines, emergency rooms, and psychiatric hospitals.

How does one intervene?

The caregiver must have a command of the concepts and techniques of assessment and a heightened awareness of self. Techniques for intervention may be considered under four major caregiver tasks:

1. Establishing a relationship with the client that will meet the client's implicit need for a helping relationship. In this transaction the caregiver will focus on building trust and will expand the caregiver-client frame of reference (Fig. 1)
2. Deciding what kind of interview is indicated

3. Employing techniques of intervention based on lethality
4. Implementing a plan of action for the client

Establishing a Relationship

The "how" of suicide prevention begins in the first contact with the client. The implicit request, "Care about me," is accompanied by the explicit request, "Help me." The client's request for help is accompanied by an implicit need for a relationship.

Case 3: Peggy

Peggy is a 19-year-old who hesitates to talk during the initial interview. She says a friend sent her and adds, "I hope you can help me." She gazes off, pauses often, sighs, and looks about to cry. She huddles in a corner of her chair and rubs the arm of the chair with her fingers. At first she says she is unable to describe how she is feeling right now:

Caregiver: I'd like you to tell me how you felt before you were feeling so miserable.
Peggy: I started college—it was so frightening—such a big place . . . [*Silence*]
Caregiver: You felt lost and scared because it was new and overwhelming and different.
Peggy: It was terrifying. I knew I could never be the super student my parents wanted, even though I was an honor student in high school. It was never enough just to be good. I don't want to be the doctor that they—that my father said I should . . . awful, so terribly bad . . . [*She points to scars on her wrists and screams.*] Please God Help Me!!! I'm scared—I'm going to kill myself. . . I've got to kill myself, I don't deserve to live! Can you help me? Can anybody really help me?

Questions for the caregiver arise at this point:

1. What does the client want and need from you?
2. What can you give this client—what can you do for this client?
3. What kind of interview is needed?
4. What intervention is indicated?

The first two questions can be dealt with as the caregiver establishes the relationship with the client. Despite the multitude of variables and individual differences a single individual may present, establishing the relationship is a necessary and powerful beginning. It is what the client wants but cannot always ask for, and it is the first and most important act of the caregiver. Eliminating this essential step will cause frustration to the caregiver and will reaffirm the client's fears of personal worthlessness and helplessness. The caregiver who wishes to support the client's feelings of self-worth begins with the process of building trust.

The Building of Trust

Establishing trust is not an easily quantified process. It begins with the first contact and becomes an ongoing process for the duration of the relationship. The caregiver begins by being there consistently and being warm, empathetic, and accepting (Carkhuff 1973). In each interaction, the caregiver listens attentively to the client's words, pauses, intonation, and meaning. Everyone's body posture and nonverbal behaviors communicate a message; the caregiver's message to the client should be, "I am listening to you—you are important to me, I want to know you." Each time the caregiver is predictable, honest, and dependable, the cumulative message to the client is, "I am trustworthy."

In the building of trust, everyday events are important. The caregiver must be prompt for appointments and prevent interruptions during telephone or office sessions. It is absolutely essential to do things on time, as promised. It is inadvisable to promise something the caregiver cannot deliver (eg, "I will have Doctor Fredericks call you in the next hour"), if you do not have the power to control Doctor Fredericks' return call, you may be chagrined to find that today is his day off). Of course, caregivers *don't have to be perfect,* but they do need to be aware that small details have an impact on trustbuilding.

Caregivers need to show acceptance of the client and their belief in the client. Interpreting to one's clients how they *really* feel or *should* feel, act, think, or behave is not therapeutic.

Caregivers need to communicate to the client their belief that the client acts in response to needs, although there are probably better ways of satisfying these needs. One begins by trusting the client to provide reliable content (what is said) and messages (how it is said and what it means). When a discrepancy between the message and the content arises, validation or confrontation is indicated. It does not build trust to announce judgmentally that a client has lied or manipulated the facts, nor is it reasonable to avoid confrontation when the issue is pertinent. It may be effective to point out that the words and meaning of the client's statements seem confusing or contradictory.

Trustbuilding progresses when the caregiver encourages the client to ventilate anger and other charged feelings and then acknowledges the client's feeling of being overwhelmed, hopeless, or afraid. At the same time, the caregiver gives assurance that things can get better—help is available or on the way and the crisis is time-limited. The client needs assurance that it was wise to reach out for help. It is important to emphasize that the caregiver will be an active, directive, and concerned helper. It is also important to remember that accepting and trusting a client does not imply a laissez-faire attitude. One does not passively allow clients to do as they please—ie, cancel appointments, arrive late, indulge in abusive language, make excessive phone calls, arrive drunk for sessions, and the like. Rather, the caregiver conveys the message that the client is a person worthy of respect, although some behaviors do not meet his needs and are unacceptable. Needless to say, a caregiver avoids creating barriers to the trustbuilding process, such as delivering long monologues or permitting the interview to become immobilized by the client's intense anxiety. It is also unwise to schedule meetings when the caregiver's illness or pain can impede the listening process and blur the focus on the client's needs. Experience with interviewing will allow the caregiver to combine the processes of trustbuilding and assessment.

In the continuing excerpt with Peggy, the therapist is concerned with trustbuilding.

Peggy: Can anybody help me? [*Sobs uncontrollably.*]
Caregiver: [*Leans forward and touches Peggy. Waits while she cries.*]
Peggy: I try so hard not to cry.
Caregiver: With all that pain and fear—it must be impossible to hold all those tears in.
Peggy: [*Sobs.*]
Caregiver: I want you to cry when that's the way you feel. Just remember, even though you feel terrible now because the crisis is so painful, things can get better.
Peggy: But I'm so awful, so bad. . .
Caregiver: A lot of people have felt the way you do and they've gotten better. I know it's hard for you to believe that now.
Peggy: Do you really think I could . . . I can do anything right?
Caregiver: Yes, you already did the first and most important thing right: You came in to get help. It must have taken a lot of energy and courage for you to get up this morning.

At this point, one may surmise that Peggy's need for trust and a relationship are being met. These are basic needs of all clients. This beginning trust makes change and growth possible.

Expanding the Common Frame of Reference
(The Caregiver-Client Framework Box)

The caregiver wants to get to know the client, to find common ground that can become a shared frame of reference for them both. The caregiver must know what meaning the client assigns to words (eg, "I feel depressed"), which may not mean what the caregiver thinks they do. The further the caregiver can expand this shared frame of reference to include feelings, values, perceptions, and needs, the greater the impact of the caregiver on the client, and the more understood and supported the client will feel. The client will begin to feel less alone.

This shared frame of reference may be conceptualized in diagrammatic form as a Caregiver-Client Framework Box (Fig. 1). The caregiver expands this framework by listening for feelings, and by establishing shared words for the feeling and its cause. For example,

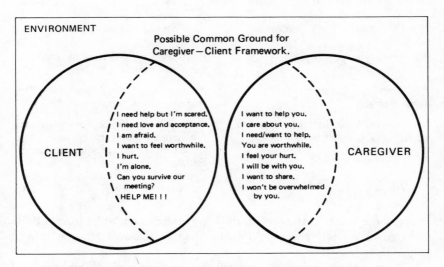

Fig. 1. Caregiver-client framework box: beginning of initial interview. Remember that the chart is static, but the process and the persons involved are dynamic. The rectangular box represents the environment which may have commonalities for the caregiver and the client. The circles represent the caregiver and the client. Each has possible commonalities; each has private areas. These possible commonalities move into the overlap area of proved commonalities by a process of identification and validation. In the caregiver client framework, the overlap is the area of concern; it describes (1) what we can talk about here; (2) who can say what (role); (3) what is recognized and responded to in each person.

when Peggy says, "It was so frightening—such a big place," in describing her reaction to school, the alert caregiver shares her fears by agreeing that they are natural: "You felt lost and scared because it was so new and different, so overwhelming.

The caregiver wants to include whatever has meaning for the client. Perhaps if clients who can't talk about feelings of anger or depression watch television serials or soap operas, they may be able to talk about their responses to similar feelings expressed in the television drama. The caregiver can then help the client discuss not only feelings of depression but also of suicide. By asking directly and non-judgmentally, "Tell me about your suicidal thoughts and feelings," the caregiver is beginning to expand the shared frame of reference to include the client's struggle with suicidal feelings. The caregiver can then lead the conversation to reasons for living and fantasies of dying.

Judgmental questions which express a moralizing viewpoint or predetermine the answers in the direction of the questioner's choice or suspicion do little but becloud the problem:

Wording of the Question	Message of the Question
You're NOT suicidal, are you???	Both phrasing and tone indicate that the answer desired is "NO."
Oh, come on [*jokingly*], you aren't really suicidal?	Again, "NO" is the response solicited by both wording and tone.
You say you're suicidal, but I want to know, what is REALLY bothering you.	Suicide is considered here the masking symptom, and the client is asked to confess the true problem. It is questionable whether a client would feel free to reiterate in reply that suicide really is the "bothering" problem.

It is easy to see that the *content* of these questions is suicide, but their *message* conflicts by saying loud and clear, "Don't tell me you're suicidal."

Nonjudgmental questions utilize the open-ended style without moralizing or directing a specific response. Here, the message is consistent and congruent with content:

Wording of the Question	Message of the Question
You've been feeling so miserable, I wonder if you have considered suicide?	Phrased as a statement, this message conveys acceptance of whatever feelings are there.

Wording of the Question	Message of the Question
I would like to hear more about your suicidal feelings.	
Please tell me about any suicidal thoughts or feelings you may have.	Note that statements encourage more verbal response than questions.
I'm concerned that you may be feeling suicidal. Are you feeling suicidal now?	

The Caregiver-Client Framework Box can be expanded by adding messages to the content (Fig. 2). This is the purpose when the caregiver says, "If I couldn't hear a word you are saying, I would still get a message that you are feeling pain and hurt." This is a useful approach to the client who is being hostile, manipulative, or angry. Responding to the client's feelings is especially helpful when these feelings are directed at the caregiver. Such client behaviors are difficult for caregiv-

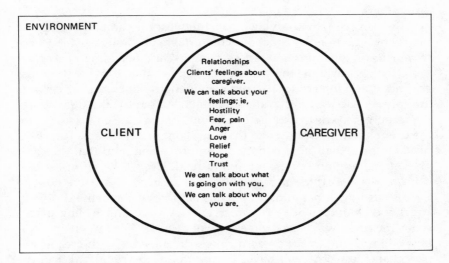

Fig. 2. Caregiver-client framework box. The rectangular box encloses the environment, which may have commonalities for the caregiver and the client. The circles represent the caregiver and client. Each circle contains possible commonalities in the overlapping area, and each has a private area. The potential commonalities are enclosed within the overlap area of proved commonalities by an expanding process of identification and validation. The overlap, or set intersection, represents the caregiver-client framework that is the area of concern. Its limits enclose (1) what we can talk about here, (2) who can say what (role assumed), and (3) what is recognized and responded to in each person by the other. *Note:* This visual rendition is necessarily static, whereas the process and persons diagrammed are dynamic phenomena in continual motion.

ers who may find themselves dealing with their own response ("Why, that guy is downright obnoxious! I don't have to put up with that. . . If he acts like that, no wonder nobody will help him.") While trying to focus on the more productive questions, "How does this behavior work for the client?" "Does it meet his needs?" "Does it succeed in getting help?" The fact is that the client's way of asking for help has probably alienated most of his friends and would-be helpers. The caregiver has to focus on what this behavior accomplishes, why the client is using it, and what it is communicating. This is not to say that the caregiver must be the perfect neutral, who neither has nor expresses feelings about clients. Nevertheless, caretakers do need to avoid being imprisoned by their negative or positive feelings about clients.

This self-awareness and controlled response will help the caregiver envision what goes on in most of the client's relationships. The way the client behaves and relates to the caregiver represents a capsule version of the client's usual behavior. The client who is often angry and hostile with the caregiver is probably angry and hostile with others.

By using certain interviewing techniques, the caregiver can direct the client who rambles on about comfortable but nongermane topics to refocus on the important issues, feelings, and needs. The caregiver must focus clearly on the goals of therapy—suicide prevention, assessment, and intervention—and avoid lengthy or confusing detours into purely social or irrelevant small talk. As part of the framework, the caregiver needs to express consistently a hope based on reality for the client's improvement, one that the client understands. The client needs to hear that there is hope for improvement and that the caregiver is helping and will continue to help. *Usually the client needs to hear this message expressed frequently and in different ways.* Here it is not the *content* that is paramount, but the *message*. If the content of help and hope conflicts with the caregiver's message and feeling of despair, the client will hear the message of despair. The caregiver's feelings will transmit to the client through the message with greater impact than the words will have. Furthermore, the client will feel the emptiness in reassurances not supported by reality. Saying "Don't worry, everything will be all right" can be more harmful than helpful, since the message conveys a denial of the client's worry and concern by the caregiver. It would be more effective to say, "I know how worried you are because you are feeling suicidal. We want to protect you from these suicidal feelings and acts. But I know how hard it is to believe you will ever feel better."

The caregiver should expand the transactional framework to include awareness of the caregiver-client relationship. Feelings and responses between caregiver and client need to be brought into the open for discussion. That is to say, the caregiver who attends to the connections between the client's content and their relationship will hear messages which express the client's feelings about the caregiver. This feedback is most effective when timed and tailored to the client's readiness, as indictd by verbal and behavioral cues presented to the caregiver.

The excerpt below illustrates the approaches that may be used to expand the caregiver-client framework, in another conversation with Peggy (Case 3):

Caregiver: Peggy, I'm glad you feel a glimmer of hope. That's very important. We need to talk now about all your feelings—the hopeful ones and the hopeless ones. We need to understand what makes you feel suicidal and how you feel and think during these periods of depression.

Peggy: Some of my thoughts are so monstrous—I could just never tell anybody.

Caregiver: You're afraid to talk about some of your ideas because they seem so dreadful. You might be afraid I'd laugh at you or despise you.

Peggy: I have never told them to anyone . . . I just couldn't tell you.

Caregiver: It's even scary to think about telling, because I might see the self you work so hard to hide from others.

Peggy: [Silence]

Caregiver: I know these feelings are hard to put into words but I'll help you when you're ready. For now, can you tell me what you think of doing when you feel like hurting yourself?

Peggy: Well, I just want everything not to be painful, or confusing, and I get to thinking that if I just go to sleep—when I wake up, everything will be clearer . . . so I take pills. Sometimes I have to hurt myself, so I cut my wrists. Sometimes I . . . [Silence]

Caregiver: You feel so miserable, lost and hurting that you take pills or cut yourself to make the misery and pain go away.

Peggy: Yes, but nobody understands why I do it. They say, "Why, you're so pretty and young, you have everything to live for—how could you want to die?" Even when I take all those pills I'm not sure I want to die, and nobody understands that, either.

Caregiver: It makes the pain worse, doesn't it, when people don't understand?

Peggy: I try so hard to explain but they just don't listen.

Caregiver: I wonder if that is partly why you're afraid to discuss your feelings here—you feel everyone will misunderstand, anyway, and will think you're bad.

Peggy: I don't want people to think I'm bad like my mother does. Even though I know I'm bad.

Caregiver: It's very hard for you to trust me. You wonder if I'll think you're bad just as your mother and others do.

Peggy: [Looks away]

Caregiver: Peggy, I think you struggle very hard to be good, but right now you're so miserable and confused and suffering that you have trouble always doing what you want to do or think you should do.

Peggy: You wouldn't think I was bad?

Caregiver: No, Peggy.

Peggy: Well . . .

Caregiver: Well, it takes time to trust someone. We'll work on that together. Now let's talk about what we have to do to protect you from these suicidal feelings. What keeps you from hurting yourself? Or feeling worse?

The process of meeting the client's basic needs consists of establishing a relationship, building trust and expanding the caregiver-client frame of reference (Fig. 1). In this process the caregiver may tailor the approach to each client. The framework box can be generalized to any client even though the approach is individualized. In determining what kind of interview is indicated, however, the caregiver must tailor the interview to the client and the particular situation.

What Kind of Interview Is Indicated

No intervention would be realistically oriented that did not include some consideration of the relatives and friends and any other key relationships of the suicidal persons. It is a basic requisite of family crisis intervention that the client be seen with the family or with significant others wherever possible.

Clinical experience indicates that involving the family is often the most valuable and productive approach to the client's problems. It is based on the concept that the suicidal person's feelings are representative of the covert struggle and feelings of other family members. When such a crisis prompts the client or family to seek help for the client, the caregiver has the opportunity to intervene at a time when the greatest change is possible (Pittman, 1966). When intervention involves the family in effecting change rather than the suicidal client alone, the caregiver has the best change of promoting the health and stability of the family unit.

When a family interview is not possible or cannot be approximated, the caregiver will conduct a crisis-oriented interview, strongly directed toward keeping the client connected with his or her family and family resources. The interview is scheduled to meet the immediacy of the client's needs and of the situation. If there is to be a delay, the client must reliably contract not to do anything self-destructive until the next interview with the caregiver.

Techniques of Intervention

Focus on the Current Hazard and Crisis.   The interview needs to focus on clarifying the hazard and crisis. Clients who digress need frequent direction toward what is pertinent to the current situation. Assess the lethality of suicidal intent as rapidly as possible.

When a client presents many problems, the caregiver helps to focus on the worst problem. When the client is confused, the caregiver helps with the one problem that can be dealt with in that session. For example:

Client: I just don't know where to begin. My daughter is pregnant and not married, I have a retarded son, my car doesn't work, and I don't have any food.
Caregiver: You do have several problems. Which one did you want to work on now?
Client: I guess the food, but my daughter is also worrying me.
Caregiver: Let's just talk about food first. How do you think you might tackle this problem?

Make Sure the Client Gains a Clear Perception of the Hazard and Crisis. The client needs you to restate the problem, showing how you perceive and evaluate the situation. It is essential to repeat this within a common frame of reference until the client hears and understands you. Be empathetic and reflective about the client's internal turmoil, but help put this turmoil into perspective.

Reduce Any Immediate Danger. Using short, clear commands, direct the client to remove or destroy any method available by which to carry out the suicidal plan:

"I want you to put the gun down so we can talk."
"I want you to flush those pills down the toilet."
"I want you to put the knife in the other room while we talk."
"I want you to take the bullets out of the gun."

Alternatively, direct the client to separate himself from the method:

"I want you to leave the gun where it is and go over to your friend's apartment."
"I want you to leave the gun here and come into the other room, where we can talk."

Have the client repeat, "I promise not to do anything self-destructive intentionally or unintentionally until I talk to you first by phone or in person." The client must repeat your exact words—a shrug, a mumbled "m-m-hm" or other gesture of assent is not acceptable. The time limit of the contract must be specific and must be clearly stated by the client.

When the client is unable to make the statement as described, the caregiver directs the client as follows: "Qualify the statement any way you wish, but repeat it as I give it to you." A client who is unable to make this contract is really telling you that safety provisions will be necessary—hospitalization, perhaps, or some other alternative must be considered.

Evaluate the Client's Need for Medication. When internal turmoil is severe, the client may need medication to reduce stress, promote sleep, or make it possible to think clearly. This medication must be prescribed by a physician who is aware or should be made aware of the suicidal crisis. It is wise to ask the physician to prescribe small, nonlethal amounts of medication and to ask a relative or friend to keep the bottle and dispense as needed. Bear in mind that although medication can provide great benefit, your decision to resort to it can also be interpreted by the client as your permission to commit suicide.

The same client may say, "They gave me the pills because they wanted me to die." As a safeguard against such a possibility, medication must be controlled and the client be made to understand that *no one* has given permission to use the medication self-destructively. In any event it is rare that medication alone has solved a suicidal crisis.

Evaluate the Client's Need for Someone Present. The client who indicates an inability to control suicidal impulses, who discloses a specific and imminent plan, or who cannot promise to avoid self-destructive behavior may be saying, "I need someone to protect me from myself." Before considering hospitalization, the caregiver may realize that this client is afraid of being alone and for the time being needs to stay with someone else. The caregiver actively helps the client to solve the problem and find someone whom he can stay with for a few days. If no such person can be found, hospitalization must be considered. In no case should the caregiver ever invite a client to become a houseguest, even as a last resort! Once the caregiver exchanges the therapeutic role for the role of host, it becomes, at the very least, infinitely harder to reach the goal of mobilizing the client's own resources.

Mobilize the Client's Internal and External Resources. Success in reducing suicidal lethality hinges on getting the client back into a network of resources where personal feelings of isolation and worthlessness diminish. Conversely, when lethality is not immediately reduced, the availability of these resources may give the client the support and hope needed to continue even for a little longer. Caregivers are advised to seek out these resources for the client, particularly in response to the client's feeling that no one cares. Several approaches may be considered in mobilizing these resources and involving others in the client's therapy.

The Hazard. When the client's perception of the hazard (defined in Chapter 3 as a clinical characteristic) is clarified, it may be possible to mobilize his or her internal strengths to manipulate, decrease, or eliminate the hazard. The threat of the hazard may be minimized when its limits are clearly outlined.

The Crisis. The crisis (also defined in Chapter 3 as a clinical characteristic) usually becomes less threatening as the client is safely surrounded and supported by persons who care and understand the former's internal turmoil. It is important that the client be made to feel confident that he or she will be helped and protected even in the event of losing control.

Significant Others. These persons need help in finding out what the client needs and learning how to direct their energies toward supporting the suicidal individual. The caregiver must decide which significant others will be able to be helpful and assist these significant others to plan for their own support so that they will not be drained by the client. Strengthen the communication between the client and these significant others. Support their relationships by directing both client and significant others toward exchanging messages of care and concern. Teach them to ask directly for what they want.

Priorities in the Organization of Resources. Organize a resource network so that the client will have direction and priorities. Make sure the client knows what resources to use first and how to make use of them. At first, the caregiver may need to contact outside resources for the client and arrange for the support being sought. The caregiver must be alert to all cues from the client which show the client's readiness to take over. The caregiver's messages must always reflect this eventually: "I will help you get started so that you can do more on your own. I will respect and care about you as you return to independence." The caregiver who consistently does everything for the client is headed for disaster by creating a totally dependent client. Even in an emergency, caregiver's must direct clients to do as much as they can for themselves (eg, first-aid measures). In areas where the client cannot be independent, caregivers use authority and direction. Unfortunately, many clients remain suicidal for fear that by surrendering their suicidal intent they risk losing the caregiver's care and concern.

The caregiver's attention to internal resources of the client is paramount to effective therapy. Confused, disoriented clients need assistance in structuring their day. Frequently the client needs help even to make a *"do list"* of what is to be done in what order and at what time of day. Simple chores often taken for granted by the caregiver (shower, hair wash, laundry, meal planning) can be overwhelming to a client until the first "do list" is launched. Simple lessons in problem solving, with the client providing the data and the caregiver helping to set priorities, are important in strengthening the client's internal resources. Often, the client has solved a problem of this kind but needs support from the caregiver. A pat on the back or a smile of encouragement may be all that is required to set the plan in action.

Harnessing Coping Devices That Have Not Disintegrated. Ask the client to search for any coping devices that may have worked in the past. Encourage problem solving that applies previous coping strategies to the current hazard. The client should also be encouraged to visualize some coping strategy that *might* work and to anticipate the consequences. The most important resource a client can have is the belief, "I can help myself." Let the client choose a coping strategy that will fit his or her lifestyle but at the same time make sure there are three choices for the solution of any problem. Having only two choices makes a client feel boxed in.

There are five common ways of harnessing the client's coping devices.

ASSIGN STRUCTURED TASKS.   Give the client tasks to do and assist in the structuring of the client's time, ie, "Go to the market now; call your mother at 10 A.M., and then do your homework." Depending on the client's needs, the caregiver will determine how detailed the directions must be, and how simple the tasks.

CONTINUE ACTIVITIES.   Daily activities need to be continued as much as possible. An immobilized client may actually require a firm command to initiate any activity. However, too much activity can be just as harmful as too little. The caregiver's goal is to assist the client in successfully modifying an exhausting schedule and to help set realistic priorities for a daily regimen of purposeful activity.

DIRECT THE CLIENT TO PLANNED AND ORGANIZED ACTION.   It may be wise to structure an entire day. Conversely, it may only be necessary to work with what the client says must be done. The client may then be able to decide personally what to do first.

Alternatively, the client may have to be directed specifically to contact certain community resources for therapy, money, or housing or directed specifically to certain activities, such as keeping a journal or diary, expressing inner feelings through painting, sculpture, or pottery making, or making social contacts with others.

EXPLORE ALTERNATIVE SOLUTIONS WITH THE CLIENT.   When the client is locked into a situation ("I have to kill myself—you see, I can't live with my husband and I can't live without him so I have to die") the caregiver explores alternatives together with the client. The alternatives may seem limited in the client's perception. The caregiver can offer other choices and can involve significant others in the search for still other possibilities. The goal here is to get the client out of the corner into which he has boxed himself.

It may also be wise to help the client perceive the secondary benefits arising from putting oneself into such a position—whether in the form of attention, help, affection, or empathy from those who respond to the dilemma.

TEACH PROBLEM-SOLVING TECHNIQUES TO THE CLIENT. Ask the client how he/she thinks the problem could be solved. Remember that the client needs *at least three* viable alternatives to avoid feeling boxed in by rigid either-or solutions. The consequences of each possible solution should be discussed. When no choice seems desirable, the client may have to choose the most palatable one. As a client once said, "I felt I was caught between a rock and a hard place. Now I see I have three choices—a rock, a hard place, and a bed of nails. Looking at it this way, the hard place doesn't seem so bad." In the final step of problem solving, the caregiver, looking back at the problem and the process, encapsulates what the client has learned from the process that will be of help in the future, what coping device has been reaffirmed or developed that will help in dealing with future hazards. Spelling this all out reinforces positive aspects of the transaction.

*****

The techniques of intervention discussed here present a range of approaches suitable to the needs of a suicidal person. Table 5 will assist the caregiver in correlating the appropriate intervention approaches with the lethality of risk assessed. It is important to note that the caregiver does not change the intervention techniques used, but rather changes their relative importance and the amount of directive guidance that must be provided as the degree of risk varies from low to high.

Table 6 indicates appropriate responses to specific presenting problems, by types of clients.

Implement a Plan of Action

As the fourth major component of intervention, the plan of action reverses the direction of the client. Effective caregivers help their clients decide what they can do. They assist in structuring or organizing their client's activities, then decide how the client will report on

TABLE 5. Intervention Techniques Based on Lethality

	LETHALITY		
TECHNIQUE	**Low**	**Moderate**	**High**
Assess emergency	No plan to suicide within next 24 hours.	No plan within next 24 hours.	Plans suicide in next 24 hours. What, when, where: What has already been done?
Focus on hazard and crisis	Primary.	Primary after emergency is ruled out.	May be secondary until client is safe.
Clarify the hazard/crisis	Assist client to arrive at clearer idea.	Client needs more help from caregiver.	Client needs most help from caregiver.
Reduce imminent danger	Help client reduce future danger. Obtain verbal contract to avoid suicide.	Help client reduce danger. Obtain verbal contract.	*Direct* client to reduce danger. Provide first aid if necessary. Obtain verbal contract.
Assess need for medication	Evaluate.	Evaluate.	Most often—but must be monitored!!
Assess need for someone to stay with client	Often a good idea to have someone available for support.	Frequently necessary.	Essential precaution to prevent hospitalization or suicide.
Mobilize internal and external resources	Very important; usually can mobilize internal resources.	Very important. Can mobilize some internal resources.	Essential. Few internal resources. *Need* help to mobilize external resources.
Contact significant others.	Important.	Very important.	Essential.
Harness coping devices	Minimal help needed.	Needs more help.	Needs commands and directions.
Give structure	Minimal help needed.	Needs more help.	Needs specific directions.
Continue daily activities	Needs encouragement.	Needs encouragement and some direction.	Needs directions and assessment of what is possible.
Direct to planned/organized action	Needs encouragement.	Needs encouragement and some direction	Needs commands.

TABLE 6. The Suicidal Person's Presenting Problems as Revealed in the First Interview

CAREGIVER'S OBJECTIVES	CLIENT'S REACTION	CAREGIVER'S RESPONSE
Angry Client		**Identify the Feeling Observed**
Assess degree of risk.	"I asked for help and you don't even know the right thing to say."	"You sound really angry."
Assess possibility of homicide.	"Who are you, anyway? Are you a shrink? How could you help? You don't know anything, anyway. You don't know how I feel or what it's like. I'll bet you're not even 20. How could you know anything about life?"	"You're wondering if I could understand what you're going through."
Allow ventilation of anger.	"I called you and you've only made me worse."	
	"What do you MEAN I'm angry?"	
	"Let me talk to someone that knows what they're doing. You're a student, right?"	
	"My husband is an S.O.B."	
	Yelling and screaming.	
	Nonverbal behaviors, such as clenching fists, pounding the desk, etc.	
Challenging Client		**Direct the Focus to the Problems**
Be alert to the person who knows jargon terms but tends to focus on the listener instead of the problems at issue.	"I don't know if you could understand. Have you ever been suicidal?"	"You're wondering if I can understand and help you."
Avoid a power or knowledge struggle.	"You just changed the subject and your voice is shaking! What's the matter, can't you take it?"	"You called for help, but are you getting what you need when we talk about me?"
Focus on the person. Assess degree of risk, capacity to ask for and get help despite the challenging approach.	"What is your background for this kind of job? Do you have a degree?"	

(Continued)

79

TABLE 6, continued

CAREGIVER'S OBJECTIVES	CLIENT'S REACTION	CAREGIVER'S RESPONSE
Challenging Client, continued	"You see, my problem is I'm in a neurotic depression. Do you know what that means?"	"I'd like to know what that means to you in this situation, or how you feel about your problem."
	Looks directly at caregiver, faces caregiver with a firm, confident posture, may sit in caregiver's chair behind desk.	
Controlling Client		
Assess degree of risk.	"Yes, therapy is a good idea, but I couldn't go back. You see, I can't afford it."	"There seems to be a screen that goes up when I suggest something. I wonder if you can hear what I'm saying?"
This is a person who will reject help, often using the "Yes, but" ploy. Client rejects all suggestions offered by the caregiver.	"Yes, I tried that, but it didn't work."	"These suggestions don't seem to be acceptable. What are you going to do?"
Point out that the client is responsible for setting goals and making choices.	"Yes, but you don't understand how my family hates me. I can't ask them for help."	"It's difficult for you to accept the help I'm offering you. You say 'Yes, but,' so you must be responsible for your own solution. What will you do?"
		"You ask me what you should do but respond to my suggestions with a 'Yes, but.' Is this what happens when other people give you advice?"
Client High on Drugs/Alcohol		
Assess to differentiate between behavior caused by drugs, alcohol, or psychosis.	*Unclear, slurred speech, repetitious.*	"Why did you call today (tonight)?"
Assess degree of risk.	*Confusion about what has already been said.*	"I wonder why your voice sounds so sleepy (slurred)? Have you taken anything?" (If so, how much, what, when, why?)
If not in emergency, ask client to call back when he or she can think more clearly.	*Inappropriate affect, silly, boisterous state.*	"Do you do this often?"
	May say, "I've had a few drinks," or agree, "Yes, I'm high (or drunk)," if asked.	
Avoid judgmental responses.	*May call from a party or a bar, the noise of which can be heard over the phone.*	"Did you take alcohol/drugs to kill yourself? Are you planning to kill yourself?"

Suspicious Client

Assess degree of risk.

Establish trust.

Rule out paranoia. Is client so fearful that basic needs for food and safety are being neglected?

Assess capacity to cope.

Rule out psychosis.

May act drunk, showing perceptual difficulties and uncoordination—shaking hands, stumbling, bumping into things—with alcohol on the breath.

"Are we being taped (listened to, watched)? Are you spying on me?"

"Everyone is against me."

"I can't give you my name or address. I don't want the State to know where I am."

"Do you think I'm paranoid?"

"Why do you want to know?"

Fearful, suspicious tone of voice.

Checks doors for locks, glances frequently at the door while talking.

"It's hard to talk to you now. I want you to call me when you are more alert (awake/straight)."

"We're not being taped. You seem afraid others are watching or listening. Do you worry about this much?"

"With these fears, how do you manage to sleep, work, or eat?" (How do you cope?)

"I want your name and address and phone number in case we're cut off or you need emergency help, but we can come back to this later . . ."

"It must be hard to get help when it's so hard to trust people."

Silent Client

Establish trust

Assess degree of risk.

Assess capacity to cope.

Get the needed information by the question method if nothing else suffices. Go through the gamut: sexual, suicide, money, job, death, failure, family, friend, anger, feeling hopeless, helpless, unloved?

"I hope you can help . . . I . . . " *Silence.*

"It's hard to talk . . . " *Silence.*

May have difficulty looking directly at caregiver. May stare at the floor or the wall.

"You're wondering if I can help. It sounds very hard for you to talk about what's bothering you."

"Would it help if I ask questions?"

"I know it's so hard to talk and ask for help when you've always been able to handle everything alone, or especially when you feel your problems are so terrible nobody could understand. What kind of problem is it?" (Itemize, allowing lots of time lapses for responses.)

(Continued)

TABLE 6, continued

CAREGIVER'S OBJECTIVES	CLIENT'S REACTION	CAREGIVER'S RESPONSE
Silent Client, continued		
		"Are there things it's easier to talk about? Maybe we could start here." (Don't get sidetracked but use your topic as an opener.)
		When seeing client face to face: "It isn't necessary to talk to get help from somebody or to feel better." (Just sit with the client.)
Clinging Client		
When client won't let you go, set limits on time.	"What should I do?"	"I want you to (dress, call your therapist, eat, etc)."
	"I know you're going to leave now; I'll be all alone and I won't know what to do."	
Assess degree of risk.	"I know you have to go but I wonder how many pills I need to . . ."	"I wonder if you really feel suicidal or if you don't just want to talk longer. Is there someone you can stay with if you are afraid to be alone now?"
Assess coping devices and direct client to use them.	"You want me to see my therapist, but you're the only one I can really talk to—you understand."	"You explained your feelings clearly to me and you can do the same with your therapist. Why don't you write them down so you won't forget?"
Give client specific directions or tasks.	"When you leave, I'm afraid I'll be so alone I'll really do something to hurt myself."	"What will you do if you get another suicidal impulse?"
	May hold onto therapist's arm or clothing.	"I really must go now. What you need to do is (specify). Talking to me any longer isn't best for you right now."
		"What you need to do now is to work on expressing those lonely feelings in another way (specify writing, gardening, phoning a friend, cleaning house, or whatever)."

progress or problems. If need be, they work out together with the client a plan for what the client will do that day and every day. In all this structuring the caregiver is as authoritative and directive as needed. A time limit or some deadline may be helpful (eg, you'll go to the bank and call me back before 2:00 P.M.).

Decide what you as the caregiver will do, and when. This will include contacting any other caregivers or agencies the client may be seeing. You will also decide when you as the caregiver report to the client.

After the client has made a contract with you not to commit a suicidal act or take a suicidal risk, for a specific period of time, decide what ongoing help or therapy may be needed and direct the client to make what arrangements may be necessary to obtain it. Note that, in intervention, a contract is a verbal agreement between caregiver and client. Usually the client promises in so many words, "I will not do anything to hurt myself accidentally or on purpose" for the time period stipulated.

The client's network of significant others needs help to plan how to assist the client. The significant others will need encouragement to form support groups for themselves. If you as the caregiver cannot help them, direct them to some other resources which may be more effective or appropriate (Table 7).

If the plan of action bogs down, seek consultation. Always use consultation when you don't know what to do. Select a consultant who is objective and who is skilled in suicide prevention. Beginning caregivers need to consult a professional more often than their more experienced colleagues.

Decide what follow-up will be appropriate and who should be responsible for it.

Once the client has agreed to a viable plan of action, be firm and consistent, directing the client to take the first step. At this point, a client may become fearful and try every delaying tactic imaginable. Be on the alert for the client who seductively drops a lethal suicidal hint five minutes before you are ready to end the session.

Once a client has been transferred to another caregiver or therapist, reinforce the referral relationship firmly. All complaints to you must be referred promptly back to the new therapist. It is inappropriate to listen to your referred client, to commiserate with him/her, or to agree that the therapist is not acceptable. The correct response is, "You really must tell your therapist how you feel." Some clients look for an ally against the therapist when the going gets rough. In such a situation, the caregiver must firmly direct the client back to the therapist. In situations where the client already has a

TABLE 7. How to Refer a Client: An Itemized Procedure

1. Determine the client's needs.
2. Determine the referral agency appropriate to the client's needs.
3. Discuss the referral with the client and why you suggest this referral. ("You say you want help in dealing with your feelings; this agency can help you.")
4. Initiate contact with the agency if the client is unable to do this.
5. Ask to speak with the intake worker and then do the following:
   a. Identify yourself, your agency, and your relationship with the client.
   b. State what the client needs:
      (1) Needs to be seen immediately, today.
      (2) Needs an appointment for therapy within a specific time.
      (3) Needs medication (new, recheck, refill).
      (4) Needs assessment and treatment.
      (5) Needs immediate protection from suicidal acts by hospitalization.
      (6) Needs a range of services (cannot feed himself or otherwise take care of himself).
   c. Identify the client:
      (1) Full name and address.
      (2) Age and sex.
      (3) Nature of current hazard and crisis.
      (4) Brief past history (should be relevant and concise).
      (5) Further information as called for.
   d. Ask the intake worker the following questions:
      (1) When will the agency accept the referral?
      (2) What does the agency do if the client misses an appointment?
      (3) Who will be the agency worker for you to contact later if necessary?
      (4) What, if anything, do you have do to to complete referral?
      (5) What does the client have to do to complete referral?
6. Make sure that the client and the referral agency really connect and get together.
7. Follow up the client's progress with the referral agency in accordance with the policy of your agency and your assessment of the client's need for follow-up.

therapist, the client must be directed back to that therapist. Here the caregiver must again be firm in reinforcing the existing therapeutic relationship.

Have the client summarize the plan of action finally worked out, including the tasks involved, the person responsible for the services referred, and a realistic follow-up date. When all this has been done, stop talking and let the client begin the tasks assigned under the plan.

Conclusion

Principles and techniques of intervention have been discussed to help the caregiver plan a successful intervention with the client. A brief comparison of the various types of facilities that offer some form of suicide prevention service may be helpful to the caregiver who seeks to connect the client with the needed resource available in the community.

All the assessment and intervention techniques discussed here are based on a crisis intervention model. However, the literature does not report research on suicidal persons who never come to the attention of the helping professions—the "silent" suicides, who might respond only to techniques not as yet developed. Nevertheless, clinical data show that the crisis intervention model offers successful approaches to those persons in suicidal crisis who have come to the attention of caregiver intervenors.

Clients who present a life style of suicide still pose a continuing problem. We do not yet know what to offer them. We have neither a cure nor a proven treatment program. Most suicide prevention programs have developed some approaches to the chronically suicidal person, but clear-cut successes are very few. For these clients the crisis intervention model has been found ineffective. Rather the rehabilitation model appears to be more appropriate for their treatment.

We believe that this situation offers a strong indication for further study on chronic suicidal populations. We need further research findings to add to those discussed in the section of Chapter 7 dealing with "The Chronically Suicidal Person." We need more concrete findings to offer frustrated staff members of emergency rooms and every other treatment facility who struggle with the enigma of the chronically suicidal person, the silent suicide, and how to help them.

WHAT TO EXPECT FROM A VARIETY OF SERVICES

A. Community Mental Health Centers

Description:
Staff of professionals and trained paraprofessional workers
Coordinates with other community agencies for needed services (eg, hospitalization)
Under local, state and federal auspices
Goal: To keep client in community
Focus: Assess and treat emotional problems and problems in living

Services:
Multidisciplinary
Group and individual therapy
Medications
Can hospitalize
May have emergency team/home visit

Services (cont.)
May have special programs for special populations
Anyone may refer
May have geographic requirements for clients
Fees: 0 to sliding scale
Usually see walk-in clients

Comments:
Emergency teams are busy and usually screen requests for home visits
Calm objective manner of staff may seem uncaring to beginning caregivers
May have special programs for adolescents, elderly, ethnic groups, etc

B. Suicide Prevention Centers

Description:
Staff of professionals and trained paraprofessional volunteers
Offers anonymity to callers
Private organization
Goals: Research, training, community-oriented services to suicidal persons
Focus: Suicide prevention (including prevention of self-destructive behaviors)

Services:
Multidisciplinary
May have group and individual therapy
Can refer for hospitalization
Fees: 0 to small; anyone may refer
May see walk-in clients

Comments:
Encourage volunteer applications
Usually offer 24-hour phone hotline

C. Hotlines (Fig. 3)

Description:
Staff: Trained volunteers and supervisors
Goals: Various (may include community referral, support, a friendly chance to talk). *May* assess for suicide; however, this is not the focus

Services:
May be open weekends and evenings
Anyone can refer

DATE: _____ TIME: _8:30 P.M.___

FIRST INTERVIEW,
TELEPHONE CONTACT

CLIENT'S IDENTIFYING DATA:

NAME: *Refuses* _____ TELEPHONE NUMBER: ( ) *Refuses*

ADDRESS: _____

AGE: 45   SEX: M   LIVING ARRANGMENTS: *Alone*

ALCHOHOL: *Social drinker before crisis. Now drinks heavily on a daily basis. Says he's had two drinks before calling.*

CURRENT RELIGION: *Catholic who hesitates to contact his church or priest.*

DRUGS: *Denies drug abuse.*

CRISIS DATA:

CURRENT HAZARD: (What made you want help today?)
"*I am 45 years old and thought I had everything to live for—a fine family, a darling 2½ year old little girl, a good job as an auto mechanic, I could fix anything and make it run, I have no reason to live—last week I killed my wife and child in a car accident, and I was driving.*"

CRISIS: (How are you feeling now? Are there any symptoms or unusual behavior?)
"*I don't know. I drink to forget. Nobody cares. I would be better off dead. I can't think of anything else but that I killed my family because I was drinking and driving. Now there is no hope for me but to kill myself and join my wife and child in death.*" (Feels alone, helpless, hopeless, ambivalent, guilty, unloved.)

PLAN: (Can you tell me how you might commit suicide?)
Method: "*I would just shoot myself—that would be the easiest way out.*"

Availability: "*I have a gun and bullets at home.*"

Lethality: "*I know how to shoot because I used to go hunting a lot. And anyway I have already taken some pills—but you don't have to know what they are.*"

When and Where: "*Well, I will just go home and shoot myself tonight.*"

HISTORY OF SUICIDAL BEHAVIOR: (Any past threats, thoughts, attempts? How lethal? Give specifics of when, where, and outcome.)
"*I have never been suicidal before or even thought about it. I only started thinking about it after the accident.*"

HISTORY OF PSYCHIATRIC TREATMENT OR MEDICAL TREATMENT: (Was past or current treatment helpful? Would you go back to that caregiver? Are you in treatment now?)
"*I have never had any treatment. Right now, I don't think anything could help. The only person I ever talked to was a priest.*"

Fig. 3. Caregiver-client information sheet illustrating typical information yielded by a telephone contact. This sheet is typical of forms regularly checked off in some telephone centers for every call received. (Continued on p. 88)

RESOURCES	SIGNIFICANT OTHERS (Name, Phone, and Relationship)	COPING DEVICES
a. *Currently asking help.* b. *Past history is stable.* c. *Had a good self image as an auto mechanic.* d. *Has friends even though he doesn't feel anyone could help at the moment.*	a. *Priest? Father O'Brien, St. Timothy's Parish* b. *Family?* } *could not* c. *Friends?* } *identify*	*Current:* a. *Drinking* b. *Talking with caregiver.* c. *Working daily* *Past:* a. *Stable employment history* b. *Religion?*

LETHALITY	HOW SOON SHOULD LETHALITY BE REVIEWED?
High emergency rating due to specific plan and method. *Low lethality is predicted if he can get over this crisis.*	*Constantly until he makes a contract not to suicide for a given period of time.* *After contract, review before contract expires.* *Review sooner if any change is noted.*

PLAN OF ACTION:
a. *Insist on a nonsuicide contract.*
b. *Encourage agreement to see caregiver or priest tomorrow.*
c. *Help client understand he is in a time-limited crisis and if he can survive this period, things can get better.*

FOLLOW-UP:
a. *As explained to client, caregiver finally got telephone number and called back every 15 minutes.*
b. *On each call, the client was told, "You are important, I don't want you to die," and plan listed above was followed.*
c. *After two hours, client agrees to a non-suicide contract and plans to visit priest the next day.*

CONSULTATION:
a. *Consultant was immediately involved because caregiver felt helpless and powerless and wanted to share the client's situation with someone else.*
b. *Caregiver shared feelings of hopelessness and desperation with Consultant and was helped to set plan of action in motion.*

Fig. 3 (cont). Caregiver-client information sheet, reverse side.

Comments:

Check to ensure that the hotline number is correct and still in existence

D. General Hospital

Description:

Staff: Medical, nursing, and auxiliary

Goals: Cure and care of medical conditions

May have emergency room and/or psychiatric unit (see E and F)

Suicidal clients may not be admitted. May admit overdose clients for limited observation. Policy dictates whether psychiatric consultation or referral or constant nursing supervision is needed or available

May require psychiatric consultation before client is discharged

Services:

May be multidisciplinary

Open weekends and evenings

May require ability to pay

Comments:

Staff are often untrained in suicide and may be frightened by suicidal clients. Emotional needs and psychopathology expressed as medical ailments may go unnoticed, unreferred, unassessed, and possibly untreated

Client is likely to be discharged without follow-up for suicidal behavior

Special programs for suicide are rare

A client who gives the staff clues about suicidal thoughts may receive a prompt transfer to another facility

Attitudes toward suicide may range from avoidance of suicidal clients to strict requirements for constant nursing supervision, etc for possible psychiatric basis for these complaints

E. Psychiatric Hospital

Description:

May be a private or a public facility or a unit of a general hospital.

Staff: Professional medical, nursing, psychiatric, and auxiliary

Goals: Cure and care of mental illness, maintenance of mental health

Focus: (1) improvement and stability so client may return to community or (2) rehabilitation or transfer to residential or sheltered care

May also have drug and alcohol programs

Description (cont.):

May have security or locked units for acutely suicidal persons. Even in this setting, there is *no* guarantee that suicide will be prevented

Persons may be involuntarily confined when deemed necessary by law (each state has varying criteria and laws for involuntary admission). There are also laws to protect a person's rights during this time

Services:

Multidisciplinary

Individual and group therapy

May have outpatient programs

May have emergency team or home visits

Open weekends and evenings

May require ability to pay

May have special programs for suicidal behavior

May see walk-in patients

Anyone may refer, but a staff psychiatrist must admit

Comments:

Friends and family may be included in treatment

Medications and dangerous objects are closely watched

Hospital policies regulating confidentiality of client's records may be more rigid

Persons under legal age may or may not be admitted

F. Emergency Rooms (usually part of General Hospitals)

Staff: Professional medical and nursing

Goals: Lifesaving measures and treatment

May require ability to pay

Policy regarding suicidal persons may require any of the following:
    Immediate medical treatment
    Notification of police
    24-hour hospitalization
    Psychiatric consultation
    Referral or transfer to psychiatric facility
    Treat medical conditions ONLY and discharge

G. Other Counseling Services

Private clinics

Colleges and universities

Churches

Women's organizations
Public health agencies
Free clinics
Helping persons or caregivers not formally identified by a facility
   or organization
Individual counselors in private practice

THREE ILLUSTRATIVE INTERVENTIONS

Case 4: Howard

Howard is a 30-year-old businessman who has been feeling sad
and upset for several months. He has been talking frequently with his
friend, Sue. He knows Sue has been working as a volunteer telephone counselor at a local crisis service for the past several months.
Prior to this conversation, however, Howard had not asked Sue for
help, nor had he shared his feelings of sadness and helplessness with
anyone.

Conversation	Assessment and Intervention
Howard: I just have to tell you something—I have to tell someone or I'll explode. You're the only one I trust, and it is a matter of life and death. But you've got to promise you won't tell anybody what I say.	
Sue: Howard, you really sound upset and serious, but you're asking me to make a promise I couldn't keep. I can only promise to respect your wishes for secrecy as long as it doesn't interfere with your safety or someone else's. If you want to tell me, you'll have to trust me. You can be sure I won't tell anybody anything about your personal business. I'd only disclose whatever is necessary for your safety or someone else's.	Responds to Howard's feelings. Responds to his message that this is important and serious.

Refuses to agree to secrecy. Sue is careful to reassure Howard that his information is *confidential* and his privacy will be respected. *However*, this agreement to respect privacy DOES NOT mean keeping a secret which endangers the health of the client or others. |
| **Howard:** You just have to promise or. . . well, you just don't care about me at all. If you were really concerned about me you'd give me your promise. | Possibly testing Sue to see if she will stick to what she said. (Can he trust her?) |

Conversation	Assessment and Intervention
Sue: I hear what you're saying, but I must be honest to the both of us. I can't agree to confidentiality before you tell me your secret. *I do want to help you* but I. . .	Sue responds to Howard's feelings and says "I want to help." Reaffirms respect for privacy and confidentiality but emphasizes she won't keep a life-endangering *secret*.
Howard: There's nobody else I can talk to . . . Well, I have these terrible feelings and I'm very frightened.	
Sue: Tell me about your feelings that are scary.	Encourages Howard to explore and share his feelings. Accepts his feelings of being frightened.
Howard: I just get so scared. I have these terrible dreams—I dream I kill myself. I'm just panicked. Lately I've been thinking about taking a lot of pills just so I can go to sleep and not have these terrible dreams.	
Sue: You have these nightmares and imagine you kill yourself. Are you feeling suicidal right now?	Restates (empathy); asks directly about suicide.
Howard: I just want to take those pills and I don't care if I wake up or not.	
Sue: You don't care if you live or die. . . Do you have a specific plan?	Although Howard's plan sounds vague, Sue asks for specifics to assess the possibility of an emergency.
Howard: Well, I'd just take those pills and never wake up. I have pills in the house—you know, a couple of bottles of sleeping pills, and I'd take all of them. I don't really have a definite time in mind but I do think about it.	
Sue: Howard, I'm very concerned about how bad you are feeling. You sound as though you have been so scared and miserable. . . Have you taken any pills to help you feel better today?	Again Sue checks for a specific plan already in action, *even though* Howard has presented a vague plan.
Howard: No.	
Sue: Good. Tell me. . . what started all these terrible feelings and how did you feel before it all started?	Focuses on the hazard and the pre-hazard state for clues in deciding whether this is a crisis or is chronic.
Howard: Well, I'd say I was my usual self before. Nothing like this ever happened before. It all started suddenly. . . about four months ago. I was having trouble at work and, well, the kids were really getting on my nerves and everything started to	

Conversation	Assessment and Intervention
cave in. Ever since then I've been scared.	
Sue: So several things started to happen about four months ago. But what happened recently that has made things so much worse? That started you thinking about suicide?	Restates (empathy). Focuses on *recent hazard*.
Howard: Well, I guess about a month ago I began thinking my wife was not really in love with me. I suspected she was going out with another guy and. . . well, now I worry that she might leave me.	
Sue: So things got worse when you became anxious that Jeanne might leave you for someone else? That must have been a frightening thought. But what happened *today* to make you talk about this now?	Restates (empathy). Focuses on immediacy of hazard. Assesses a possible low-lethality attempt, *but* clarification is needed.
Howard: Well, last night I really scared myself. I took three of those sleeping pills. They didn't hurt me but the idea really shook me up. Not only that, but ever since I began worrying about Jeanne I've been having these dreams and thinking constantly about killing myself and even. . .	
Sue: You worry about suicide and even. . .	Restates so that Howard will continue.
Howard: And I even think about killing Jeanne and the kids.	
Sue: It sounds to me as though all these things are overwhelming you at once. First it was work and the kids, then you became afraid that Jeanne might leave you, and now the thoughts of suicide and killing. What has kept you from carrying out your thoughts?	Accepts feelings. Restates and asks for Howard's coping devices.
Howard: I don't know. . . I guess I just keep busy and it helps to be able to tell you—just to tell somebody I can trust and get it off my chest.	
Sue: I can imagine how terrible it's been for you. You told me you have trouble sleeping. Have you had trouble with other things like eating or concentrating?	Focuses on crisis symptoms and extent of disturbance.

Conversation	Assessment and Intervention
Howard: It's been a nightmare. I don't even know how I manage. I only get a few hour's sleep and hardly eat anything. It's awfully hard to concentrate at work but my boss thought I had the flu like everyone else.	
Sue: Well, let's see if I understand what you've said so far. Until four months ago, things were O.K. Then trouble with work and the kids got to be a problem, but you were still handling things. About a month ago, you became anxious about Jeanne's leaving you for someone else and then you began having nightmares of suicide and murder. Now everything is sort of caving in and you feel like exploding. You aren't eating, sleeping, or concentrating and you're frightened—you need to talk to someone.	Gives a clear perception of hazard and crisis in summarizing Howard's problems sequentially.
Howard: Yeah... When you put it all together like that, it's a lot less confusing and not so scary.	
Sue: Well, I think it is very frightening, even though talking about it makes things a bit clearer. I think you realized how frightening and dangerous your feelings of suicide were and that's why you wanted to tell me about them.	Shares her concern and her feelings (warmth, congruence).
Howard: You may be right... I was sort of afraid to tell you but then I was too scared not to.	
Sue: I'm very glad you did tell me. I think you were really giving me a message: You were overwhelmed by your feelings and frightened by your suicidal thoughts and you wanted to get help.	States message—responds with her honest feelings.
Howard: I really was scared.	
Sue: You were wise to be frightened by your thoughts and it's important that you wanted to get help. It's important for you to know that many people are frightened by suicidal thoughts, but they can get help to deal with these frightening thoughts.	Reinforces coping. Gives information. Gives hope.

Conversation	Assessment and Intervention
Howard: Is that really true? Many people? I thought I was the only one with such awful, sinful ideas.	
Sue: It is true. You're not the only one who has thoughts of suicide or murder. And you can be helped to get better, just as others have been helped.	
Howard: I don't know how anything like this could get better.	
Sue: Howard, what I see going on is that right now you are in a crisis. If we can help you during this period when the crisis is at its worst, then you can feel better. What you need is the right kind of help so you won't go through this frightening experience alone and so you can be helped to control your suicidal impulses.	Gives a clear perception of limited crisis. Gives hope. Offers an appropriate referral and implies she will remain with him as a supportive friend.
Howard: Oh, I couldn't tell anybody but you. Nobody else would understand. Anyway, I don't have any money and I just couldn't let Jeanne know, or the kids.	
Sue: Howard, I know a really good therapist who would understand and would want to help. I can call and let him know you're going to call for an appointment. He works at a community mental health center where they charge you what you're able to pay. I know how difficult it is to go. But you must. I want you to promise me that you won't do anything unintentionally or on purpose to hurt yourself until you see him for that appointment.	Responds to Howard's feelings but reinforces therapeutic plan. Attempts to make the contract (Howard's promise not to suicide).
Howard: I can't. You're the only one I can talk to.	
Sue: Howard! I really want you to promise me right now!	Gives firm, clear command.
Howard: I just can't Sue—you are the only one I could talk to.	
Sue: I can be your friend, Howard, but I can't be your only confidante or your caregiver. Would it help if I went with you to the office for the first appointment?	Clearly states her role.

Conversation	Assessment and Intervention
Howard: Yeah... I guess if you could come with me it would help. I promise not to do anything till then.	
Sue: Good. But I want you to repeat the exact words of the promise.	Insists on *clear, complete* verbal contract.
Howard: I promise not to do anything unintentionally or on purpose to hurt myself or anyone else till I talk to the therapist.	
Sue: I'm glad you made the promise. I can feel more comfortable. Now—what are you going to do to keep yourself together till the appointment?	Focuses on coping strategies and assessing the need for structure.
Howard: Well, if I keep real busy at work, I feel better.	
Sue: Good. What else? How about friends or family—can they help?	Moves to bring in significant others.
Howard: Well, I'm afraid to tell Jeanne. When I'm away from the house at night I'm sure she is going out with that guy.	
Sue: Well, if keeping busy helps, how about if you continue working during the daytime and then keep occupied with Jeanne and the kids at night?	Responds to feelings by suggesting new coping which involves family.
Howard: I wonder... what could I do? It's so hard for me to think of anything.	
Sue: What do you usually do?	
Howard: I don't do much of—well, Jeanne sometimes makes dinner for a few friends, and the kids like picnics and movies.	
Sue: Well, a dinner party usually takes some time to plan. What could you do for tonight—maybe go out for dinner?	Focuses on a realistic plan.
Howard: We could go out for dinner, I guess ...	
Sue: That's a good idea. Then you might even want to plan a small dinner party for next week.	Reinforces Howard's coping and encourages planning for the future.
Howard: Yeah.	
Sue: Maybe after dinner tonight you might go to a movie.	Suggests activities for the agitated client. Keeping busy helps decrease agitation.
Howard: Jeanne might like that.	
Sue: That sounds like a good plan for	

Conversation

tonight. How about the weekend?

Howard: Well, the kids want to go camping but I've been putting them off. I just don't think I could.

Sue: What about a barbecue or picnic in the backyard?

Howard: Well, that's a pretty safe thing. . . it's not too hard. I think I could do that with Jeanne and then I wouldn't have to worry about pulling it off.

Sue: Howard, you say planning is hard for you, but this sounds like a good plan for tonight and a good plan for the weekend. Maybe you could sit down with the whole family and plan what you would like to do Monday.

Howard: Maybe we could . . .

Sue: I mean it's nice to know you don't have to carry the whole load. The family can help with the planning and help with the work. That's how families take care of each other. When you feel a little less afraid, maybe you can share what you've been going through with them so they can help you through the rest.

Howard: That's O.K. too. I've got some other ideas already.

Sue: It sounds great. You have a fine plan for now—but there's one other thing I wanted to ask you—do you have any other friends to talk to?

Howard: No, just you.

Sue: Well, I'd feel more comfortable if you had other friends besides me.

Howard: Well, I will have this man, this therapist you recommended. . .

Sue: Yes, that's good, but in a time of crisis you need support from all the friends you can muster. Aren't there any other friends you could call on for help right now? Although it would be hard, I'd like you to consider involving Jeanne and the kids in your crisis.

Assessment and Intervention

Reinforces message that Howard can plan and cope with family's help.

Reinforces message of the helping family by extending family help to include not only planning and activities but sharing the emotional load.

Responds with independent message that he can handle this task.
Reinforces plan and moves to significant others not in the family.

Good sign; Howard is beginning to think of the therapist Sue has referred him to.
Attempts to extend Howard's contacts, but seeing that there are none—for the present—returns to family and tries to hook them in as Howard's emotional supports.

Conversation	Assessment and Intervention
Howard: That really upsets me.	
Sue: Yes, but they care about you and they'd want to help.	Reinforces family image as caring and cooperative.
Howard: That's true. . .	
Sue: I was just wondering if maybe the whole family isn't in crisis and feeling as miserable as you are—perhaps you were just the first to reach out for help.	Considers possibility of family crisis instead of just individual crisis.
Howard: Do you think so?	Reinforces client's internal resources.
Sue: It's very likely they need help as much as you do and all of you are protecting each other from the same secret.	Focuses on family as a unit and implies the benefits of family therapy.
Howard: Well, I'll have to think about that.	
Sue: Maybe they need your strength and approval to be able to ask for help. But if you all worked on the crisis together, you could support each other and work through the crisis better.	Reinforces family strength and unity in emotional crisis.
Howard: I wonder. . .	
Sue: I think you should wonder about it and check it out with the family. Do you want to call the therapist I recommended and set up the appointment?	
Howard: Yes. But I need his phone number and the address.	
Sue: O.K. I'll give you his business card with all that information. When you make the appointment, you should mention your thoughts about including the family. You need to discuss this with the therapist.	Encourages Howard's calling and making appointment as a coping mechanism. Reinforces role of therapist.
Howard: O.K. The more I think about it the better it sounds. But it's all so scary. . .	
Sue: Well, the therapist will help you. You won't have to do it alone. One final thing—if you have any trouble reaching the therapist or setting up an appointment, will you let me know so I can help?	Reinforces role of therapist. Reinforces support that she cares about Howard.
Howard: You'll be the first to know.	
Sue: Good. I'll look forward to hearing how it goes.	
Howard: O.K. Thanks.	

Case 5: Darcy

Darcy and Marion are co-workers in the same department. They have worked together for about two years. Marion describes Darcy as "Quite competent and capable of assuming greater responsibilities. As far as personality goes, however, Darcy is really moody. She doesn't seem to have any friends in the department, although she is superficially friendly to everybody. It is interesting that she really becomes flustered under pressure. She has a lot of potential for someone who is only 30 years old but she really needs to work on her relationships with others."

Lately, Marion has become increasingly concerned about Darcy's moods. Darcy frequently looks tearful, very sad, and distressed. She seems not to be as neat about her appearance as she used to be. During the past two weeks, Marion has made several subtle comments to give Darcy the message, "I'd like to help." Darcy responds both to the message and to Marion's invitations to coffee with such comments as "It doesn't matter anymore."

Today, Marion thinks Darcy is acting strangely. She is torn between respecting Darcy's privacy and responding to Darcy's obvious misery and need for help.

Conversation	Assessment and Intervention
Marion: Darcy, I'm really concerned about you. What do you mean, "It doesn't matter anymore"?	Takes the initiative, asking for clarification.
Darcy: Just that. Can't you mind your own business?	
Marion: I'm not trying to annoy you or butt in, but I am concerned. You look as though you're going to cry. I'm worried that you may feel so miserable, you'll think nobody could possibly help you.	
Darcy: Who asked you to be a shrink?	
Marion: Nobody, but you do seem to be asking for help, and I feel terrible that you are so unhappy. I'd like to help.	
Darcy: [Shrugs]	
Marion: I wonder if you've been finding it difficult to do things you usually do—like eating, being with other people. . .	Offers an easy topic to discuss.

Conversation	Assessment and Intervention
Darcy: Well, food just doesn't interest me and I've not been doing things with others—well, except my boyfriend. Even that just isn't the same.	
Marion: Could you tell me how it's different now?	Asks for detail.
Darcy: Well, I used to look forward to being with him. Now, it's kind of a bore but it's worse being without him.	
Marion: So what you're saying is that things are different now. Things you used to like are a bore but you still don't want to be alone.	Clarifies and reflects.
Darcy: Yeah.	
Marion: That sounds pretty depressing. I wonder if you've thought what would happen if things go on like this? If you could change anything, what would you change?	Reflects and asks for idea of the future.
Darcy: Well, nothing's going to change, I know that. So things will go on like this and I know I won't be able to take it.	
Marion: So things will get so bad you can't stand them—then what will you do?	Reflects.
Darcy: I don't know, something terrible.	
Marion: When you say "something terrible," I imagine all sorts of things. Do you mean you would think about suicide?	Asks directly about suicide even though Darcy initially rebuffs her. Shares her concern.
Darcy: Who asked you to be so nosy?	
Marion: Nobody, but I'm worried that you might feel so miserable that you might think of hurting yourself. I really want to know if you're thinking of suicide right now.	Shares concern and asks directly about suicide.
Darcy: Yeah, but what can you do about it?	
Marion: I can listen—sometimes you feel better when you can talk to somebody. I care about how you're feeling.	Offers help. Accepts feelings and suicidal thoughts. Counters Darcy's helplessness with offer of help.

Conversation	Assessment and Intervention
Darcy: I've already talked and talked and talked. . . I still think I'd be better off dead.	Clarifies and then focuses on specific plan of suicide.
Marion: You feel that living isn't worth it. Maybe you have a plan—for instance, if you wanted to end it all now, what would you do?	
Darcy: I have a gun and bullets at home and if my boyfriend really leaves next week like he said, then that's *it!*	Darcy identifies plan which is highly lethal, and also identifies the hazard.
Marion: It sounds like you're really desperate, that without him life isn't worth it.	Restates feelings.
Darcy: Right.	
Marion: Have you ever felt this miserable or depressed before?	Focuses on past history.
Darcy: Well, yes—I guess off and on for several years I have these really blue spells.	
Marion: Sounds as though it's been hard for you. Have you tried suicide before?	Focuses on coping and assesses past suicide attempts.
Darcy: Not really. I've just thought about it a lot.	
Marion: Things have been really hard for you, Darcy. I just wonder what has kept you going?	Focuses on coping.
Darcy: I guess I've always managed because I had someone to hang on to. Now my boyfriend is the only one left and, well, if he goes too. . .	
Marion: I see. You feel that he's your last support and if you lose him, you couldn't find another support or go on.	Restates for empathy.
Darcy: He's the only reason I go on living.	
Marion: I wonder. You say you've talked and talked about this; but have you tried any sort of therapy or found anything at all that helps?	Searches for other coping.
Darcy: Oh, sure. I went to someone for therapy once, but I didn't seem to get any better so I stopped going. It doesn't matter what I do, anyway—it won't change anything.	

Conversation	Assessment and Intervention
Marion: You feel nothing you do is important and no one can help you. Hasn't anyone else been helpful before—a teacher . . . friend . . . relative . . . priest . . . neighbor?	Searches for coping and helps Darcy identify significant others.
Darcy: Nobody.	
Marion: It seems you've always had to rely on yourself. What do you do for yourself when you get to feeling like this?	Searches for coping in past.
Darcy: Well, when I feel good I like painting and making things and cooking but when I feel down I don't feel like doing anything.	
Marion: Well, what about work? Doesn't that help you keep going?	Helps Darcy identify coping.
Darcy: Yes, but it's getting harder and harder to get here, and if I keep getting sick and taking sick time and coming in late, they'll surely fire me—I just know it.	Discovers that Darcy's one last coping device may be in danger of disintegrating.
Marion: So what you're saying is that it's been harder and harder to get to work. Are other things hard, too? Any trouble sleeping or eating?	Assesses for other symptoms of crisis.
Darcy: Yes. I just don't seem to have any appetite and I don't sleep very well.	
Marion: What about other things? Do you get any pleasure from drinking, sex, or things you used to enjoy?	Assesses degree of crisis and extent of alcohol use.
Darcy: No, that's why my boyfriend is planning to leave me. I do drink—more and more. I keep hoping I'll feel better but I only feel worse.	
Marion: Darcy, you sound to me like a person who is depressed, the way you describe yourself. Would you say that's about right?	Offers clear picture of the crisis. Asks for validation.
Darcy: I guess so. I sure feel awful enough. . .	
Marion: You know, Darcy, I think you really need to consult somebody to see if you can't get some relief so you can sleep and start to feel better. Most important, I don't want you to kill yourself. I want	Even though Darcy seems very negative about talking, Marion offers the idea of treatment to help with personal difficulties. Thus Marion shares Darcy's feelings, suggests therapy, and gives hope.

Conversation   **Assessment and Intervention**

you to get some help so you can be
protected from your suicidal impulses and get through this crisis.

Darcy: Why would you care about
me?

Marion: Because you are someone I   Reaffirms message, "You can trust
am concerned about, and I think   me—I care."
your death would be a terrible
waste. You need some help to get   Gives hope and a clear picture of a
over this crisis.   time-limited ordeal.

Darcy: I don't know . . . do you really think—?

Marion: Yes, I really do. I've seen   Gives hope.
people who felt hopeless and
overwhelmed by suicidal feelings,
and I've seen them get better. They
were glad they took the risk and
tried therapy again. Anyway, I
think you've been trying to tell me
for sometime you want help.

Darcy: I don't know, maybe. . . . I
just didn't think anyone cared.

Marion: That's what happens when   Restates feelings to expand care-
you feel worthless and so very   giver-client frame of reference.
alone.

Darcy: Yes, that's the worst part.

Marion: Darcy, I want you to live.   Asks for promise to decrease danger
And I want you to promise me   and remove method.
you'll give that gun and the bullets
to someone else for now so you
won't have them around the house
while you're feeling so down.

Darcy: I couldn't give the gun away.

Marion: Well, could you give me the   Asks again for promise to remove
bullets? I'd feel you were much   method.
safer this way.

Darcy: Well, maybe. . . I'll have to
think about it.

Marion: Then I want you to promise   Asks for contract not to suicide.
me something else. Promise me
you won't do anything to hurt
yourself accidentally or on purpose
unless you call the suicide prevention center or your caregiver first.

Darcy: I don't think I can say that.

Marion: Well, then, qualify it if you   Encourages Darcy to make promise
must, but I want you to promise me   *specific.*
now!

Darcy: Well. . . I promise not to do
anything accidentally or on pur-

Conversation	Assessment and Intervention
pose until Friday of next week, the day Frank said he'd leave.	
Marion: Thank you. I really feel a lot safer. It's important to you and to me that you gave me your promise. Now. What person would you feel comfortable seeing? I mean about your problem sleeping and your depression?	Responds to Darcy's promise by sharing feelings. Focuses on referral.
Darcy: Do you think I should go back to the person I was seeing— you know, the one I stopped seeing?	
Marion: If that person can treat your depression and help you sleep, why yes, I think it's important to go back.	Encourages return to original caregiver.
Darcy: I'm kind of scared to call. Would you call for me and make the appointment?	
Marion: How about if we make the appointment together? You have to help set up the appointment so it's at a time when you can get there.	Responds to feelings by offering to help but encourages independence by helping, not doing it for Darcy.
Darcy: Let's call now before I lose my nerve.	
Marion: O.K. I am really so glad you're going to try this again, Darcy. I know it will help you to feel less alone.	
[The appointment is made for the following day.]	
Marion: Darcy, I'm so relieved to know you have an appointment for tomorrow. How are you going to manage until then? Will you be with your boyfriend tonight?	Focuses on structure and need to be with someone until appointment.
Darcy: Yes, we're having dinner with friends.	
Marion: O.K. I imagine you'll feel better as long as you aren't alone. But remember, if you start thinking about suicide or get an impulse to commit suicide, call the suicide prevention center any time, day or night. Now—have you changed your mind about giving me the bullets?	
Darcy: No, I just can't go that far. I have to keep the gun and the bullets.	

Conversation	Assessment and Intervention
Marion: Well, I can understand that they are important to you, but I trust your promise and I know you'll keep it. I just hope you'll decide to give the bullets to someone else as soon as you feel up to it.	Accepts feelings. Reinforces promise and trusts Darcy to fulfill promise.
Darcy: Yeah, I guess you could call them my security blanket.	Leaves the door open for removing bullets when possible.
Marion: Well, maybe you can trade them in soon for a safer security blanket. Now, what do you plan to say at your appointment tomorrow?	Gives hope. Asks Darcy to give a clear perception of the hazard and crisis and state what she wants from caregiver.
Darcy: I think I'm going to say I'm depressed right now, and I'm afraid my boyfriend will desert me. I guess I have never done anything about my down periods in the past. They keep haunting me. This seems to be the worst time up to now because I plan to shoot myself next Friday if my boyfriend leaves me. But I promise not to do anything before then. I hope I can get some help so I can sleep better and start feeling better. I'm not sure I can get rid of these depressions but I am willing to go back to my therapist and talk about them even though I'm kind of scared to go.	
Marion: You can really make your thoughts and feelings clear, Darcy. I think it must be pretty scary to go back to the therapist you stopped seeing, but you already know one thing. You know that this therapist won't reject you the way you think your boyfriend will. I felt good after our telephone call when you got such a warm welcome from your therapist. He was really concerned about you and wanted to see you as soon as possible.	Reinforces internal coping. Accepts feeling. Reinforces new caregiver as warm, concerned, trustworthy.

Case 6: Lynn T

Report	Assessment	Intervention
Lynn was a 21-year-old college student. She got along well with the other students and with her teachers,	Recent life style stable.	

Report	Assessment	Intervention

who considered her to be reasonably successful, personable, and stable.

Four months before graduation, her classmate Marie made an appointment to speak with one of their teachers. Marie told the teacher that within the past few weeks, Lynn had become increasingly withdrawn and tearful, spending much of her time in her room.

Isolation/withdrawal noted.

She would not talk to anyone about what was disturbing her and made vague statements like "It just doesn't matter anymore" and "Nobody cares, anyway."

Possible suicidal clues presented.

Although Marie could not say why, she was uneasy and fearful that Lynn might be thinking about suicide. She had attempted to be helpful but saw no improvement in Lynn after three weeks of trying. Now she felt frustrated and helpless. She didn't know what to do and had come to the teacher to ask for advice.

Feelings of hopelessness.

Classmate and teacher are resources.

Lynn was maintaining a B average in school, attended class regularly, and completed all assignments. She had not missed any days at her part-time job.

Strengths: constructive coping still intact; also ability to maintain daily activities.

Determine if any further evaluation and intervention is necessary and who should do it.

Recently, however, she had expressed doubt about her ability to function after graduation in "the real world." Her mood and behavior were described as apathetic and depressed. Although considered attractive by others, Lynn had recently made several statements referring to herself as ugly, and had also expressed self-doubt because she had no boyfriend and dated only occasionally.

When questioned by her friends and family about what was wrong, Lynn's usual reply was that she didn't want to talk about it, at which point she would either leave the house or lock herself in her room.

Lynn had no known history of emotional disturbance. She lived at home with her parents and had several

Report	Assessment	Intervention

friends. Although she did communicate to some degree with her friends, she refused to talk with her parents at all, and expressed a great deal of hostility toward them, stating that they didn't understand her and weren't interested in her, anyway. There were two younger brothers at home. Classmates had suggested that Lynn make an appointment with the school counseling service but she rejected this idea with a considerable show of anger.

Assessment: Living with significant others but communication broken off; some withdrawal but still in contact with friends.

After this talk with Marie, the teacher decided to speak to Lynn directly and asked that she come to his office after class.

Intervention: Once having determined that intervention is indicated, begin immediately.

Upon her arrival, Lynn was openly antagonistic. She told the teacher he was interfering in a matter that was none of his business and said she felt betrayed that her friend had revealed such personal information to another.

Assessment: Is hostile, rejecting help.

In the face of her open hostility, the teacher related his genuine concern and that of her friend.

Intervention: Start building a relationship.

Lynn insisted that she didn't want to talk about any of her problems, but the teacher was persistent. He reassured Lynn that whatever personal distress she was feeling, this would not affect the faculty's evaluation of her classwork.

Intervention: Determine what the client needs. Determine what the caregiver can do.

Upon hearing this, Lynn looked somewhat relieved, then indicated she would talk only if she could be assured that the information be kept confidential.

The teacher replied that he did not expect Lynn to divulge very personal and confidential information to him, but that he was worried about her and wanted to help. He pointed out that he could not promise to keep a secret that might be harmful to her.

Intervention: Refuse complicity in harmful secrets but offer assurance that help is available.

The teacher then asked Lynn directly if she had been thinking about suicide. The girl responded with an angry yes.

Assessment: Need to determine suicidal intent.

Intervention: Ask directly about suicidal intent.

Report	Assessment	Intervention
Upon further questioning it developed that for the past two weeks Lynn had been preoccupied continually with thoughts about killing herself, but she would say nothing further.	Need to identify the hazard and recent feelings and symptoms.	
Although clearly exhausted, she continued to refuse all his offers to help, repeating that no one really cared about her. When the teacher showed he understood, however, she mentioned that her parents showed no concern for her.	Feelings of rejection from parents.	Show acceptance and understanding of client's feelings.
Apparently this feeling on her part was one of a longstanding nature, as there had been no recent change in the relationship, from what the teacher could gather.		
After he determined that Lynn would be alone at home until late that evening, the teacher summoned Marie from class and asked her to accompany Lynn home and stay with her that evening. Although Lynn objected verbally to this arrangement, she left the office with Marie.	Resources are still available.	Caregiver is active and directive; provides resource.
An hour later the teacher telephoned Lynn. Although still hostile, she was more willing to talk by that time. Again he questioned her about her suicidal ideation. She admitted that she had been thinking about crashing her car into something, but had no more specific details to offer.	Suicide plan vague, but available and lethal.	
Throughout the conversation Lynn kept saying that she didn't really want to talk about anything and wished people would stop bothering her. Nevertheless the teacher maintained his attitude of concern and firmly informed Lynn that he would continue to "bother" her as long as she was in distress.	Verbal message says "Leave me alone"—nonverbal behavior says "Help me."	Continue with messages that caregiver is listening and is concerned; and that help is available.
It is important to note that despite her continued objections, Lynn did continue the conversation, even if somewhat reluctantly.	Client does not recognize she is signaling for help.	Focus on current stress.
Lynn could not really say what was wrong. She felt depressed, hopeless, and rejected.	Depression, feelings of hopelessness.	

Report	Assessment	Intervention
Although in reality Lynn's schoolwork had been satisfactory, she felt that she had done poorly.	Inaccurate perception of events.	
At the same time, she was concerned about what she would do after graduation. She felt as though she had worked and studied hard for four years and no one had ever appreciated her accomplishments.		Facilitate the expression of feelings by questioning.
Lynn couldn't remember when she started to feel this way but it seemed like a long time. She was unable to identify any recent event that might have prompted the recent increase of symptoms, and appeared reluctant even to think about it.	No identifiable hazard can be found.	Attempt to identify and clarify hazard.
Yet in the face of her anger and their frequent misunderstandings, Lynn said that she loved her parents.		
By this time Lynn was much more willing to talk. However, she vehemently rejected the teacher's suggestion that she seek professional help.	Rejects professional help, so other resources must be found.	
He then advised her that her parents and her academic advisor would be contacted. Lynn agreed to turn her car keys over to Marie, and she promised to attend class the next morning. Marie offered to drive her to school.		Mobilize available resources; and reduce immediate danger by removing method and availability. Consult with others, providing additional resource and reassurance and maintaining hope.
The teacher then telephoned Lynn's academic advisor, who in turn called Lynn to let her know that he, too, was concerned and anxious to help in any way possible. He reassured Lynn that her personal problems would not prevent her from graduating if she was able to continue with her work.		
A telephone call was then made to Lynn's home.		Continue to mobilize additonal resources.
Rather than the rejecting, disinterested mother Lynn had described, Mrs. T was genuinely concerned about her daughter, as was Mr. T, and both parents seemed relieved to talk about their anxiety about their daughter. They indicated that they had not been able to communicate with Lynn for several months, had become increasingly worried about her be-	Inaccurate perception of significant others.	Provide support for significant others.

Report	Assessment	Intervention

havior, and were nearly frantic about what to do.

Family relationships had been stable until recently. There was no past history of serious problems and there had been no previous suicide attempts. Although communication was disrupted, both Mr. and Mrs. T seemed quite perceptive and were well aware of many of the feelings that Lynn had expressed, even of her suicidal thoughts.

No psychiatric history, and no previous suicidal attempts.

Because of Lynn's hostility and her refusal to talk, they felt helpless. They both indicated their willingness to play a supportive role and to urge Lynn to seek counseling. Both offered to attend sessions with her should this prove desirable.

Significant others willing and able to help.

Although Lynn continued to express hostility and reject all offers of help, the teacher called or saw her daily for the next week. He also spoke briefly to her parents and to Marie every other day or so to offer his support and minimize their feelings of helplessness.

Continue intervention as long as situation is not resolved, and provide support for other caregivers.

In this same period, Lynn and her parents revealed that she had been disturbed by feelings of low self-esteem for several years. Despite evidence to the contrary, she felt that she was worthless, a failure, ugly, and unloved.

Self-deprecating feelings of long standing.

In attempts to dissipate these negative feelings, Lynn was reminded of specific past successes that she had accomplished.

And notwithstanding her depression she was urged to continue her attendance at school and at her job.

She was able to do this, although her general mood and behavior did not change and her suicidal ideation remained the same. In fact, she thought frequently about killing herself—sometimes with her car—but her plans were vague and not well formulated.

Symptoms remain the same; no change in suicidal ideation or plan.

Report	Assessment	Intervention

Each day, however, she renewed verbally her promise that she would not do anything to hurt herself for the next 24 hours and that if she did feel the impulse to do anything of the kind, she would talk to someone before taking action.

Intervention: Obtain verbal contract; reduce immediate danger.

The teacher-caregiver was not a qualified therapist, and was experienced only in counseling students about academic problems. His role here was not to deal with the longstanding problems, but to prevent a suicide. His aims were to protect Lynn from self-destructive behavior, provide support, mobilize her resources, and get her to accept professional help. A month later, Lynn was still rejecting suggestions for counseling because "it wouldn't do any good." She felt that seeking professional help would only confirm her feelings that she was a failure who couldn't handle her own problems. She believed that there was a stigma attached to consulting a professional counselor and could not be persuaded otherwise. Her hostility decreased considerably during this period but she began at the same time to express feelings of worthlessness and extreme guilt at the trouble she had caused everyone and because of her angry remarks to those who had first tried to help her.

Intervention: Clarifying role of caregiver, and clarifying client goals.

Assessment: Hostility decreased, feelings of guilt and worthlessness increased.

Nevertheless, with the consistent and persistent support of family, friends, and faculty, Lynn's suicidal ideation decreased. She remained depressed but was able to continue attending class until graduation.

Assessment: Decreased suicidal ideation.

Assessment: Depressed mood continues but daily life stable.

Afterward, however, Lynn cut off communication with the teacher-caregiver and her classmate who had been the first to try to help her.

Several months later a friend reported that Lynn was working in another state. No further information was available on the long-term outcome of the intervention.

REFERENCES

Aguilera DC, Messick JM, Farrell MS: Crisis Intervention: Theory and Methodology. St Louis, Mosby, 1970

Carkhuff RR: The Art of Helping: An Introduction to Life Skills. Amherst, Mass, Human Resources Development Press, 1973

Drye RC, Goulding RI, Goulding ME: No suicide decisions: patient monitoring of suicide risk. Am J Psychiatry 130:171, February 1973

Delbridge PM: Identifying the suicidal person in the community. Nurs Digest, November/December 1975, p 36

Fisher A: Suicide and Crisis Intervention: A Survey and Guide to Services. New York, Springer, 1972

Kovacs M, Beck AT, Weissman A: Hopelessness: an indicator of suicidal risk. Suicide 5:98, 1975

Motto JA: The recognition and management of the suicidal patient. In Flack FF, Draghi SC (eds): Nature and Treatment of Depression. New York, Wiley, 1976

Pittman FS, DeYoung C, Flomenhaft K, Kaplan D, Langsley DG: Crisis intervention therapy. Curr Psychiatr Ther 6:187, 1966

Pretzel P: Understanding and Counseling the Suicidal Person. New York, Abingdon Press, 1972

Roffman JG: Hospitalization of the suicidal client. Crisis Intervention (Buffalo NY: Suicide Prevention and Crisis Services) 5:1, 1974

Savage M: Addicted to Suicide. Santa Barbara, Calif, Copra Press, 1975

Schwartz DA, Finn DE, Slawson PF: Suicide in the Psychiatric Hospital. Am J Psychiatry 132:150, February 1975

Tabachnick N: Interpersonal relations in suicide attempts. Arch Gen Psychiatry 4:16, January 1961

Social and Rehabilitation Service, Youth Development and Delinquency Prevention Administration: Hotline for Youth, DHEW Pub No SRS 72-26006. Washington, DC, 20402, USDHEW

Watzlawick P, Beavin JH, Jackson D: Pragmatics of Human Communication. New York, Norton, 1967

Weissman A: Epidemiology of suicide attempts. Arch Gen Psychol 30:738, June 1974

Wold C: Subgroupings of suicidal people. Omega 2:19, 1971

Chapter 5
Survivor-Victims of Suicide

Who suffers more in a war —the fallen victim, who survives only in the memory of the survivors, or the survivors, who die daily in remembering? The future development of the suicide intervention process will show increased emphasis on areas of prevention with families of suicidal persons. As for now it must be concerned with "postvention" for the survivors.

REVIEW OF THE LITERATURE

Barbara Bell Foglia

Only recently has it been recognized that the experience of the individual who has lost a loved one through suicide is unique. And only recently has this come to the attention of researchers in the area of suicide. A review of the research literature reveals a small but provocative number of research studies concerned with some aspect of the experience of families and/or individuals bereaved by a suicide. In comparing these studies, one must remember that the particular pattern of emotional reaction to suicide and the quality of response differ with each survivor, depending on such factors as the previous experiences of the surviving individual, the relationship between the survivor and the deceased, and the circumstances surrounding the suicide. Thus the surviving individual's response to the crisis of suicide will be shaped by that person's total past experiences and the coping mechanisms developed as a result of these experiences.

Past experience is of particular significance in relation to the

113

phenomenon of suicide. Frequently the family which experiences a suicide has experienced other difficulties involving maladaptive coping mechanisms such as marital problems, emotional or psychologic disturbances, or failures in communication. This is not to say that all families of a suicide experience all of these problems. Indeed, some families may not have experienced any of them. They are mentioned simply to show that one cannot attribute all the reactions of the bereaved solely to the fact of the suicide itself. Like any other human reaction, response to the crisis of suicide must be viewed in the fullest context of the forces which have fashioned it.

Children as Survivors

In 1966, Albert Cain and Irene Fast published the findings of a study completed on 45 disturbed children, all of whom had one parent who had died as a result of suicide.* Although each child's response was unique, two crucial factors were identified as constants in the disturbed reactions of each child to the parent's suicide: (1) feelings of guilt in the child and (2) distortions in communication between adults and the child about the suicide.

In each case, the child's guilt regarding the parent's suicide was so intense that superego distortions were readily discernible in the child's psychopathology, reflected in statements of guilt and self-recrimination, depression, masochistic character development, self-destructive behavior, and reaction formation resulting in passivity and inhibition. The expression of these distortions varied considerably from one child to another, depending on such factors as the personality of the child prior to the suicide, the personality of the surviving parent, the nature of the suicide and the child's involvement in it, the child's age, and so on.

Similarly, the basis for the guilt feelings held by the child varied with each child. In some instances it originated in hostile feelings toward the suicidal parent entertained by the child before the suicide. In others, the child had misbehaved immediately before the suicide and in consequence felt actually responsible for it. Another constellation of guilts revolved around the suicidal act itself. Many of the children studied felt that in some way they should have been able to pre-

---

*The sample consisted of 32 boys and 13 girls. There were twice as many fathers as there were mothers among the parent suicides. Fifteen percent of the children were under 3 years old at the time of suicide; 30 percent were 3 to 6 years old; 40 percent were 6 to 12 years old; and 15 percent were over 12 years of age.

vent the parent's suicide (eg, they should have been at home instead of out playing). These children blamed themselves for not knowing whom to call upon after discovering the suicide, not running fast enough for help, or not opening the windows of a gas-filled room. This particular focus of guilt was clearly evidenced by the unwavering insistence of these children that the fault was theirs.

The second major area in the disturbed reactions to parental suicide was distortion in communication between adults and the child about the suicide. In all but a few cases, the surviving parent avoided communicating directly with the child about the suicide. Distortion in communication not only occurred in the form of such evasions and in suddenly hushed conversations with others at the child's approach, but frequently consisted of outright lying to the child.

Cain and Fast (1966) cite several instances where the child actually witnessed the suicide of the parent or was the first to discover the body. Yet when the child confronted the surviving parent with this direct experience, the parent in most cases countered that the child was confused or had had a bad dream, and that the suicided parent had actually died in a car accident or from a heart attack. In some cases, the harmful effect on the child of such conflicting responses was compounded by differing accounts of the cause of death at different times, and by other marked inconsistencies among the statements of relatives, neighbors, teachers, and schoolmates regarding the cause of death.

Cain and Fast (1966) concluded that these distortions in communication contributed directly to a number of pathogenic elements in the children. Because these children had no opportunity to discuss their experiences and to relieve their feelings of guilt, many of them devised fantasies about the suicide, while others acquired open distrust of the surviving parent as a result of the latter's lying and evasions. Because of the inconsistencies in what the children were permitted or not permitted to know and discuss, many of them developed stammers, stutters, shyness, a reticence to speak, and/or learning disabilities. Most of them came to distrust the reality of their own experience. Perhaps the most complex reaction to these distortions in communication occured in the form of ego-splitting in which the child compartmentalized each set of contradictory beliefs about the parent's death with its own defensive configurations and fantasies, yet both existing side by side.

In their contacts with the parents of these children Cain and Fast (1972) noted a number of suicide-based pathogenic patterns lived out after the suicide. The chief source of these enduring disturbed reactions were identified as (1) the intense guilt evoked by the suicide; (2) the typical shame, denial, and concealment often associated with the suicide, which inhibited or distorted the normal mourning process; and (3) the response of the community, which conveyed implicit accusation rather than emotional support for the suicide's surviving spouse.

In a separate study, Cain and Fast (1966) explored the phenomenon of identification by the child, later on in adult life, with the suicidal parent. They found four major types of identification.

Direct Identification with the Parent in the Suicidal Act. This reaction manifested itself in the child who later commits suicide in a manner similar to or identical with that of the parents, or in the child who assumes perceived characteristics of the dead parent (eg, the constant deep breathing and gasping of the boy who found his mother in a gas-filled room).

Resignation of the Child to a Fate of Death by Suicide. This reaction was illustrated by a small number of children, who, when grown, harbored a sincere belief that they would eventually die by suicide. While some of them had actively sought treatment in order to be rescued from this fate, the others were passively resigned in their conviction that the future could not be altered.

The Child's Continuing Fears of His or Her Suicidal Impulses. Although some of the children studied never came close to a suicidal act or experienced an impulse to commit suicide, others had to be constantly on guard to avoid certain occasions or environments triggering a suicidal impulse. These were the survivors who were particularly prone to panic on the anniversary of the parent's suicide.

Masked Manifestations of the Child's Identification with the Suicided Parent. Initially, these subjects had no conscious memory or knowledge of the parent's suicide. However, they were all prone to various phobias otherwise unexplained, such as fear of heights or fear of driving. Gradually, the cause of the phobia was uncovered in each case by psychotherapy and the patient had to begin working through the crisis of the suicide. In some instances this new awareness increased the risk of a dangerous suicidal crisis. In fact, these findings suggest that identification with the suicided parent can impel the survivor making such identification also to commit suicide within anywhere from a few days' time to three or four decades later.

* * * * *

T. L. Dorpat (1972) completed a study of 17 patients treated in adulthood by psychoanalysis and psychotherapy. These patients had been selected for this study by virtue of the fact that during childhood each of them had lost a parent by suicide. Most of them had experienced emotionally disturbing events prior to the parent's suicide, such as episodes revealing prolonged marital discord between the parents, multiple suicide gestures or threats by the suicidal parent, or loss of the nonsuicidal parent by death, separation, or divorce prior to or within a year after the suicide.

Prominent among the psychologic findings which Dorpat noted in these patients were guilt over the parental suicide, depression, morbid preoccupation with suicide, self-destructive behavior, absence of grief, and developmental arrest. The results of this study indicated that these individuals had responded to the overwhelming trauma of parental suicide by premature crystallization of rigid defensive maneuvers (chiefly denial) rather than by developing a broader and more flexible range of adaptive and defensive capacities.

In the research cited thus far, the samples consist exclusively of a clinical population. Furthermore, they are retrospective studies in which the suicide may have occurred as long ago as several decades before the study was undertaken. For these reasons, caution must be exercised in generalizing research results. Not only are the samples biased toward pathologic reactions to suicide, but further difficulties are posed in ascertaining whether the suicidal act was merely one symptom of an already disturbed family or in fact was the actual cause of the maladaptive responses noted. In any event, it is likely that these families are to be located toward the more disturbed end of the mental health spectrum of all families who have experienced a suicide.

Twelve Widows of Suicides

Studies have been conducted on individuals who have utilized more adaptive, integrative modes of coping with the suicide of a loved one. Noteworthy among these is a study by Samuel Wallace published in 1973. Wallace conducted a year-long case study of 12 Boston women who had lost their husbands through suicide, with the purpose of evaluating the influence of the marital relationship on the suicidal act and the effect of the suicide on the widow survivor.

Each of the women in the study responded to this death crisis differently—some with intense grief, others with feelings of guilt, and still others with a sigh of relief. Although a variety of other dynamics may have influenced each widow's response to the suicide, Wallace found the essential differences among them to be dictated by the emotional investment of each woman in her relationship with her husband.

Wallace identified three groups in this sample of 12 widows: Members of the first group (seven widows) had separated themselves socially from the husband's existence and were leading independent lives of their own. All seven of these women had essentially completed their period of mourning for the loss of a valued relationship. Similarly those of the second group (two widows) had experienced several phases of anticipatory grief, as each had been involved in a marriage in which the husband's ill health suggested his impending death. Those in the third group (three widows) had been caught unprepared for death, suicide being even further from their anticipations than other forms of death. Wallace noted that only for these three widows did bereavement follow its classic pattern.

In all three groups each widow had her own special needs, problems, and methods of coping with the experience of her husband's suicide, some coping more effectively than others. Yet all of them experienced feelings of isolation. For some, this was an isolation initially self-imposed in an effort to rest and reflect while searching for an explanation of the event. However, when these widows did seek support from friends or relatives, they discovered that those they approached often were reluctant to become involved. Most of these women related how outcast, rejected, alone, and hurt they felt. They had been abandoned to their forbidden thoughts and feelings, left alone to find their own solutions. In view of this very real isolation, perhaps it is not surprising that four of these women contemplated, and one actually attempted, suicide.

Families of Five Adolescent Suicides

A report by Herzog and Resnik (1967) describes a preliminary retrospective study of the families of adolescent suicides that took place in Philadelphia during 1965 and 1966. During this period a total of nine adolescents committed suicide but only seven families were available, two families having moved out of the community. Within the seven families available for study considerable difficulty was encountered in obtaining permission for interviews with the surviving parents, and in no family was access to the siblings of the deceased granted to the investigators. Thus, the observations of Herzog and Resnik are based on interviews from a total of five of the original nine families recorded.

The findings of the author's preliminary study indicate that the parents of adolescent suicides (1) refuse to think of the death as a suicide, preferring to consider it an accident; (2) feel hostile toward persons who designate the cause of their child's death as suicide; (3) feel long-lasting guilt about the death of their child. Another striking observation was the frequent signs of family disruption noted among the parents of the suicide. Along with other implications, this latter finding illustrates again the necessity of evaluating family relationships as they were before the suicide when attempting to analyze the responses of the surviving family members to the suicide.

In this study Herzog and Resnik observed that the immediate parental response to the sudden loss of the child appeared to be overwhelming hostility and denial followed by guilt and depression. Projection of this hostility upon society as personified by the medical examiner, police, or physician was common. Herzog and Resnik noted that this defense seemed to allow the surviving parents to externalize the stress immediately, though temporarily. The more successfully the parents projected their guilt, the less they had to face within themselves.

It is interesting to note that despite the resistance of the parents to the research interview and the projection of their guilt and hostility, all of those interviewed said that they would have appreciated having a professionally trained person to talk to immediately following the suicide. The researchers state their opinion that this is the best time to begin intervention with the survivors so that rapport can be established before the development of defensive reactions.

Significant Others as Survivors

A study conducted by James Henslin in 1967 consisted of interviews with 58 persons connected with 25 suicides. Henslin found that the significant others who interpreted the cause of the suicide as lying outside themselves did not seem to experience severe adjustment problems. Conversely, those who felt they had somehow caused or contributed to the suicide, or who believed they could somehow have prevented it, encountered significant problems in adjusting to the suicidal death.

Augenbraun and Neuringer (1972) seem to support these findings as a result of their own casework experiences. They conclude that there is little need for psychotherapy for the survivor who has the capacity to develop efficient adaptive defenses. This is most likely to occur in situations where the relationship between the deceased and the survivor was a positive one with minimal ambivalence, and where the fact of suicide can be attributed to circumstances outside the control of the survivor. More frequently, however, the survivor has been involved in a conflicted relationship with the deceased, and the act of suicide itself may be considered, in part, one outcome of this conflict. The survivor is then subject to overwhelming stress which may contribute to the development of several maladaptive coping mechanisms. In all such instances psychologic intervention is indicated, as it may forestall the onset of a serious psychologic disturbance.

Postvention for the Survivors

From this review of the research literature, it becomes apparent that individuals react to the crisis of suicide in patterns of response that vary from maladaptive defensive maneuvers to efficient adaptive coping mechanisms. It further reveals that there are a multitude of dynamic forces which may influence the response of any person bereaved by suicide. All these studies seem to be in consistent agreement, however, that some sort of mental health intervention should be available to the survivors of suicide. Edwin Shneidman (1973) has dubbed this type of preventive consultation "postvention."

According to Shneidman, postvention is comprised of those activities following the death of a significant other by suicide that serve to assist the survivors in coping with their emotional and psychologic response to the loss. Shneidman maintains that the focus of postvention is not limited to the initial stages of shock and disbelief, but rather is directed toward bereavement as it is experienced in daily living by the survivor. Thus postvention should typically extend over the first critical year following the loss of a significant other by suicide.

Shneidman's concept of postvention is one which borrows many characteristics from psychotherapy—talk, opportunity for ventilation of feelings, interpretation of the event, reassurance, direction, and even gentle confrontation. Thus postvention affords an opportunity for the expression of guarded emotions, especially of those negative affective states such as anger, guilt, and shame. This process brings a measure of stability to the grieving person's life and at the very least provides a genuine interpersonal relationship in which honest thoughts and feelings can be expressed.

Harvey Resnik (1969) has further attempted to conceptualize the sequential phases of postvention, which he calls "psychological re-synthesis." The three sequential phases of psychologic resynthesis are (1) psychologic resuscitation, (2) psychologic rehabilitation, (3) psychologic renewal.

Phase 1: Resuscitation. This consists of the immediate response of the intervenor to the psychologic crisis of the survivor of a suicide. Resnik states that within 24 hours of the suicide a supportive visit should be scheduled with the survivors to assist them in withstanding the initial shock of their grief. As noted, immediate contact between the surviving family members and the intervenor also makes possible the development of rapport before the survivors can begin to elaborate rigid defenses. Once a helping relationship has been established, a return visit should be made by the caregiver within a matter of days in order to provide supplementary information and to encourage verbalization. At this time the survivors are frequently preoccupied with feelings of responsibility for the suicide, evidenced by such reactions as feelings of blame or guilt for acts or failures to act. This phase of psychologic resuscitation may continue for several weeks.

Phase 2: Resynthesis. This consists of psychologic rehabilitation. Resnik describes this as the process which helps survivors to learn new ways of coping with their loss. The major and most difficult task of this phase is to prevent the perpetuation or development of family pathology. Resnik maintains that this can be facilitated by the intervenor who fosters the exploration of guilt before gross distortions can develop. This second phase may last for several months, during which time the caregiver's contacts remain regular but unstructured.

Phase 3: Renewal. This consists of what Resnik describes as the forfeit of grief and its attendant bondage to the suicide, during which the substitution of new object relationships and new contacts is made in part. This phase generally occurs at any time from about six months and onward following the suicidal death. Meetings during this phase are initiated only as the survivors desire them. This phase is terminated by the intervenor's communication with the family on the first anniversary of the suicide.

Resnik acknowledges that this final communication reopens the mourning process with all of its pain, but only for a short time, and this hurt is countered by the fact that the intervenor has shown an awareness of the importance of the date and is reaffirming the availability of help, which can be most reassuring to the survivors. At this time the process of psychologic renewal passes wholly into the hands of the survivors.

Thus the concept of psychologic resynthesis, with its three component phases, represents a beginning effort in the profession to identify the steps by which postventive intervention can meaningfully assist the surviving members of a family to cope with the reality of suicide.

Toward a Workable Postvention Procedure

Before a program of postvention can be initiated successfully, it seems essential to direct reflection and research to a number of variables in the therapeutic situation. For example, what professional background should the intervenor possess (eg, mental health professional, visiting nurse, minister, or perhaps supervised volunteer)? From what organizational framework should services be offered (eg, suicide prevention center, community mental health clinic, medical examiner's office, religious organization)? And what is the most appropriate setting for the delivery of services?

It has been suggested that the intervenor not be perceived by the survivor(s) as an investigator, but rather as an interested and compassionate person. Thus the intervenor's association with the medical examiner's office might pose a barrier at the outset, before the opportunity is presented to establish a working relationship with the survivors. Similarly, direct association of the intervenor with a mental health facility might inhibit successful postvention. For example, a surviving family member who is invited to a community mental health clinic might interpret the invitation as implying blame for the suicide or as an inference of mental illness in the family, particularly at a time when the survivor's own feelings might be colored by such fears.

This brings attention to the survivor's potential resistance to postvention from any source. Despite the agreement among researchers that preventive intervention is desirable for the high-risk group of the suicide's survivors, the proposed recipients may not concur. Considering the social stigma that is attached to a suicide and the resulting vagueness with which the family shrouds the event, it should not be surprising that many surviving family members retreat from overtures of postvention.

One solution previously discussed, is to initiate intervention as soon as possible following the suicide, preferably within 24 hours. Another possibility might be to make the initial contact in the survivor's home. Not only does the home provide a setting in which the survivor will probably feel less threatened, but it could also provide additional information by permitting the caregiver to observe at first hand how the survivors are responding (eg, how the home is being managed, whether belongings of the deceased are in evidence, how the family members interact, etc). Still another approach might be to utilize a supervised volunteer who is also the survivor of a suicide, an approach similar to that of the widow-to-widow program in Boston (Silverman, 1969).

In a broader sense, perhaps, postvention efforts should also be focused on a program of suicide education for the community at large. In a more immediate approach, educational endeavors might wisely be directed toward individuals in the community who are most likely to encounter and perhaps influence the survivors—health professionals, teachers, religious officials, police, social services, and the like.

There is also a need for further research into the effects of suicide upon the surviving family members and the development of a fully effective means of intervening to the survivor's best advantage. Although the research already completed in this area is illuminating, it is only a beginning. There are many gaps yet to be explored. For example, there is a need to study survivors quite early in their post-suicidal period, because, as already mentioned, too many reports provide data from retrospective studies of survivor reactions to a suicide which may have occurred years or even decades earlier. During the time intervening between the event and the investigation, it is not unreasonable to expect some distortion in the individual's memory of initial response to the suicide. Similarly, maladaptive defense mechanisms of survivors may have become rigid, further beclouding the issue. Another research approach, based on longitudinal studies of survivors, might provide additional insight into the frequent changes in the survivor's pattern of adjustment over the years. There is also a need to explore the separate but related issue of the dynamics of family interaction before the suicide, in order to gain a more realistic perception of the response of family members to the suicidal death.

Even more important would be studies on the nonpathologic survivors of suicide. Because most of the published studies of survivors have taken their samples exclusively from a population of individuals actively involved in psychotherapy, these studies afford little insight into the dynamics of successful modes of coping with suicide. Not only would studies utilizing nonpatient populations contribute to a more complete and accurate understanding of the survivor experi-

ence, but they might also greatly enlarge the assessment and intervention repertoire of the intervenor working with survivors.

It is apparent, then, that many questions remain unanswered in
this area. Yet inroads have been made. Survivors have finally been
recognized as a potentially high-risk group for the development of
psychologic and emotional difficulties. Further, there is general
agreement among researchers that a program of preventive intervention for the survivors is desirable both as a means of providing comprehensive preventive mental health care in the community, and
specifically as a means of suicide prevention. Our review of the research literature reveals not only a growing appreciation in the
caretaking professions of a serious phenomenon previously unrecognized, but also a whole area in the mental health field which by its
very nature demands continuing professional scrutiny and investigation.

A PROGRAM IN POSTVENTION

Donna Ziebarth Junghardt

Using the definition of postvention from the preceding section, I
should like to describe one innovative project based on this kind of
postvention. One of the programs currently under way in the San
Bernardino County Department of Public Health in California is the
Suicide Survivor Follow-up Program. The purpose of this program is
to bring support and comfort to members of the suicide victim's family, as well as to gain specific information about psychologic counseling.

It is essential to this kind of postvention program that the
coroner's office collaborate with both local departments of mental and
public health by forwarding at once a copy of the death certificate of
each recorded suicide to the local district office of the health department. As a mental health nurse working in the health department,
my task is to contact the family immediately after the head of the
household has received the family's copy of the death certificate.

The advantage to the community of having a mental health nurse
in the health department is obvious. Since all death certificates are
filed at the branch offices, we have the earliest access to the official
information on all deaths in the area. Also, mental health/public
health nurses are accustomed to making home visits and we usually
are able to gain entry into the home when others may be turned
away. Approaching the family of a suicide victim is at best very

difficult, especially for a total stranger. But to approach family members offering them crisis intervention treatment makes the situation even more difficult. They may feel they have no need for help, since they aren't the one who committed suicide. Contrast this response with that of the distressed individual or family who calls or visits a clinic recognizing and verbalizing a conscious need for help!

The suicide survivor program in San Bernadino has been expanded to provide crisis intervention treatment for family members and often for friends, the employer, or others closely associated with the suicide victim. The primary goal is to help these survivors recover from the intense and difficult grief process which is often more troublesome at every stage than the typical nonsuicidal grief experience. The suicide of a loved one or a close associate carried with it a unique burden of guilt and shame for those left behind.

Early Professional Contact Desirable

Research studies reveal that many suicide survivors have stated that they would have responded to a trained professional had one offered to help them with their feelings at the time of the event. Yet most survivors of suicide never take the initiative of seeking out such help. Therefore, they must be sought out by the mental health nurse. We have found that this first contact with a caregiver is most effective when made 24 to 48 hours after the suicide, and *before* the funeral. If intervention can be initiated at this time, a supportive relationship will be under way while the family is still in shock. At such times most people are quite willing and even eager to talk to an understanding, gentle "outsider." This outsider should not be associated with the official team investigating the suicide—the police, the coroner, the insurance company investigator, etc. She needs to be objective but not distraught, as the family members or friends may be. This contact serves as a cathartic, therapeutic experience for the family and gives the nurse the opportunity to establish rapport before denial and resistance set in. If this first contact is delayed even a week, it is much more difficult and sometimes impossible by that time to reach the family in any meaningful way.

The Postvention Process

The counseling for the family (or any significant others) may be divided into the three phases of Resnik's *psychologic resynthesis*, described in the preceding section. The first phase, that of *psychologic resuscitation*, begins with the initial visit to the survivors' home. Sometimes when information is sketchy, the cause of death may not be officially determined as suicide, but listed as a possible suicide pending further investigation. In either event, the initial home visit is made promptly—just as soon as the information is received from the coroner's office. The goals of this initial contact are

1. To establish rapport with the survivors
2. To help the survivors withstand the initial shock of their immense loss
3. To help the survivors become aware of their basic emotions at this time—their feelings of confusion, guilt, and blame, and often their strong feelings of hostility and perhaps severe depression

Some families cannot bear to face the fact of suicide in the short time between the death of the victim and the funeral. They simply cannot discuss it. I've found that they appreciate being allowed to arrive at the full realization of their loss in their own good time. The mental health nurse respects this defense and makes no attempt to tear it down. A person has a defense for a very good reason—he needs it. He should never be forced "to face the facts" before he is ready to do so. Sometimes one survivor, or a whole family, cannot accept the fact that this death is a suicide. They prefer to believe it was a homocide or an accident or someone else's fault. It is overwhelming to admit that a member of one's own family deliberately killed himself.

The second stage, *psychologic rehabilitation*, takes place over the next few months. I usually try to meet with the family again immediately after the funeral in launching this phase of the postvention. The goals here are

1. To make a contract with the family establishing regular meeting times with them, either with individual members alone or in group as a unit, and either in the home or at the office (sometimes a combination of these), covering the first six months of the first year following the suicide
2. To support the reintegration of the family
3. To help the family deal with the period of mourning and the grief process, and to help them understand the dynamics of grieving
4. To deal with whatever emotions or social problems or crises may arise during this period

These meetings will probably not be held on a weekly or other unitized interval over the whole period. I have found it necessary to visit most families as many as two or three times the first week, then weekly for the next three or four weeks. After the initial crisis period of approximately six weeks has passed, the remaining visits may be scheduled in one of two ways—either "on call," with the family calling me whenever they feel they need to meet, or set up in advance at two- or three-week intervals. I have found that after six weeks most families are functioning pretty well on their own and need only occasional sessions, perhaps to reaffirm new coping devices, or to reopen communication between two family members.

After the six-month anniversary of the suicide, the phase of *psychologic renewal* begins to unfold. The family is regaining its integrity and the mental health nurse is now available only upon request. Most families in my experience have not requested appointments beyond this time.

At the time of the first anniversary of the suicide, it is a good idea to revisit the family once more and to reevaluate any continuing problems. They may need further therapy as a family unit, or one member may need referral for longer-term individual therapy. After this visit, the contract that was made between the parties has been fulfilled.

Case 7: Dick

Marge Jackson and her husband, Dick, have been separated for several years. He drank heavily and frequently drove over to her home, where he would start yelling, berating her and their three children. Marge also had a drinking problem. Susan, the eldest child, had just turned 18, but because of her poor school attendance was still a junior in high school. Richard, 16, the only son, was a sophomore. Barbara, 10 years old and in the fourth grade, was the only one who was doing well at school. One night Barbara and Richard had a fight and Barb yelled at her brother, "I wish you were dead." Richard had also been having trouble dealing with his parents' fighting and only the month before had run between them to prevent his father from hitting his mother. Jackson turned on the boy and began to beat him instead of the mother. Richard was left with a black eye and swollen bruises on his face.

Richard's girlfriend, Linda, was using drugs and had been in trouble both at school and at home. At this time, Richard's father was living with Linda's mother and this presented enormous difficulties for the teenage pair, who had been "steadies" for a year. Richard and Linda were having frequent quarrels. Richard was furious that his father was living with Linda's mother. On this particular evening, Marge remembers that Richard was at home. He had acted worried but had been quietly listening to records until the phone rang. It was Linda. Marge could hear Richard pleading with her not to break up with him again but she hung up on him. He dashed back into his room, grabbed a jacket, and stormed out of the house. He yelled behind him that he was "going to see some guys." It was about 9:00 P.M.

Marge had a couple of drinks, and then she and the girls went to bed. She was awakened in the middle of the night by police pounding on the door. She remembers only vaguely what they said except that "they told me Richard was dead. He had hanged himself with his own belt in an orange grove only half a mile away."

One day later, after receiving a copy of the death certificate, I planned to make a home visit to the Jacksons that same day. The funeral was to be held two days from then. Arriving at the address listed as the home of Richard's mother, I saw the curbs on both sides of the street lined with cars. This was not unusual. Relatives and friends often hover about before the funeral. Afterward the family is left alone and people find it increasingly difficult to talk to family members about the tragedy. Although I have made many home visits, I think that first encounter at the door of a family of a suicide victim is probably one of the most difficult. It is literally necessary to "talk your way inside."

This first visit to the Jacksons was a failure. I was met at the door by three or four "protecting" relatives, who told me that the family was much too upset to talk to anyone. I explained the purpose of my visit, left my card, and asked when I would be able to see Mrs. Jackson. They answered vaguely, "Probably some time this afternoon," so I pressed for a specific time, and we finally agreed that I could return about 3:00 P.M.

At 3:00 P.M. I was met at the door by Marge Jackson, who was in her bathrobe looking very disheveled and upset. Four women were in the living room still "guarding" Marge and her older daughter, Susan. The youngest child, Barbara, was not at home. At the start of the interview, the other women did most of the talking, saying that this was certainly not a suicide, "Richard would never do anything like that." When Marge saw that I remained noncommittal and did not try to argue, she began to open up. Eventually some of her protectors left the room when they realized that I was not going to hurt anyone.

Marge's initial reaction to the event seemed to be a combination of shock, confusion, and a terrible sense of abandonment. Apparently, after her separation from her husband, she had relied on Richard a good deal. She, too, however, was adamant in her insistence that this was not a suicide. After talking with many of Richard's friends, she discovered that he had been arguing with two strange young men outside a nearby market. She firmly stated he had been murdered, but when she attempted to obtain more details from the police, she had been rebuffed by their blunt statement that this was "an open and shut case of suicide."

In the first weeks of counseling, my visits with the family had much the same content. Richard had been murdered, and the police weren't going to do anything about it. The possibility of suicide was never discussed. It was possible, however, to get Marge to talk about Barbara. Barbara had been sent away to stay with relatives during the funeral. Marge mentioned that now Barb seemed afraid at night; she would never go into Richard's room (which incidentally was still exactly as he had left it). Barb's grades in school were failing and she seemed to dread going to school.

Marge and I talked about how Barbara might be trying to tell her family nonverbally that she needed help because she was very upset. Marge was afraid of "babying her" by leaving a night light on or spending time with her in her bedroom after the lights were out. Marge had avoided any discussion with Barbara's teacher about what the child was going through, even though the other children at school were known to be teasing her about her "crazy brother who killed himself." We also discussed the possibility of impulsiveness in Barbara's behavior.

Barbara's suicide attempt two months later made her mother realize that it was time to face the facts and stop some of her obsessive talking about "the murder." She realized that she couldn't continue to carry on as she had been doing because she had to deal with the needs of her daughters. Actually, 18-year-old Susan proved to be the strongest member of this family. She seemed to understand Barbara's misery and was the one who saved her life. Barbara's suicide attempt was well planned. No doubt it would have succeeded had Susan not realized from our family counseling sessions the need to be aware of any changes in the behavior of the others.

Barbara had taken with her every available pill in the house before Susan drove her to a slumber party. Their mother was out of town for the night. The child would have been in a strange home where the adults were not attuned to her natural behavior, and, once having taken the pills, she probably would have gone to sleep and just never awakened. However, Susan noticed in the car that Barb's speech was "different," so she stopped the car on the freeway. She told Barb they would not budge until Barb told her what was going on, so the child tearfully told her everything.

Susan did not return home to double check the story, nor did she try to contact their mother. Because of our many family sessions, which had increased her sensitivity to her family, she drove directly to the emergency ward of the nearest hospital, where Barbara's stomach was pumped after discovered that she had taken ten times the lethal dose of her mother's tranquilizers. During Barbara's two-week stay in the hospital, I spoke with her physician and daily with her mother. Her suicide note was a poem to her dead brother in which she described her terrible loneliness for him and her desire to see him. In the final sentence, she said she was coming to see him as soon as she could. To Barbara, her only chance for a reunion with her brother was to die!

After Barbara returned home from the hospital, all three family members seemed much closer to each other. They began to think of themselves as a family again. They cleaned out Richard's room, even though it was a painful experience. They read his unmailed letters stating that he didn't want to live without Linda. At last they began to accept the fact that Richard had done what he had wanted to do and their own hostility and agitation gradually diminished.

At the six-month anniversary of Richard's suicide, we reviewed the family's progress. They were able to see many areas in which there was improvement. For one thing, Barbara's grades in school had returned to normal. Susan decided to finish high school at night and go to a beauty college during the day. Marge and Dick were still quarreling, but Marge was developing some insight into how she contributed to their fighting instead of considering herself always the martyr. Her drinking had lessened, too.

Six months later at the yearly evaluation, I found the Jackson family much the same as they had been six months before, except that Susan was planning to be married. The family did not call me for further appointments and the case was closed.

Principles Underlying Postvention

Special considerations should be borne in mind when dealing with the survivors of a suicide victim:

Family Members Need to Accept the Suicide in Their Own Time.   Acceptance of the fact of suicide is a difficult but critical task. Some survivors get so locked into their doubts by such questions as "Did he or didn't he?" "Was it an accident?" "Was it homicide?" that they never arrive at the process of normal grieving. They play Sherlock Holmes by expending their energy in going out and doing their own "investigating."

Should We Convince the Family of the Value of Crisis Intervention? Usually the clinching argument for parents of young children is that family sessions will help them understand the symbolic and nonverbal clues their children may be giving them when they are unable to talk about their distress.

One of the most difficult problems in communication is that of reaching the father of the suicide teenager. After three years of working with suicide survivors, I find that the parents of a teenager who has committed suicide find it very difficult to share their grief. They seem to withdraw into separate shells of guilt and self-doubt. Even when one parent is willing to try counselling, it is rare that they both are. Each parent, I am sure, must do a good deal of conscious and unconscious blaming of the other parent as well as himself for the tragedy.

Family Members Need to Learn That Grief Is Self-Limiting. They need constant reassurance so that everyone will keep working at the resolution of their grief. They need to be told repeatedly that what they're going through is a self-limiting process and that if they are able to work on their feelings as they arise and deal with them, not push them away or refuse to acknowledge them, their terribly painful emotions of grief and loss will subside. The grief process does eventually resolve itself. Parents of a suicide do not have to look forward to a lifetime of feeling so terrible that they cannot really carry on with their normal activities.

Family Members Need to Learn How Children Grieve. In families with very young surviving children, I have found that the surviving parent or parents usually appreciate being told how a child handles grief and loss, and how a child may display depression. The parents are of course quick to realize that a child of five years or younger usually does not come up to you and say, "Mommy, I feel sad about Daddy's dying." But children do tell their parents in many ways about their sadness, and also about their anger that a parent is gone. Sometimes this response shows itself in regressive changes of behavior (such as temper tantrums in a usually even-tempered child, sudden inability to get along in school, or just plain misery).

Goal of the San Bernardino Program

The main goal of the Suicide Survivor Follow-up Program of San Bernardino is to help the children. If a professional caregiver intervenes at the time of a parent's death, perhaps we can spare the child some of the long-term destructive effects of losing a parent through suicide. Adults who as children lost a parent by suicide fill their waking thoughts with ideas of suicide. Therapists have cited patients who couldn't remember a conscious moment in which they didn't want to die. In such cases, when probing back, the therapist has often found that, as a young child, this adult had lost a parent through suicide or even natural causes. Somehow, in dealing with grief caused by the parent's death, the coping mechanism of the patient incorporated this concept of living with death. One therapist I know recalled a patient in her forties who told him that the thought of killing herself never left her mind—she knew it was something she had to do. The therapist was able to "postpone" her suicide by showing her that her own three children would have to go through the same kind of hell she herself had gone through her entire lifetime if she carried out her compulsive intent, and for the same reason.

REFERENCES

Augenbraun B, Neuringer C: Helping survivors with the impact of a suicide. In Cain A (ed): Survivors of Suicide. Springfield, Bannerstone House, 1972

Cain A, Fast I: Children's disturbed reactions to parent suicide. Am J Orthopsychiatry 36:873, October 1966

———: The legacy of suicide. In Cain A (ed): Survivors of Suicide. Springfield, Bannerstone House, 1972

Dorpat T: Psychological effects of parental suicide on surviving children. In Cain A (ed): Survivors of Suicide. Springfield, Bannerstone House, 1972

Henslin J: Strategies of adjustment. In Cain A (ed): Survivors of Suicide. Springfield, Bannerstone House, 1972

Herzog A, Resnik H: A clinical study of parental response to adolescent death by suicide. In Farberow N (ed): Proc 4th Int Conf Suicide Prevention. Los Angeles, Delmar, 1967

Resnik H: Psychological resynthesis: a clinical approach to the survivors of a death by suicide. In Shneidman E, Ortega M (eds): Aspects of Depression. Boston, Little, Brown 1969

Shneidman E: Deaths of Man. New York, Quadrangle (NY Times Book Co), 1973

Silverman PR: The widow-to-widow program: an experiment in preventive intervention. Ment Hyg 53:333, 1969

Wallace S: After Suicide. New York, Wiley, 1973

Welu TC: Broadening the focus of suicide prevention activities utilizing the public health model. Am J Public Health 12:62, 1972

Welu TC: Pathological bereavement: a plan for its prevention. In Schoenberg B et al (eds): Bereavement: Its Psychosocial Aspects. New York, Columbia Univ Press, 1975

CHAPTER 6

Variables in Suicide Statistics, Including Ethnic Aspects

Interpretation of statistics is at best difficult. Suicide statistics present additional dilemmas specific to the subject. It is important to clarify the meaning of statistical data assembled on suicide in order to help the caregivers to be critical consumers of suicide literature. For example, the ethnic variables in suicide statistics call for close attention. Although a comprehensive chapter on ethnic variables including each ethnic group is certainly desirable, it is only feasible to present a small section of the ethnic picture. It is hoped that this exposure will encourage caregivers to explore the area of ethnic aspects in more depth.

VARIABLES IN SUICIDE STATISTICS

Corrine L. Hatton
Sharon McBride Valente
Alice Rink

Suicide statistics measure the distribution, or frequency of the occurrence, of suicide in a population. By studying such numerical data, it should be possible to establish the causes of suicide. Measuring the incidence of an event such as suicide in the population can help investigators assess the extent and magnitude of the problem. Suicide statistics can be studied to determine which members of a population are more likely to commit suicide than others. The study of suicide in a population makes possible general association between suicide and the personal characteristics of individuals who kill themselves. Some of the characteristics selected for this purpose are age, sex, marital status, occupation, religion, and ethnic origin. Their measurement for a population provides a body of knowledge from which to ascertain the etiology of suicide, with the ultimate goals of control and prevention.

Based on findings from the data assembled, programs can be organized to prevent or reduce the occurrence of suicide. They are of great importance in the location and operation of suicide prevention centers, in the provision of suicide prevention services by various community mental health facilities, and as part of the curriculum content of certain college courses. Subsequent to the use of these statistics by the community, analysis of increases and decreases in the suicide rates can also help to determine the effectiveness of the programs undertaken.

Problems of Interpretation

By law, the death certificate must contain a statement about the *cause* of death—for example, pneumonia, acute morphine poisoning, gunshot wound of the head. Most states further require that the *mode* of death be certified as natural, accidental, suicidal, or homicidal. This classification is usually abbreviated as *NASH*. The mode of death is unrelated to the cause of death. A death described as "equivocal" is a death where the mode is unclear or uncertain. This is a problem which arises often in distinguishing between the modes of accident and those of suicide. The cause of death may be easily established, but whether death occurred by accident or by suicide may remain in doubt. The Los Angeles Suicide Prevention Center has a team that is utilized by the coroner's office to investigate certain equivocal deaths. Team recommendations regarding the mode of certification are then reported to the coroner.

The following examples (Allen, 1973; Litman, 1963; Litman et al, 1968) present situations where the cause of death was clear, but the mode was uncertain or highly questionable:

Example 1:

Laborer, 25-year-old male. Cause of death "severe contusions of brain due to fractured skull." Decedent lived with wife and her parents. Wife stated subject was a mental patient and had attempted self-destruction in the past. Subject drove pickup truck into a wall at 6:50 A.M.; there were no skid marks. *Mode of death certified as undetermined.*

Example 2:

Male 46 years old, real estate broker. Cause of death (1) bilateral extensive bronchial pneumonia, (2) extensive brain damage, (3) secobarbital intoxication. Subject was admitted to the hospital after ingesting 30 sleeping tablets (Seconal). He died 10 days later. Although subject was having some "family differences at home," his wife denied suicide. *Mode of death certified as undetermined.*

Example 3:

Female 48 years old. Cause of death lacerated lung, fractured ribs—was a patient in a mental hospital and "jumped or fell" from a second-story lavatory window. *Mode of death certified as undetermined.*

Example 4:

A married man stayed out late drinking with friends from work about once a month. To avoid his angry wife when he came home late at night, he habitually went to sleep in his car, parked in his garage, and in the winter would sometimes run the motor of the car to keep warm. One morning he was found dead of carbon monoxide poisoning. *Mode of death certified as accidental.*

Example 5:

An alcoholic with cirrhosis of the liver was warned that alcohol would surely kill him. He continued to drink heavily and soon died. *Mode of death certified as natural.*

Example 6:

A woman took a considerable quantity of barbiturates at 4:30 P.M. and fell asleep in front of the refrigerator on the kitchen floor. She knew that every working day for the last three years her husband had come home at 5 P.M. and went straight to the refrigerator for a beer. There was thus a strong possibility that she would be rescued. However, her husband was delayed and did not reach home until 7:30 P.M., when he found her unconscious. She later died at the hospital. *Mode of death certified as suicide.*

These examples clearly illustrate the difficulty in compiling accurate statistics on suicide. There is thus a discrepancy of undetermined magnitude between the reported number of suicides and the actual number of suicides. We can only be certain that the recorded number of suicides is actually the minimum number of suicides committed.

There are many sources of error to avoid in the interpretation of statistics. Comparisons of groups of suicides may differ in so many respects that a comparison of their rates does not reveal which factors are significant in explaining the differences found. Statistics may not always reflect reality or represent changes in suicide rates where changes are recorded. These changes may represent a change in community attitudes, change in the methods used by the coroner for examination, or the adoption of a more accurate system for recording deaths. Some investigators suggest that the high suicide rates in some communities are a reflection of the number of autopsies and toxicologic examinations performed by the coroner's office, resulting in an increase in the number of suicides that are discovered and reported.

Coroners often consider it their primary responsibility to rule out homicide. If homicide is not confirmed by the coroner's examination, further investigation to assess the possibility of suicide may be minimal. A determination of suicide depends on the findings of the medical examiner or police authority, who decides when a death will be certified as suicide. The responsible official may be reluctant to certify a death as a suicide unless evidence establishes this fact beyond the shadow of a doubt. Litman (1963) reports that in one city, authorities certified a death as a suicide only if there was a verifiable handwritten suicide note (in Los Angeles it is estimated that about one-third of the city's suicide victims leave such notes).

In order to certify suicide as the cause of death, the responsible officials must know the intention of the victim, for it is the intent which distinguishes suicide from the other modes of death. Even where reliable information is available, we can sometimes only speculate about the decedent's actual intention to commit suicide, and even when the cause of death is clearly established, the intention of the victim may remain in doubt.

Relevant information may not be available to officials. Often it can only be provided by friends or family members well acquainted with the deceased. Family and friends may either not have accurate information or may distort or conceal evidence of suicide. Survivors, who frequently experience feelings of denial about the event, may be reluctant to reveal information pointing to suicide.

Further complications arise when a person is found dead in a strange community or has severed family and social connections. There may be no one who accurately knows the age, marital status, occupation, and other vital statistics of the dead person. Furthermore, distinguishing individual characteristics may be either unknown or incorrectly classified.

Geographic variations also affect suicide statistics. Legal and social customs vary in different communities. Important differences exist in the definition and recording and reporting of a death as suicide. Moreover, the kind of death which is subject to legal and medical investigations varies from state to state. As long as these national and international inconsistencies exist, accurate comparison and analysis of statistics will not be possible.

Although specific characteristics of the deceased may be accurately recorded, interpretation may be misleading. For example, knowing the marital status of the decedent at the time of death tells us only that, and not whether the individual has maintained a stable marriage over a long period of time, or has never been married, or has been involved in numerous relationships. Again, stated religion at the time of death does not indicate how religious preference has affected the individual's life, whether religious beliefs or activities were part of it, or whether the decedent may in fact have been an atheist. We don't know whether the Spanish surnamed individual was a recent immigrant or was well integrated into the community. Further distortion may occur here because Spanish surname does not indicate whether the cultural characteristics of the individuals reflect Mexican, Puerto Rican, Cuban, or some other Latin American heritage. There are also widely divergent cultural characteristics among persons classified only as Oriental. Many other examples of relevant ethnic variables could be cited, but the point to be made is that a person's vital statistics at the time of death yield only a limited amount of information about that person.

The Psychological Autopsy

The problems of accurately defining and reporting suicide are mutiple. With increasing use of the psychological autopsy, however, certification has become less difficult. The psychological autopsy is an attempt to assess the intention of the deceased and the role he played in his own death. As a result of the application of this method, some accidental deaths are found to result from self-destructive behavior, while other deaths, at the time thought to be obvious suicides, turn out to be questionable.

The investigation team conducting the psychological autopsy has been trained in the field of human behavior. Members obtain information by interviewing people who knew the deceased, such as spouses, parents, children, physicians, neighbors, and clergymen. Where available, records of the deceased which may be found in hospitals, clinics, social agencies, and other repositories, are examined. The team focuses particularly on the decedent's lifestyle just prior to death. Data are obtained on life history, personality, mental health status, medical history, quality of communication with others, and other interpersonal activities. This information is then added to the other data already available to the coroner, along with the team's recommendation of the modes of death indicated for the certification (Farberow et al, 1971).

This method of investigation has resulted in more accurate certification of modes of death, but as Weisman (1974) points out, "The material comes from secondary sources, people who knew the victim, not, of course, from the victim himself. This leaves a gap between what others say about a person after a tragic act, and what the person might have said about himself."

ETHNIC ASPECTS OF SUICIDE STATISTICS

Jan Green

The information on which this discussion is based has been accumulated through clinical experience and from the statistics gathered at the Los Angeles Suicide Prevention Center with the aid of the Medical Examiner-Coroner's Office of Los Angeles County.*

In all probability, there are discrepancies between the published number of suicides and the actual statistics. All we can be certain of is that the published number of suicides is the minimum number of suicides.

Because of differences in investigation and reporting, suicide statistics vary from community to community. We at the Center feel that we have been able to keep accurate records for our community because of our association with the County Coroner's Office. The Suicide Prevention Center has a team that is called upon by the Coroner's Office to investigate equivocal deaths which could be attributed to suicide. A psychological autopsy is conducted, and recommendations of the mode of certification are given to the Coroner's Office.

---

*The Los Angeles Suicide Prevention Center has been fortunate in its close working relationship with the coroner's office, starting in 1960, when Dr. Theodore Curphey was coroner, and continuing with Dr. Thomas Noguchi since 1967. The accuracy of the Center's records reflects the cooperative nature of this effort.

Naturally, the focus of the Center is on preventing suicide. In order to set up and evaluate our emergency services for suicidal individuals, however, we have found it necessary to study the committed suicide.

Over the past decade, the study of ethnic variables in suicide rates has notably increased. Since suicidal persons are found in all ethnic groups, the caregiver needs to develop an awareness of these variables. At the same time, we must realize that although statistics indicate a higher incidence of suicide in older Caucasian men than in others measured by age, race, and sex, this act is nevertheless committed by all races, all ages, and both sexes. Of the people who call the Los Angeles Suicide Prevention Center, 82 percent are Anglo-white, 13 percent are Black, 4 percent have Spanish surnames, 0.3 percent are Oriental, and 0.2 percent are American Indian. These percentages are based on data reported by the callers. They correspond closely with the statistics of committed suicides in Los Angeles County (Wold, 1974).

The Shifting of Ethnic Proportions

Historically, it would appear that suicide has been primarily a Caucasian problem. In 1960, for instance, the Black population in Los Angeles County comprised 7.6 percent of the total population but accounted for only 2 percent of all suicides, with a rate of 4.3 per 100,000. Persons with Spanish surnames (mostly Mexican-American) made up 9.5 percent of the population but accounted for only 3 percent of all suicides, with a suicide rate of 6.9 per 100,000. Anglo-whites for that same year made up 80.8 percent of all county residents, but were responsible for 92 percent of all suicides, with a rate of 22.3 per 100,000. The county average rate was 15.9 per 100,000.

More recent population figures (1970 census) and suicide statistics compiled by the Los Angeles Coroner's Office (1972–73) began to show somewhat different proportions (Figs. 4 and 6). The Black population had increased to 11 percent and Black suicides are now 7 percent of the total. The rate for this group has jumped to 11.8 per 100,000—an increase of 174 percent in a fairly short period of time.

According to the *Research Coordinator*, Anglo-whites have decreased from 80.8 percent of the total population in 1960 to 68.1 percent (*Reasearch Coordinator*, 1970). However, this group still accounts for 85 percent of all suicides and has a suicide rate of 23.8 per 100,000. Persons with Spanish surnames still account for only 6 percent of yearly suicides, with a rate of 7.1 per 100,000. Orientals (including Japanese, Chinese, Filipinos, and Koreans) make up 3 percent of the population and 2 percent of all suicides.

One of the major significant differences in the incidence of suicide among different ethnic groups is the age factor (Figs. 4, 5, 7). Whites seem to become more suicidal with advancing years; 60 percent of all white suicides were 40 years old or older. Among Black suicides, however, only 25 percent were over 39, and 44 percent were specifically in the age group 20 through 29 years. Similarly, suicides with Spanish surnames were younger at the time of death: 65 percent of them were 39 years of age or less, with 35 percent in the 20–29 group. On the other hand, the suicide rate of Orientals in this country resembles that of Anglo-whites. Although only 3 percent of the population, Orientals account for 25 percent of all suicides, with a rate of 22.1 per 100,000 (1972–73 figures). But as with other minority groups,

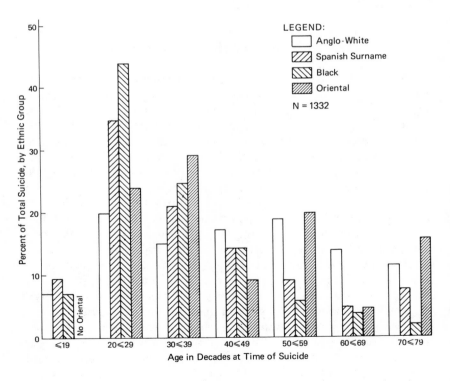

Fig. 4. Suicide in Los Angeles County, 1972–73, by age groups, in decades at time of suicide.

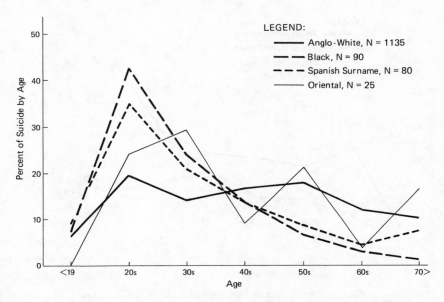

Fig. 5. Suicide in Los Angeles County, 1972–73, by age groups, in decades at time of suicide.

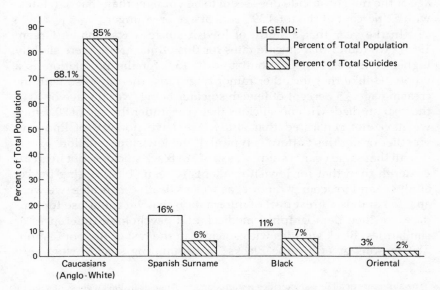

Fig. 6. Comparison of ethnic composition of Los Angeles County with suicide percentages (1973–73 statistics).

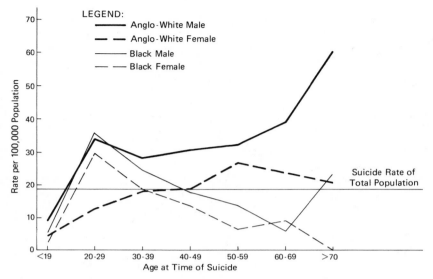

Fig. 7. Suicide rate in Los Angeles County, 1972–73.

age at the time of suicide does seem to be younger than that of whites, with 52 percent of the total 39 years of age or younger.

In the year that a study of Jewish suicides was made (Green, 1968)* we found that suicide rates for this ethnic group were slightly higher (16.5 per 100,000) compared to 15.9 for the population as a whole. Unlike that for other minority groups, the rate rose with increasing age: 75 percent of Jewish suicides being over the age of 40 in the year studied, with no suicides that year under the age of 20. Since we have not replicated that study, we have no way of knowing whether or not this pattern is typical of the Jewish population.

In that same year, a study was made of Black suicides, but in greater depth than that for Jewish residents (Green, 1968). Using police, autopsy, and toxicology reports, as well as death certificates, we were able to compile a great deal of information that we could use to compare, for their demographic, medical, and psychologic differences or similarities, Black suicides with suicides in the rest of the population. The reasons given by the Blacks for committing suicide were very

---

*The survivors of all Jewish suicides reported in Los Angeles in 1968 were contacted by telephone and a questionnaire on each was completed by the interviewer as part of the survey conducted.

similar to those given by the general population: poor health, mental as well as physical, heading the list. A more detailed comparison of Black suicides compared with all others in Los Angeles County is given in Table 8.

It is dramatically apparent from an examination of these county-wide statistics that continuing research and clinical investigation are needed to give us clearer guidelines to successful suicide assessment and intervention, particularly where ethnic variables must be taken into consideration.

BLACK SUICIDE

Elsie R. Christian

A Review of the Literature

Although numerous articles and books have been published about the Black population in the past ten to fifteen years, social scientists have almost totally neglected the topic of Black suicide until very recently. Suicide rates have been lower for Blacks than for whites, but this fact in itself would point to Black suicide as worthy of study. Indeed, it appears to this writer that all aspects of Black mortality require attention and investigation by those concerned with preserving life.

Much of the literature on Black suicide explores the reasons for the comparatively low Black rate by focusing on the relationship between suicide and economics, power and position. In 1938, Prudhomme, a psychoanalyst, was one of the first to observe that the rate of Black suicide attempts was as high as or even higher than that of whites. His theory was that these attempts were impulsive hysterical reactions brought on by social oppression. He concluded that as Blacks became assimilated into the dominant society their suicide rate would approach that of whites (Prudhomme, 1938).

In 1954, Andrew Henry and James Short, postulating a view similar to Prudhomme's, suggested that unfavorable economic conditions of society exerted a greater influence on white suicide than on Black because Blacks had been conditioned to accept a subordinate position in society along with its accompanying low income. They found that Black suicide was less sensitive to the business cycle than white suicide. However, they noted a greater sensitivity to the

TABLE 8. Black Suicides Compared with All Others,
Los Angeles County, 1972–73

DESCRIPTION	BLACKS (%)	TOTAL OTHER (%)
Reason for Suicide		
Poor health	33	40
Love trouble	29	26
Financial	10	5
Death of a loved one	3	5
Don't know	25	24
Sex		
Male	67	60
Female	33	40
Marital Status		
Single	29	19
Married	36	37
Divorced/separated	29	29
Widowed	3	10
Unknown	3	5
Method Used		
Gun	35	35
Barbiturate overdose	32	39
Hanging	8	7
Carbon monoxide poisoning	8	7
Jumping from a height	6	3
Ingestion of nonbarbiturate substance	8	3
Other method, not specified	3	6
Employment Status		
Employed	84	84
Unemployed	15	5
Retired	1	11
Professional other than medical	5	7
Medical Doctor	2	1
Registered Nurse	2	2
Clerical	11	11
Skilled labor	21	24
Unskilled labor	13	6
Student	6	4
Police/armed guard	5	2
Entertainer	3	2
Small business owner	6	4
Housewife	13*	19†
Medical History		
Private physician (M.D.)	32	40
Psychiatric therapy	17	9
Depression	59	53
Alcoholism	8	14
Drug addiction	6	5
Schizophrenia	6	3
Chronic instability	29	13
Special Interest		
Left suicide note	17	36
Had been drinking	21	28
Murder-suicide	5	1
Previous attempt on record	21	18
Previous LASPC contact	3	3

*Percentage of female Black suicides.   †Percentage of female "Total Other" suicides.

economic cycle after 1923 as evidenced by nonwhite suicides and correlated this increase in the suicide rate with the expansion of economic and social opportunities open to minorities since that date (Henry and Short, 1954).

The current literature on Black suicide recognizes the fallacy in the widespread belief that Black suicide is rare. In fact, there has been such an increase in Black suicide rates nationally that the once-popular myth that poor people rarely kill themselves has been disproved. Recent examination of early statistical data also shows that young Blacks have been committing suicide at a high rate for much of this century. Currently, it is becoming apparent that the suicide rates for Black youth—especially Black females—are increasing rapidly. Herbert Hendin, a psychoanalyst, pointed out in his book, *Black Suicide*, that "in the United States the highest suicide rate is found among the lowest social classes" (Hendin, 1969, p 133). This author also found that the rates of suicide among young Black men in New York City have been higher than those for young whites since 1920.

The major portion of Hendin's own research on Black suicide was devoted to the study of a small group of Black suicide attempters in New York. He found that the members of this group showed feelings of rage and worthlessness resulting from the larger society's rejection of Blacks. He concluded that the self-hatred he observed in some of his subjects was attributable to the fact that Blacks are encouraged to become upwardly mobile but are prevented by racial discrimination from succeeding. Hendin concluded that "Blacks who survive the dangerous years between 20 and 35 have made some accommodation with life—a compromise that usually had to include a scaling down of their aspirations" (Hendin, 1969, p 145).

Warren Breed, in a study of Black suicide, investigated the reaction of Blacks to feelings of powerlessness and discrimination. In an article entitled, "The Negro and Fatalistic Suicide" (1970), Breed attempted to show a correlation between the severe regulation of minorities and suicide. His research involved the study of 42 Black male suicides in New Orleans. Study findings indicated that over two-thirds of the victims had experienced conflict with the police and other authorities. Breed suggested that some of the victims had an extreme fear of the police, and some had experienced conflicts with persons in other official capacities. His findings indicated that some of his subjects committed suicide as a result of their conflicts with authority, but he took into consideration the fact that other stresses might also have been involved.

Breed suggests that these suicides can be categorized as

fatalistic—that is, as suicides resulting from excessive regulation by society. This category of suicide is one of four that were formulated by Durkheim, the noted sociologist. Durkheim used this category in assessing the causes for suicide among slaves but felt it had no contemporary importance (Durkheim, 1951 trans). However, Breed has extended its use to categorize suicide by persons who live under severe authority, such as Blacks.

Similarly, in his study of suicides in the Chicago area, Ronald Maris (1969) found that the Black suicides were predominantly fatalistic in attitude. He considered external constraint or hyperregulation a factor in most of the Black suicides he studied. However, he pointed out that the frustration felt by Blacks when prevented from achieving status was more often evidenced as aggression externally directed rather than self-directed. Maris theorizes that this externalized response accounts for the low Black suicide rate in the area he studied, at the same time recognizing that although strong external constraints are generally found to be the cause of the lower suicide rate among Blacks, they can be the reason for some Black suicides as well (Maris, 1969).

Richard Seiden, a clinical psychologist, has discussed the pressures of urban living in the Black community as related to suicide. Specifically, he stresses unemployment as a major problem for the lower-class urban Black:

Although the rate of unemployment has increased across the board nationally, its effects in the black community have been devastating, with unemployment approximately twice as high for blacks as for whites. [Seiden, 1972, p 5]

The problems of urban dwelling for Blacks were described by Lacy Banks in an article about the recent rise in Black suicides:

For blacks, the rage peaks early in life. Young blacks become aware of their condition and are faced with the challenge of an adjustment that means yielding to their rage or scaling down their aspirations. [Banks, 1970, p 78]

Jack Gibbs and Walter Martin, authors of *Status Integration and Suicide* (1964), suggested that the suicide rate of a population varies inversely with the stability and durability of social relationships in that population. This theory, based on the sociologic theory of status, role, and role conflict, is designed to predict suicide rates for various population groups. The hypothesis is that a population which enjoys a high degree of status integration will show a low degree of status incompatibility and a small number of conflicting roles; therefore, the stability and durability of its social relationships would not be threatened.

According to this theory, Gibbs and Martin indicated that Blacks would show a high degree of status integration. However, as the educational and occupational options available to Blacks increase, there should be a corresponding decrease in role and status compatibility. Likewise, we may anticipate some deterioration in the stability and durability of social relationships among Blacks and a consequent increase in suicide rates.

Some experts in suicidology believe that suicide occurs as a result of loss. Warren Breed considers loss the least-explored cause of death yet a very significant factor in suicide. He explained that loss can be loss of position, loss of mutuality (social relationships), or loss of person (love). By loss of person, Breed means an actual, threatened, or imagined physical or emotional rejection or abandonment by a loved one. (Breed does not include in his category "loss of person" the loss suffered by one person as a result of the death of another.) According to Breed, the suicide victim must feel the loss and be aware of it. Also, it is necessary that others are also aware of the loss, so that it causes the victim embarrassment or humiliation. This negatively affects the self concept in that the victim feels the loss of prestige in the eyes of others (Breed, 1967).

Until recently the theory of loss was invoked to explain suicide in general and suicide was not associated with ethnic factors. However, the writer recently found a strong correlation between Black suicides and loss (Christian, 1973). The research involved the study of half of all Black suicides in Los Angeles County for the year 1971. The most frequent motive for the individual's suicide which could be ascertained from the findings was loss of love. The results of this study led the writer to believe that the loss of a love relationship may have special significance for those who have no money or other ego supports such as position or prestige (Christian, 1973).

The research on Black suicide so far is sparse, speculative, and limited in scope, but it does indicate that some social scientists are concerned about the problem. While the authors whose work is discussed here have made honest attempts to explain Black suicide, it is evident that further research is needed. Certainly, future research on Black suicide should be conducted by persons who have an understanding of Black attitudes, values, and lifestyles, as well as a knowledge of suicide.

Assessing Suicidal Risk

Once the characteristics associated with Black suicide attempters and victims are identified, we may be able to discern a high-risk group of suicidal Blacks. We are interested in examining the traits of those already known to be at high risk and discovering the motivation behind their suicidal impulses. The paucity of research and literature on Black suicides makes our task more difficult. The reader should bear in mind, then, that the conclusions drawn here are based on few studies and much speculation.

In assessing suicide potential among Blacks, the questions arise, are the characteristics of Black and white suicidal persons significantly different? If so, how are these differences manifested?

We already know that since the early 1900s Blacks attempted suicide more frequently than whites, while at the same time the suicide rate for Blacks was lower than for whites. Ronald Maris has suggested that the unsuccessful suicide attempts among Blacks are in reality a "cry for help," an attempt to draw attention to the subject by alarming others. Maris noted that these suicidal gestures often resulted from a marital estrangement, concluding that these attempts were made in a crisis situation that could be resolved over time (Maris, 1969).

Racial Differences among Attempters.   In a study conducted on a group of white and nonwhite suicide attempters in Monroe County, New York, the researchers found that there were major differences between the nonwhites and the whites. They found that nonwhites had a much higher rate of attempted suicide than whites. In fact, the ratio of nonwhite women to nonwhite men attempters was 6:1, while the ratio of white women to white men attempters was 3:1. The findings also indicated that nonwhite attempters were younger than their white counterparts.

The findings of a five-year follow-up on the Monroe County study revealed that none of the nonwhites had actually committed suicide, while almost a third (32 percent) of the whites had done so. However, 11 percent of the nonwhite attempters had died of other causes within the five-year interval between the original study and the follow-up. The causes of these nonsuicidal deaths is not given in the follow-up report, but all of them occurred within the 25 to 44 year age group. It is interesting also that the age of death of these non-suicided subjects considerably predates their normal life expectancy (Pederson et al, 1973).

While these findings are significant, we cannot conclude that nonwhite attempters will not eventually commit suicide. It may be that factors are operating in the situation of the attempters different from those at work in the situation of victims. Apparently some of the attempters were in a crisis situation that they were able somehow to overcome. Perhaps those who died during the five-year span used other means of self-destruction. None of these possibilities can be determined at this time.

One conclusion of the Monroe County study was that "since nonwhites who commit suicide do not as often have a history of attempts, the attempts [of nonwhites] may not be as predictive of future suicides as they are for whites" (Pederson et al, 1973, p 1075). These investigators also warn their readers that "the suicide attempts of whites and nonwhites form two distinct patterns and should not be looked upon or investigated as a common problem with similar motives or prognoses" (Pederson et al, 1973, p 1076).

We can speculate that the Black attempters may be acting on impulses in crisis situations and may be less likely to be chronically suicidal, their need being to alert others to their pain. An individual's acting-out behavior draws attention to his need for reassurance that he is desirable, is worthy of love, and is significant to those around him. It is necessary to examine the current crisis of these persons (eg, failure in social relationships, or economic frustrations) for the specific cause of their depression and suicidal feelings. In addition, this group of Black suicide attempters needs to be examined for other patterns of self-destructive behavior.

The Factor of Youth.   Another characteristic of Black suicide is that it occurs predominantly among the young. The trend toward increasingly youthful suicides has prompted concern among professionals in the health field with the specific issue of Black suicide. One of these, Dr. James Comer, stated that "suicide among young blacks is a national health crisis" (Comer, 1973, p 42). What are the causes of the increase?

Hendin postulated that the aspirations of Blacks peak during their youth. Frustration of these aspirations is a contributing factor to Black suicides (Hendin, 1969). Other authors have echoed Hendin's view, pointing out that failure in competition or achievement can lead to feelings of worthlessness. As mentioned at the outset, older Blacks have learned how to cope with their inability to achieve and have scaled down their aspirations accordingly or have blamed the system rather than themselves for their lack of success. Persons in the latter category have successfully handled the rage felt by many young Blacks living in a poor urban area.

However, many young people who are raised in depressed living conditions feel that they cannot achieve because of their personal deficiencies—they blame themselves for their inability to succeed. The psychodynamics of these young people are explained by a generally held view that they become enraged. This rage can be handled in many ways. It is either directed outward, at society, or inward, at themselves. Alvin Poussaint, a psychiatrist, suggested some of the ways in which this rage may be dealt with—through suppression and compliance, through militance or self-destruction, through sublimation (via creative competitive activities), through identification (with the oppressor), or through chronic resentment (Poussaint, 1967).

Mental health workers should realize that many young Blacks are angry, frustrated, and often afraid. Anger and frustration experienced in the search for employment may be compounded by feelings of inadequacy in love relationships. And as previously mentioned, termination of a love relationship is found to play an important role in Black suicides. In an interview for *Ebony*, the director of the Suicide Prevention Center in Washington, D.C., reported that while most suicidal callers were concerned about loss of prestige and social position, the Black callers were concerned about the loss of a lover (Banks, 1970).

In a study of Black suicide victims in Los Angeles County in 1971, the writer came to a similar conclusion. She found that often the suicide was the result of a threatened or actual dissolution of a love relationship. It seemed to her that many of the victims could have been asking for help from those close to them, as several had told some significant person in their lives of their intent to commit suicide (Christian, 1973).

In *Childhood and Society* (1963) Erik Erikson writes that during the stage of young adulthood, the need for satisfactory relations with a sexual partner, which includes intimacy and mutual trust, is of the utmost importance to the individual. In the absence of a concrete affiliation which is satisfactory to the subject, isolation may occur.

The Black Female Suicide.   As part of the increase in suicide among Black youth, the rising rate of Black female suicide in the past 20 years has become a major concern. The rates of Black women in the 20–35 age bracket have increased 80 percent, much more rapidly than the rates for Black males, white males, or white females (Slater, 1973). The research of Nancy Allen, public health educator, revealed that the Black female suicide rate in the state of California was highest in the 20–24 age range in 1970, constituting a marked increase over the 1960 rate. Allen concludes that

The increasing number of black women between 20 and 24 who commit suicide—a rate of 30.2 in 1970 as compared to white female rate of 13.6 per

100,000—suggests special psychosociologic pressures for these individuals. [*Allen, 1973, p 12*]

There has been a great deal of speculation about the cause of this increase in the Black female suicide rate. In an article on the rise of Black female suicides, Dr. Ronald Maris offers his opinion that "hopelessness and isolation resulting from failed social relationships often lead to suicide" (Slater, 1973, p 160).

Dr. James Comer suggested several possibilities. He cited as one the weakening ties of Black women to the church. For Black women, the church has long been a caring and protective institution which conferred on them a sense of belonging and worth that they did not get in the larger society. As Comer puts it:

The church and involvement in the life of the black community provided a place where an individual could participate and be accepted and valued by criteria of their own community rather than that of total society. [Comer, 1973, p 43].

For Blacks who feel powerless in the larger society, the Black community provided a shelter in the past. However, as the Black community grows and becomes diffuse, there is a loss of unity and closeness formerly shared by its members. Some urban communities have grown to the point that the individual can easily "get lost" in the community. Perhaps the problem is greater for the Black woman than for the Black man because the woman is more often at home with her children and has fewer social outlets. A young Black woman who is not fulfilled by outside employment or by some community or church involvement may place great importance on her relationships with significant others. In her limited world these social relationships take on heroic proportions. Failure or just lack of success in one or more of these relationships can leave her feeling rejected and isolated.

Dr. Floyd Wylie, a psychologist, offers another view about the increase in Black female suicides. He suggests that Black females may be negatively affected by the Moynihan theory that "female head-of-the-household families are pathological." In his opinion, "Belief in this 'lie' may be having detrimental psychic results" on young Black females who come from such homes (in Slater, 1973, p 160).

Socioeconomic Factors.   Although Black suicide victims and attempters are found at all socioeconomic levels, the majority are in the lower socioeconomic strata of the community. Taking into consideration the fact that not all suicides or suicide attempts are recorded as such, those least likely to be discovered are at the upper socioeconomic levels who have the influence necessary to prevent

disclosure. These "hidden" suicides may account for the comparatively greater incidence of suicide among poorer Blacks.

Other suicides may be concealed in homicide statistics. These
hidden cases would most likely be found among young males. The
victim-precipitated homicide in which the victim brings about his
own death by provoking someone into killing him is well known in
the Black community. This method of setting up one's own demise
allows the victim to die a hero. Suicide is viewed by many in the Black
community as an unacceptable way of coping. In the eyes of these
persons, it may be preferable to antagonize another or to precipitate
an argument in which one's opponent is goaded into striking the
death blow.

Although some social scientists overestimate the actual number
of persons who "set up" their own deaths in this manner, victim-
precipitated homicides certainly are a concern for those interested in
curbing suicidal behavior. Gang activity in the Black community is
often associated with this type of suicide. Indeed, young gang members do place themselves in positions where they are at a perilous disadvantage with the police and with rival gangs. However, the naïveté
of youth must be considered here. More than a death wish, these
youngsters may be driven by a sense of invincibility and "machismo."

Suicidal behavior may also be seen in alcoholism and other drug
abuse. Many persons use drugs to facilitate their ability to cope with
life. Some of them have in fact given up on life and have taken a slow
route to suicide, one which is more acceptable to them than a sudden
forceful act. These persons are long-term sufferers, those who have
not developed adequate coping skills. The health worker in the Black
community must bear in mind that persons evidencing these self-
destructive patterns need attention as much as does the person who
threatens or attempts suicide.

Among Blacks, who are in the high-risk group? Can we describe
the typical suicidal Black? The victim is a young person of low income, unskilled, and more likely a male, who has not previously attempted suicide. He is dissatisfied with his employment (or lack of it)
and has suffered a romantic crisis. He is despondent because he believes he is a failure and he sees no hope for the future. He is a person
who places a great deal of emphasis on the here and now. He wants
to succeed in his various roles. However, societal directives to become
a successful lover, parent, and provider may be in conflict with
societal barriers which stand between the victim and the opportunity
to express himself in these roles. This individual becomes angry,
often feels incompetent, and has little self-esteem.

This description by no means incorporates all of the many other suicidal syndromes to be found across the whole spectrum of Black suicide victims. It does not include the terminally ill patients, the psychotics, and the children who commit suicide, the characteristics and motivation of whom are more likely to parallel those of the white suicide and less likely to be associated with ethnic differences.

Intervention

Intervention with the Black suicidal person proceeds along the same lines as intervention with the non-Black. However, the helping process can be facilitated by the caregiver's knowledge of the life-styles, values, and attitudes prevailing in the Black community, especially when it is a non-Black mental health worker who is assisting a Black suicidal client. In this connection, special attention is directed toward proper use of resources available in the Black community and techniques of therapeutic intervention which are effective with Black clients.

If the helping person decides to refer the client to a mental health agency, that agency should be chosen with care. Many Black persons have had negative experiences with social welfare agencies and clinics. They often encounter long waits and impersonal agency personnel. Moreover, therapy and mental health counseling can elicit fear from the individual of being branded by the stigma of mental illness. To help the client who is apprehensive about seeking help from a mental health agency, the caregiver should encourage candid discussion of preconceived notions about therapy or counseling. The caregiver can be extremely helpful by preparing the client for the therapeutic situation. If referral is made, the caregiver should discuss the reason for the referral with the client. All too frequently, however, referral is used by caregivers as a way of avoiding a subject which is uncomfortable for them. Small wonder that the client may perceive in the referral an avoidance of his problem or a personal rejection.

The caregiver may also solicit assistance for the client from friends, relatives, and other nonprofessional resources in the community. Many persons in the Black community are not aware of the resource available to them in a situation of crisis with a suicidal person. It is important to utilize fully the caring systems of the community for all persons needing help. The caregiver should prepare the client's relatives and any other resources for their helping role with the suicidal client.

A study conducted in 1971 yielded surprising information about attitudes toward various sources of suicide help on the part of four ethnic groups in low-income and lower-middle–income areas of Los Angeles. When asked whom they would call for help if they knew someone who was considering suicide, 44 percent of the Black respondents said they would call the police, while 26 percent said they would call a relative. Significantly fewer said they would call a minister, a physician, or the Suicide Prevention Center. When asked whether they had heard of the Suicide Prevention Center, 65 percent of respondent Blacks replied they had not. It is significant that although 35 percent of those interviewed had heard of the Center, only 15 percent said they would contact the Center, a physician, or a psychiatrist for help in a suicide crisis (Reynolds, 1974). These findings indicate (1) ignorance in a community of the mental health resources available to it, and (2) poor utilization of the professional help available to suicidal persons.

Frequently the caregiver looks to the family of the suicidal person for assistance. He may be astonished, however, to find that the Black suicidal person enjoys a complete network of family and other social relationships. This situation differs from that of the typical white suicide victims, where we find greater social isolation. With Black victims, it is not so much the lack of contact with others, but the quality of the contacts which, in fact, may be the problem. Frequently, Black suicides are triggered by a plummeting personal relationship, and the caregiver should use caution, when seeking the assistance of family members, to be sure that the person considered a likely resource is not the source of the problem. Once it can be established that their involvement will not be detrimental to the client, family members can be very supportive to the suicidal client.

The caregiver should become thoroughly familiar with the community organizations he may use as resources in serving persons who need social involvement as a part of therapy. Craft workshops or welfare self-help groups can provide the suicidal client with an effective social outlet as well as involvement in a meaningful, productive activity. The church, a possible resource, has traditionally been a caregiving system in the Black community. The church gives the individual a sense of belonging as well as of being a member of a closely knit group. Church involvement can extend the opportunity to occupy positions of status and worth which are especially valuable to those who do not hold prestigious positions elsewhere in the community.

Intervention also may involve engaging the client in therapy or counseling, which presents special problems where a non-Black mental health worker is attempting to engage a Black suicidal client in the therapeutic relationship. Of course, the non-Black caregiver employs basically the same skills and techniques with the Black client as with the non-Black client, but certain dynamics may arise in this cross-ethnic situation that should be considered in advance.

First of all, it is important for the caregiver *not* to deny race as a factor in their relationship. Because of the socialization process which takes place from childhood on, color and ethnic origins must be regarded as important variables in any relationship (Simmons, 1963; Brown, 1950; Gochros, 1966). Esther Fibush, a family service caseworker, gets closer to the point: "The worker cannot afford to remain unaware of the myriad subtle and covert emotional reactions that can be triggered within himself and the Negro client by the racial difference" (Fibush, 1965, pp 271–72).

The caregiver's understanding of his or her own attitudes and values may also help to avoid problems in the client caregiver relationship. Julia Bloch, a psychiatric social worker, points out that some of these problems erupt in the process of countertransference.* She cautions the mental health worker not to misinterpret the client's dynamics by assuming hypersensitivity or racial paranoia. A client's guarded responses may indicate only that he has had previous negative experiences with whites in positions of authority. Bloch cites the example of the Black professional who objected to a caregiver's calling him by his first name. The client believed this was an example of white condescension. His desire to be addressed more formally is typical of the feelings held in the Black community. This reaction may have resulted from the Southern experience, where whites spoke and referred to Blacks by their first names to indicate their lack of status. Even today many Blacks prefer to be addressed by their surnames, especially in nonsocial situations, as a symbol of respect and politeness.

Bloch has suggested that the caregiver be aware of these differences in socioeconomic and cultural background between himself or herself and the client and of the caregiver's possible bias toward middle-class values and attitudes. A caregiver may construe a client's behavior as pathologic because the latter's values and attitudes are foreign to the caregiver's experience. Instead, the caregiver should consider whether the client's behavior is not consistent with the

---

*Countertransference is defined in the *Dictionary of Behavioral Science* as "unconscious feelings evoked in the psychoanalyst by the patient which may adversely affect the necessary objective attitude to the patient and interfere with the treatment" (Wolman, 1973).

client's subculture. Some of the survival mechanisms in the Black community which enable individuals to cope are unacceptable by white middle-class standards.

Another important point made by Bloch (1968) is that coping mechanisms (eg, Tom-ing) can be emotionally self-destructive as well as helpful for Blacks. For example, the caregiver may be flattered or amused by the client's ingratiating attitude, not perceiving it as unhealthy. Yet this attitude may in reality reflect the client's view of whites as superior and hence be indicative of the client's lack of ego strength and low self-esteem.

A problem situation arises when the caregiver is intimidated by the client's expression of antiwhite sentiments or his membership in "antiwhite" organizations. Bloch suggests in her article that aggression directed at whites can be very healthy for Blacks when handled constructively. In fact, the mental health worker should consider the client's attitudes and behavior in terms of how helpful or detrimental they are for the client. For instance, the client may be going through a phase of antiwhite sentiment in order to accept his Blackness, in which event it can be considered a constructive phase. Bloch emphasized that the caregiver should be consciously aware of subjective attitudes toward a Black client, particularly in the areas of the client's sexuality and aggressiveness. These are two areas in which the stereotypes and myths devised by whites about Blacks persist to this day (Bloch, 1968).

It should be obvious that the caregiver must never use Black dialect in attempting to establish rapport. Artificial usage of Black dialect is offensive to many Blacks. The underlying message to the client is that the caregiver is not comfortable using his normal speech patterns with a Black client. Another possibility is that the caregiver is trying to show off, to be "hip." In either case the caregiver is not acting as a good role model for the client.

In her article, Fibush discussed the guilt feelings that can be activated in the caregiver working with the Black client. She states that the worker encumbered by prejudice but who will be honest enough to admit this, should disqualify himself or herself from working with the client. Usually, however, "difference in race arouses only minor feelings of uneasiness and discomfort, suggesting that their underlying anxiety or guilt is consciously being denied or suppressed" (Fibush, 1965, p 276). She suggests that these guilt feelings may result from previous experiences of the worker, such as acquiescing in practices of discrimination or segregation. If the worker can recognize the existence of these feelings, they are not likely to interfere with therapy.

In certain situations it may be necessary to explore race openly with the client. According to Jean Gochros, a psychiatric social worker,

. . . even the skilled worker may fail to bring up "race", either because there is not a good relationship with the client or because there is one. The end result is that the worker seldom, if ever, seems to find any reason for exploring the subject. [Gochros, 1966, p29]

While so far the discussion has emphasized the emotional and social overtones of race as a factor in the client-caregiver relationship, by no means does this imply that problem situations are to be anticipated in every case. The skilled caregiver will be able to evaluate each situation as it arises to determine how the racial factor will affect the client-caregiver relationship.

Future Needs for the Black Population

The economic situation plays an important role in the mental health of those who live in this society. If unemployment continues to increase, we may anticipate that frustration and depression will increase among the Black population as well as in the total society. Although Henry and Short did find that Blacks were not affected by the economic conditions of society as much as whites, several factors are making it more difficult for Blacks to weather the economic storm of the 1970s.

First of all, in previous economic slumps the majority of Blacks lived in Southern rural areas where they grew at least some of their own food and found shelter more easily accessible. Currently, most Blacks reside in urban areas, where food must usually be purchased in stores and housing is more difficult to obtain. Second, the standard of living for Blacks is higher now than formerly. Black expectations are correspondingly greater and aspirations are higher than in the past. Third, Blacks now tend to internalize their aggression more than in the past. Previously, when they failed to succeed economically, aggression was directed outward toward others.

Greater attention needs to be directed toward Black male-female relationships. As we have seen, for people who have little status or few other ego supports, a love relationship has special significance. This relationship can provide the individual with self-esteem, shared intimacy, and a feeling of being worthwhile, but a disruption of this relationship can be devastating. Thus, we know that a disproportionately high rate of Black homicides, injuries, and suicides results from quarrels and disruptions in love relationships. Mental health personnel must begin to work with young people as early as adolescence, encouraging them to examine their expectations, values, and attitudes about sex, dating, love relationships, and marriage. Early couseling on these topics may lead to greater understanding between the sexes.

It is necessary to bring to people in the community and in the helping occupations an awareness of suicide as a reality in the Black community and one which calls for preventive intervention as well as suicide prevention and crisis intervention. By such awareness, mental health personnel and interested others will be able to identify those persons in the Black community who are chronically despondent and depressed, who show no sense of purpose or direction. Such persons should be offered the mental health services they need. In communities that do not have crisis intervention or suicide prevention services, mental health personnel can expand the scope of existing caring systems of the community such as the hospitals, clinics, and churches.

Nevertheless, much of the anger, frustration and depression in the Black population arises from poverty, bad housing, and unemployment. The angry person usually directs his anger either outward—often toward those closest to him—or inward—toward himself in self-destructive behavior. In either case, there is a great loss, not only to those affected personally, but to the community. While it is incumbent on those in the helping occupations to reach into the community in order to identify and assist these persons, we must initiate action to eradicate the social conditions that keep Blacks at a socioeconomic disadvantage within the larger society.

REFERENCES

Allen NH: Suicide in California, 1960–1970. Sacramento, State of California Department of Public Health Monograph, 1973
Banks L: Black suicide. Ebony, May 1970, pp 76–84
Bloch JB: The white worker and the Negro client in psychotherapy. Social Work 13:36, 1968
Breed W: The Negro and fatalistic suicide. Pacific Sociol Rev 13: 152, 1970
———: Suicide and loss in social interaction. In ES (ed): Essays in Self-Destruction. New York, Science House, 1967, pp 188–202
Brown LB: Race as a factor in establishing a casework relationship. Soc Casework 31:91, 1950
Christian ER: A Perspective on the Phenomenon of Black Suicide. Unpublished dissertation, Los Angeles, Calif, University of California, 1973
Comer JP: Black suicide: a hidden crisis. Urban Health 2:41, 1973
Durkheim E: Suicide. In Simpson G (ed): Suicide. Spaulding JA, Simpson G (trans). New York, Free Press, 1951

Erikson E: Childhood and Society. New York, Norton, 1963

Farberow NL, Neuringer C: The social scientist as coroner's deputy. J Forensic Sci 16:1, January 1971

Fibush E: The white worker and the Negro client. Soc Casework 46:271, 1965

Gibbe JP, Martin WT: Status Integration and Suicide. Eugene, Ore, Univ of Oregon Books, 1964

Gochros J: Recognition and use of anger in Negro clients. Social Work 11:28, 1966

Green J: Unpublished study conducted at Suicide Prevention Center, Los Angeles, 1968

———: Unpublished study conducted at Suicide Prevention Center, Los Angeles, 1968.

Hendin H: Black Suicide. New York, Harper & Row, 1971

Henry AF, Short JF, Jr: Suicide and Homicide. New York, Free Press of Glencoe, 1954

Litman RE: Psychological-psychiatric aspects in certifying modes of death. (Case Studies 5 and 6). J Forensic Sci 13:46, January 1968

———, Curphey T, Shneidman E, Farberow N, Tabachnik N: Investigations of equivocal suicides (Case Study 4). JAMA 184:924, 1973

Maris RW: Social Forces in Urban Suicide. Illinois, Dorsey Press, 1969

Pederson AM, Awad GA, Kindler AR: Epidemiological differences between white and nonwhite suicide attempters. Am J Psychiatry 130:1071, 1973

Pouissaint AF: A Negro psychiatrist explains the Negro psyche. NY Times Magazine, August 20, 1967, pp 4–7

Prudhomme C: The problem of suicide in the American Negro. Psychoanal Rev 25:374, 1938

Research Coordinator. Published by the Research Coordinating Committee of Los Angeles County, December 1970

Reynolds DK: Suicide Among Ethnic Groups in Los Angeles with Focus on Japanese Americans. Presentation at California Senate Hearing on Suicide, Sacramento, Calif, April 6, 1974

Seiden RH: Why are suicides of young blacks increasing? HSMHA Health Rep. 87:3, 1972

Simmons LC: Jim Crow: implications for social work. Soc Work 8:24, 1963

Slater J: Suicide: a growing menace to black women. Ebony, September 1973, pp 152–60

Wold C: Unpublished study conducted at the Suicide Prevention Center, Los Angeles, 1974

Weisman AD: The Realization of Death. New York, Jason Aronson, 1974, p 27

Wolman BB: Dictionary of Behavioral Science. New York, Van Nostrand/Reinhold, 1973

Chapter 7
Special Needs

There are four areas of suicidal behavior that are particularly poignant for caregivers: children, adolescents, chronically suicidal persons, and emergencies. When we consider any one of these areas, we realize that our knowledge is in an embryonic phase of development. Yet some guidelines can be offered the caregiver confronted with a case in any of these areas of special need.

SUICIDE IN CHILDREN

Corrine Loing Hatton
Sharon McBride Valente
Alice Rink

Statistics indicate that children complete a small number of suicides in comparison with other age groups of the population. It is important to bear in mind, however, that suicide threats and attempts are frequent among children. The suicide of a child is such a tragic event that the study of children who commit suicide is of paramount importance. Unfortunately, research in this area is scant and what there is only serves to highlight certain theories and suggest questions for further study.

Incidence before Age 12

Children have a concept of death that is quite distorted when compared to adult ideas of death. When a number of 6-to-11-year-olds were questioned about death, 50 percent of them described death as a reversible event (McIntyre and Angle, 1970).

Children appear today to believe that death is a going to sleep. They believe you can wake up again, just like the actors on television. They see death as an outside force that does something to them rather than as a process that occurs from within. In other words, they rarely see themselves as a possible agent of their own death (Shaffer, 1974). Although we may speculate on the nature of these distortions, it is not clear how they protect a child from contemplating suicide.

It is understandable that the younger the child, the more restricted his access to and mastery over the means for suicide. For a young child to succeed in committing suicide, such adjuncts as secrecy, privacy, and opportunity must be available. Furthermore, the child must be able to plan and deliberate effectively. Moreover, some degree of skill and coordination is necessary to the fulfillment of many suicidal plans. For example, hanging requires some technical sophistication—the place must be carefully selected and premature discovery prevented (Shaffer, 1974). Self-electrocution and drowning require comparatively elaborate and well thought-out plans. If a plastic bag is chosen for suffocation, the child must select a secluded place for the act and a time when the chances of discovery are slight.

Thus, it is not surprising that the younger the child, the more he attempts suicide by jumping out of a window or in front of a car. These are impulsive and open behaviors, they are not secretive. It is sad, though, that when these open behaviors are a cry for help, all too often they are ignored. One parent said, "Joey didn't really want to hang himself, he was just experimenting." Another parent said, "Judy didn't jump in front of that car on purpose, she just forgot to look where she was going." Another parent repeated a prevailing myth when she remarked, "My daughter couldn't have drowned on purpose in the pool. Children just *never* get depressed, or suicidal."

Most people ask whether children's suicides are not always done on impulse, and it is important to note that among child suicides studied few completed deaths were clearly impulsive. In fact, in most cases, there is evidence of prior planning. In two out of three suicides by self-inflicted gunshot wounds, the child was drunk at the time; in three out of four overdoses, the child had told someone about the overdose before losing consciousness (Shaffer, 1974). There is in all this behavior a clear indication of the ambivalence of suicide.

Place of Family Dynamics in Assessment

A child may often use suicide as a means of acting out the stress or tension of the family. Thus, a suicidal child is a family problem.

The family stress or tension may be relieved when the child's problem can be the focus of family scrutiny. Families may avoid dealing with marital troubles or other adult problems by focusing their attention on the child's problem. The child may gain some feeling of importance when the suicidal problem is the one thing that unites the parents and directs their energies back to the child. The child may also find that suicidal behavior is one sure way of getting everyone's attention. Almost every child learns at a very early age that even the negative attention provoked by screaming or yelling is much better than being ignored.

The child may learn patterns of coping that include suicide or other less lethal kinds of self-destructive behavior. Is it unreasonable that a child who sees patterns of alcohol abuse and dependence on pills from aspirin to tranquilizers may learn these behaviors while still a child? Indeed, there is clinical evidence to show that the risk of suicide is greater among individuals in whose family some member has already committed suicide. The child has been given a role model and may imitate this self-destructive behavior that has occurred in the family. Some suicidal behaviors can be traced to the child's antecedent loss of a parent at a very early age (Adam, 1974).

Suicidal behavior is also thought by some investigators (Bowlby, 1973) to stem in part from early parental threats of abandonment or sickness—"If you're not a good boy, Mommy will get sick"; "You'll be sorry you made Mommy get sick and go away." In later years the child may mimic this threat by saying, "If you don't give me some chocolate pie, I'll get sick and you'll be sorry." In the child's mind, getting sick and dying may mean the same as Mommy's earlier threat of getting sick and going away. One questions whether this early pattern of threats may not inspire a pattern of self-destructive threats on the part of the child leading to self-destructive behavior. On the other hand, many children who have experienced the same parental threats have not evidenced suicidal behavior. It is currently unclear what other factors might account for the difference in the two reactions. This problem calls for further study, especially of nonsuicidal children exposed to this pattern of parental threats.

The child's suicidal behaviors may be functional for the family and possibly in some ways for the child as well. Certainly suicide is rarely if ever just the child's problem. This is not to say that the parents are to blame for the suicidal feelings or behaviors of the child. Rather it is an attempt to focus on suicide as a problem of the family. Scapegoating either the parent or the child only creates a barrier that makes it difficult to observe how the suicidal behavior functions in the family system.

Aids in the Assessment of Suicidal Children

One cannot lump children of various ages together when assessing their suicide proneness. In order to assess the risk of suicide in any given child, one needs to know the personal history of growth and development of that child, the norms for the child's age group, and what the child's behavior means to the child. It is also important to know the child's normal behavior patterns.

Art and Play. These two outlets are often more expressive media for the child than words, and in consequence may be powerful assessment tools in the hands of the skilled intervenor. Since the child thinks in images before putting them into words, artwork may express the child's feelings more directly and more immediately than any verbal translation.

Play may help the child who is unaware of his feelings, or too confused by them to express them safely. In such situations, art and play are the first avenues of expression for the early years.

Clues to Suicide Intent of School-Age Children. School teachers report self-destructive behavior in the classroom. One child whose behavior was reported was forcing staples into his hands. Other children have been reported who have cut themselves with scissors. Reports of children running in front of cars are even more common.

One may question whether such children really want to die and whether they understand the finality of death. One may also ask whether these behaviors are not the child's desperate attempts to get attention. Nevertheless, the fact is that if the desired attention or response is not forthcoming, this self-abusive behavior may spiral, increasing in frequency and lethality. Death may be the result.

One teacher reported that some of her fifth-grade pupils' compositions revealed suicidal ideation. At least three of them wrote that they were afraid of killing themselves. It is significant that these children presented behaviors which were noticed. Attention and concern should also be given the child who is silent, withdrawn, or unable to get attention. This child's plight may be more tragic than that of the more openly suicidal child since the former is unable to signal his need for help. We may find out about this child only after the suicide, just in time to say, "But if I had only known, I could have done something!"

Defining Suicide in Children. There is no definition of suicide applicable to children which helps to answer such questions as, when is a poisoning an accident and when is it a suicide? Obviously any definition of suicide must take into consideration the developmental stage of the child. One would hardly consider a 2½ year-old's running into the roadway a suicide attempt. At 2½ years of age, a child is not expected to be totally responsible for or in control of impulsive acts and fully cognizant of dangerous situations. A definition of suicide applicable to a child would have to be based on clear-cut criteria for self-destructive acts, intentionality, and a child's concept of death and suicide. Such a definition might help clarify the relationship to child suicide of accident-proneness in children.

It is clear that further research and study are indicated. Perhaps research will lead to refinements in our assessment process that will make it possible to identify precursors of suicidal intent in addition to those already observed, such as preoccupation with death in one's writing, self-mutilation, such as biting or burning parts of the body, or other physically damaging behavior, such as frequent overdosing with aspirin or a parent's pills or excessive drinking.

Case 8: John

John was the 7-year-old son of a turbulent marriage. His early years, when he lived with an alcoholic mother and a shy, retiring father, were chaotic. John didn't realize at this time that his father also drank heavily. Since his father was absent so often, John probably didn't have many opportunities to see him drunk.

John remembers being confused by his mother's unpredictable behavior. He always felt he was bad because he had to be punished and yelled at so much. His older sister was very quiet. She left to live with their father immediately after the divorce. John, however, was only 4 at the time of the divorce and he stayed with his mother. He remembers her drinking bouts, when he was left to feed himself or go hungry. Above all, he remembers that he had to keep out of his mother's way or bear the brunt of her wrath.

When his mother was committed to a psychiatric hospital, John went to live with his father. Compared to the stormy times with Mom, these days with Dad were the good days, when they had a happy time. Then Dad married Susan. When Susan became John's stepmother John remembers that life got worse. Dad's drinking got worse too. Susan's kids were the "good kids" and John was "a terrible brat." Again, he was punished frequently, and Susan made sure that he did all the cleaning, washing, and cooking she could push off on him. John was continually disappointed that Dad never supported him. He just stood by and passively watched Susan berate him.

John was not allowed to have friends or to play. He reported that when he was seven, Susan killed his stray cat. One day he felt so hopeless that he went into the garage and took down the snail pesticide that was stored on the shelf. He decided to swallow it and end all this misery. He was sure that things would never get any better and he just couldn't stand any more. As he was pulling the box down from the shelf, he heard a familiar voice yelling. Susan had walked in and started screaming, "What do you think you're doing?" John doesn't remember what he said, but he knows that no one ever asked about or discovered his thoughts of suicide. Then and there, however, he decided he was so bad that suicide wouldn't work for him.

ADOLESCENT SUICIDE

Michael L. Peck

It has long been recognized that the adolescent lives in a continuous state of turmoil. Psychologists have voiced the opinion that the internal pressures may be greater in adolescence than in any other period of human development. A clinically oriented approach to suicidal behavior in adolescents and their therapeutic responses may afford an understanding of the dynamics of suicide specific to this period of ferment and growth.

College students live under a great variety of pressures, including the pressures generated by the phenomenon of adolescence, by the high expectancies of early adulthood, and by the stresses of competition and achievement which are unique to the college milieu. Studies of suicidal behavior on the college campus have led to the conclusion that suicide is a serious public health problem which in the college setting, ranks as the third leading cause of death and, on some campuses, the second leading cause (Seiden, 1969; Lyman, 1961).

Suicide at any age is always a tragic event for the survivors. Guilt, grief, and shame are feelings commonly experienced by survivors, who lament the needless waste and unfulfilled promise of the deceased. When the death of a young person has been self-inflicted, these reactions are understandably accentuated. The question that haunts everyone is, why should an adolescent on the threshold of adulthood and with a potentially bright future suddenly terminate his life?

Nature and Scope of the Problem

In 1967 in Los Angeles County, researchers at the Los Angeles Suicide Prevention Center found the suicide rate of 15-to-19-year-olds to be 9 per 100,000. By 1971, the rate for the same age group had increased to 19 per 100,000, the highest rate for this age group yet recorded in the United States. The age group of the 20-to-29-year-olds showed an equally dramatic increase in Los Angeles County, moving from a rate of 18.3 per 100,000 in 1960 to 31 per 100,000 in 1965 and 41 per 100,000 in 1970. This sharp rise resulted in suicide a rate for this 20-to-29-year-old group higher than that for either the 30-to-39- or the 40-to-49-year groups. At age 50 and over, the suicide rate climbs to equal and then surpasses that of the 20-to-29-year group (Peck and Litman, 1974). This appears to be the first such bimodal distribution that has ever occured in United States suicide statistics.

The increase in adolescent rates is most dramatic in that it cuts across racial and ethnic lines. In the past, the suicide rate among Blacks was considerably lower than among whites. However, in the past five years the rate among young Blacks has risen to the point where it is higher than that of whites, although the rate for Blacks over age 30 remains relatively low. The same is reported from our studies of the Mexican-American communities of Los Angeles. We find that the suicide rate among young Chicanos has risen dramatically in recent years and is nearly as high as that for the same-age white population, whereas suicide among the older Mexican-American population is still as rare as it has always been (Peck and Litman, 1974).

Increased suicide rates among young women have also been shown in the current data. Until 1965, the rate for men in this younger age group had been twice that and in some periods three times greater than that for young women. In recent years, however, the rates for women have risen even more rapidly than those for men. Although the overall rate for women in this age group is still lower than that for men, the gap has been closed so far that recently women accounted for more than 40 percent of all suicides (Peck and Litman, 1974).

Even more startling is the dramatic rise in the suicide rate for young Black women, which in the past few years has become even higher than that for Black men in the same age group. This is a remarkable finding, since it contradicts a former truism of suicide statistics that male suicide rates are invariably higher than female rates.

Profiles of the Suicidal Adolescent

There are important differences between adolescents who threaten and attempt suicide and those who commit suicide. At the same time, one needs to be aware of the similarities shared by these two groups. The adolescent who commits suicide is more likely to be a male than a female and to come from an intact middle-class family with few gross disturbances like mental illness, alcoholism, or psychiatric problems. The adolescent who is a student tends to earn average grades in college. The sterotyped picture of the "brillant but neurotic" student or the failing student is not supported by one study (Peck and Schrut, 1971). The student who commits suicide shows a pattern in early adolescence, and perhaps as far back as preadolescence, of spending much of his spare time alone. While this tendency was seen in all the suicidal groups as opposed to the nonsuicidal group, it was most pronounced in the group whose members had committed suicide (Peck and Schrut, 1971).

Some early findings (Schrut, 1964, 1968) indicate that where the history of the student is one of progressive or continuing isolation from early childhood to adolescence, the prognosis for suicide is more negative, but where the history is one of relating fairly well at some point early in life and then withdrawing toward social isolation during adolescence, the prognosis is less serious. These studies also suggest that the amount and kind of solitary activities are significant for prognosis. They further indicate that children who had a poor emotional relationship with significant others in early childhood are more likely than their peers to become suicidal as adolescents and young adults.

Clinical evidence that young people who commit suicide have had difficulty communicating with others before their suicide is borne out by the Suicide Prevention Center's records. They tend to be less communicative than adolescents who attempt suicide but do not actually commit the act. Since boys tend to be less communicative than girls generally, this may explain the larger ratio of boys over girls who commit suicide. On the other hand, the isolation and withdrawal of the victim is so great that by the time the adolescent arrives at the suicidal act, he feels that he has no one with whom he can communicate.

Adolescents who committed suicide were essentially more isolated, felt more hopeless, and were less likely to send out communication signals for help than those who did not. This is consistent with the character of a large number of suicidal adolescents, whose ability to relate to others was minimal and who were unable or less likely to ask for help than their less suicidal counterparts, even by means of threatened or attempted suicide. The boys who commit suicide are different from the adolescent girls, who are most likely to signal for help by threatening or attempting suicide. The majority of those comprising the suicide-attempt sample in the Suicide Prevention Center's studies were female, in direct contrast to the sex ratio of the committed suicide sample (Peck and Schrut, 1971).

Females, in contrast to males, characteristically are able not only to ask for medical help but also to ask for any kind of help they may need and to communicate their anxieties and fears to significant others. Moreover males tend more to harbor feelings of sexual inadequacy or feelings of insecurity about their masculinity and consider it shameful to admit to such feelings. These differences between the sexes seem to hold true for college-age students as well as for younger adolescents.

In a more recent study of adolescent suicides completed at the Suicide Prevention Center (Peck and Litman, 1974) it was found that among those adolescents in the study sample who committed suicide, 40 to 50 percent were abusing alcohol and/or drugs at the time of their death. In the period covered, many other factors seemed to contribute to the overall suicidal intent of these victims. Nearly two-thirds of them reported that they were not on good terms with their family, and nearly 90 percent felt that their family did not understand them. Not being appreciated or understood by one's family seems to be the most common feeling selected out from the continuing chaos and unhappiness in the suicidal youngster's life.

A surprisingly large percentage of this group (42 percent) reported physical fights with family members. In fact a considerable amount of physical and assaultive behavior among family members of this group was also reported.

At one time nearly two-thirds of the group had some form of therapy or counseling, while one-third had been hospitalized for mental or emotional problems. The most common diagnostic category assigned members of this sample was depression. It is clear from the fighting reported and from the substance abuse by almost half of them that several substitute forms of acting-out were resorted to by many of those studied. In any case, suicidal youngsters, regardless of the specific psychodynamic trigger identified, tend to have one thing in common—a nagging lack of optimism and hope for the future and an overwhelming sense of unhappiness.

Psychodynamics of the Adolescent and His Family

It might be useful to search out the antecedents which explain how the youngsters who actually committed suicide got to that point. Since other Suicide Prevention Center studies have revealed no major overt disturbances in the parents, how can the parents still be seen by the investigators as playing an important contributory role in the suicide? Study of the individual histories in the committed-suicide sample revealed a pattern among the parents of much striving for success for themselves and great pressure on their children to be successful. While this in itself is not abnormal, it might be seen as a compensation among this group of parents for their own feelings of insecurity, inadequacy, and failure. They may see their children as an extension of their fantasized successes and therefore are likely to screen out all other kinds of communications, especially those that might suggest their failure as parents. The children of such parents learn early that only by effective projection of their parent's fantasies will they win parental approval. These parents have great personal expectations of their children and place a heavy responsibility on them to perform.

The failure of a child of such parents to live up to parental expectations is often experienced as a great humiliation by the child, whose superego may continue to make its own demands, which may be far greater than those the parents are actually making on the beleagured adolescent. The parental expectations felt by the child who commits suicide are usually far greater than the wishes for success that most parents have for their children. These expectations add up to a total lack of acceptance of the child as the individual he (or she) really is.

Children who commit suicide find that their efforts to express their feelings of unhappiness, frustration, or failure are totally unacceptable to their parents. Such feelings are ignored or denied, or are met by defensive hostility. Such a response often drives the child into further isolation, reinforced by the feeling that something is terribly wrong with him.

Certain specific, clear-cut differences were found at the Los Angeles Suicide Prevention Center between the committed-suicide group and the other groups of suicidal adolescents. Greater frequency of psychiatric hospitalization, combined with a higher rating of emotional disturbance and fewer prior suicide attempts marked the history of the adolescents who committed suicide. These findings suggest a higher incidence of diagnosed psychotic disorders in the committed-suicide group compared with the other groups.

From work done at the Center, there is some clinical evidence that a suicidal person who is also diagnosed as psychotic is a higher suicide risk than a suicidal individual not so diagnosed (Farberow et al, 1968). There is evidence that the adolescent who commits suicide has a greater predisposition toward self-destruction and therefore requires less overt stress than his colleagues to initiate the suicide act. This evidence was confirmed in some degree by the fact that the loss or threatened loss of a loved one operated less often as the precipitating stress or "trigger"among those in the committed-suicide group than it did in the attempts of those in the suicidal groups. While this particular example may be an artifact of other data (eg, those in the committed-suicide group are more likely not to have a loved one to begin with), stress was reported to be higher among persons who attempted suicide. The reaction of the latter groups was to communicate their suicidal intent openly—verbally or behaviorally—to let others know the psychologic pain they were experiencing, and thus ultimately to reduce the stress they were feeling.

The group of suicide attempters contained a much higher number of females than males. This probably represents the general picture among adolescents. Two earlier studies showed that female adolescents have the highest suicide attempt rates (Jacobziner, 1965; Haider, 1968). Still another study showed that female adolescents have a relatively low suicide rate, far lower than males of similar age (Seiden, 1969), again finding that young females are better able to communicate their emotional pain to others in an attempt to alleviate stress.

We may speculate that the psychodynamics of the adolescents who attempted suicide differed, in relation to their childhood experiences with their parents, from those of the adolescents who committed suicide. Attempters may have seen their parents as being unresponsive to their needs rather than as denying their needs and may have used their parents as fantasized projections of themselves to the extent that they would become unconscious projections of their parents. The parents of the suicide attempters were seen as more passive and as having relatively little in the way of concrete goals for their children. These parents tend simply not to respond supportively or enthusiastically to the success or failure of their child.

Clinical Evaluation and Intervention

A suicidal crisis calls for active intervention. In such a state, precisely when the suicide risk is high, the adolescent is often immobilized by the crisis, unable to utilize alternatives to suicide. Under such circumstances the suicide plan may develop a life of its own outside the control of the individual. At such times even the therapist and important others in the life of the client may become immobilized. If the therapist has been seeing the client on a long-term ongoing basis, the therapist's stance may have been an inactive one having the long-range goal of self-reliance. The therapist may therefore have been nondirective, rather encouraging the client's own sense of responsibility and personal initative. However, during a serious suicide crisis, where the risk of death is great, the therapist is called upon to initiate an emergency response. The response should, of course, be appropriate to the individual situation but, in general, it involves the mobilization by the therapist of new resources in effecting immediate important changes in the client's life situation.

When the client is exhausted and unable to carry out an alternative to suicide, there is no substitute for hospitalization. At these times the therapist is well advised to seek formal or informal consultation with a colleague. Often a colleague, who is not involved in the situation or subject to the paralyzing forces bearing toward immobilization, can help to formulate a creative alternative plan that will successfully substitute for the plan of suicide. At these times of acute crisis, involving the family members or other people important in the life of the client, although seemingly a breach of the therapeutic contract, may prove not only to be life-saving but may be understood and welcomed by the client.

On the other hand, the therapist who is confronted with a client who experiences chronic or frequently recurring suicidal episodes needs to weigh carefully the appropriateness of an emergency response to a current suicidal episode. If the risk is neither immediate nor high the therapist may well be most effective by focusing on the long-range rehabilitative features of the plan of therapy. On the other hand, a serious suicide episode or suicide attempt by a client during the course of long-term therapy more often requires immediate reassessment of current therapy patterns and usually a consultation with another professional.

Case 9: Joan

Joan is a 16-year-old first seen following a telephone call by her stepfather, who described her as very manipulative, impossible to live with, and very unhappy. She was now threatening to injure herself. At the outset of the office interview, it was obvious that there were many conflicts between Joan and her stepfather. Mr. R stated that he had married Joan's mother one year ago, when Joan was 15. Although Joan still loved her natural father, who had died three years earlier, she seemed to welcome and accept Mr. R into the family. Their relations were reportedly quite positive for about five months. At this point the usual family problems began to develop. Disputes over discipline and conflicts over who would gain mother's attention became more frequent and aggravated the situation. Mrs. R was described by her husband as trying to settle these conflicts fairly and objectively, but Joan's demands were insatiable.

According to Mr. R, matters became worse about five months earlier, when Joan began behaving erratically, manifesting severe mood swings, with sleep and eating irregularities. She began talking about her unhappiness. It all came to a head when Joan ingested a handful of aspirin tablets in front of her mother and stepfather, two days before help was sought. The reason given by Joan for this behavior was that she was miserable and wanted to die.

Joan's version of the preceding year was not unlike her stepfather's. From her point of view, however, she described her unhappiness as beginning about ten months before when she became aware that her stepfather was taking more and more of her mother's time. The final event that contributed to her increasing unhappiness and depression occurred about three months before the interview when she learned that most of her friends were going to attend a different high school several miles away, while she would have to attend the high school nearest her home, where she would know relatively few students. Joan said this was really the reason for her unhappiness, and if somehow she could attend high school with her close friends, the issues in the home would be less unpleasant.

At this point, the therapist inquired where Mrs. R was and why she could not come to the session. Mr. R replied that Mrs. R was not well, but hopefully she would come to the next session. The therapist then offered the encouraging opinion that things could be worked out but that both Joan and her family might need to be somewhat more flexible in trying new ways of dealing with Joan's unhappiness and the repercussions it was having in the family. They all agreed, and the therapist suggested that Mr. and Mrs. R might discuss with Joan the possibility of going to the high school of her choice if it could be arranged with the school administration. Provided that Joan could take care of her own transportation, Mr. R thought this plan might be acceptable to the school authorities. He and Joan agreed to discuss it that night with Mrs. R and an appointment was made for the entire family to come in the following week.

Joan and Mr. R returned, but without Mrs. R, who was still not well enough to come. This time, the therapist chose to interview Joan alone first. She seemed as depressed as she had been the week before and expressed no feelings of relief from her unhappiness or the hope that relief was in sight. When the therapist inquired about her school situation, Joan reported that she would be able to attend the high school of her choice. Although this had made her feel better at the time, she had been unhappy and depressed ever since. When the therapist asked how her mother viewed all this, Joan burst into tears.

Joan explained that her mother was very ill, and in fact was going to die within the year. She had tried hard not to worry or upset her mother but couldn't ignore the terrible feelings of depression and fear that had swamped her ever since she had found out about her mother's condition several months ago. She viewed herself as being abandoned, and because of her tenuous relationship with her stepfather, felt that she would have no place to live and that no one would accept her. It was clear to the therapist that Joan's depression stemmed from the anticipation of loss and the subsequent feelings of insecurity and abandonment. Further, Joan was frustrated by the collusion among all the other family members in not discussing Mrs. R's impending death. The suicidal gesture on Joan's part represented an attempt to get this particular issue out in the open.

The therapist called Mr. R into the office and told him what she and Joan had been discussing. Although Mr. R seemed somewhat surprised and disappointed that Joan had revealed this family secret, he readily agreed to a family conference with the therapist which would be held at home, since Mrs. R was too ill to travel.

At this point the goals changed rapidly. Arrangements for short-term changes in Joan's environment in order to relieve her symptoms gave way to a family discussion focusing on the long-term future of this girl, to determine what would happen to her after her mother died.

In all, eight family sessions were held. The therapist learned that Joan's anxiety was warranted. Her stepfather did not want her if her mother was no longer in the picture. However, inquiry as to whom she could live with revealed an aunt and uncle who were warm and enthusiastic about having Joan live with them. Following this, several individual sessions were conducted with Joan alone which focused on her feelings of loss—first occasioned by her father's death three years before and now by her mother's anticipated death, and compounding her feelings of insecurity. However, Joan's knowledge that she would have a home where she would be genuinely welcome was a critical factor in alleviating her depression. Together, Joan and the therapist decided to terminate therapy after about six months. By that time she felt much better and more competent to deal with her future. She no longer had chronic feelings of hopelessness and unhappiness.

Four months later, Joan's mother died and Joan moved in with her aunt and uncle. She appeared to handle the crisis quite well and appropriately experienced several weeks of grief and mourning without suffering a clinical depression. She did not express suicidal feelings.

Comments on the Intervention. The first decision made by the therapist was to see Mr. R and Joan together for the first interview. This probably delayed obtaining the critical information about the impending death of Joan's mother.

During the second interview, a decision was made by the therapist to see Joan alone, which permitted the girl to reveal her real problem. It was apparent that in the presence of her stepfather Joan felt constrained to collude with the family in keeping her mother's condition a secret. Complete family participation could not have been effected had not the conspiracy of silence, so frustrating to Joan, been broken up almost at the outset.

The next decision made by the therapist concerned Joan's suicidal behavior and the accompanying risk. The therapist, in evaluating Joan's suicide potential, decided that the immediate risk was low. He correctly interpreted the suicidal gesture as a bid for communication rather than the expression of a strong desire to end her life. Because of this, customary suicide prevention precautions, such as enjoining the family to watch Joan closely, effecting the removal of dangerous implements from the home, prescribing antidepressant medication, or hospitalization, were ruled out. Furthermore, it was unnecessary to schedule an appointment for the next day as in a more serious emergency. In the case of any adolescent who represents a high suicide risk, when the danger is acute and no significant relief is experienced after the initial interview, all of these recourses must be considered important in reducing risk.

The therapist's next decision was suggesting a family discussion that night, when the discussion would be oriented toward manipulating the environment (changing high schools) in order to relieve Joan's unhappy feelings. This was an important decision even though it did not directly alleviate her unhappiness, because it made Joan realize that the therapist took her seriously, was interested in her, and was willing to intervene actively on her behalf. It is quite possible that this decision laid the ground for Joan's feeling of trust in the therapist so that at the first opportunity, which was the next session, she could reveal what was really troubling her in a one-to-one interview and feel confident that he would respond with concern and action on her behalf.

The therapist's next important decision was to see Joan alone for further therapy.

The last important decision, and the one which relieved Joan's feelings of frustration and hopelessness, was the therapist's decision to conduct the family therapy sessions in the home, where he could initiate open discussion of vital issues. The therapist's active approach was maintained throughout these sessions, which were oriented toward helping the family find solutions to Joan's problems. Had the therapist decided on the alternative of remaining in his office milieu and seeing Joan alone, or seeing Joan and her stepfather occasionally, it is unlikely that her problems could have been resolved as rapidly and as effectively.

Conclusion

It can be seen from the foregoing discussion that suicide is a major public health problem which can strike almost anywhere. The recent increase in suicide among young people is further cause for concern. Fortunately, it has been demonstrated that suicidal problems among young people can be understood and ameliorated by the application of research and training. Certainly, those who work with suicidal adolescents find their efforts measurably rewarding in terms of emergencies satisfactorily met and lives saved.

THE CHRONICALLY SUICIDAL PERSON

Carl I. Wold
Robert E. Litman

For the most part, current antisuicide efforts are based on the model of crisis intervention. Within this conceptual framework, an antisuicidal response calls for immediate establishment of a relationship with the suicidal person, an evaluation of suicidal risk based on past and present ways of coping with stress, and an action-oriented response that mobilizes the help needed. The importance of distinguishing between the suicidal individual in acute crisis and the one who leads a "career of suicide" has been recognized (Litman et al, 1974).

Desperate people with a significant potential for committing suicide are identified by health service providers, personnel in civil and criminal justice systems, telephone counseling service workers, and other community resource workers. About half of those classified in this group of recognized potential suicides are in crisis. They lead relatively stable lives but are currently responding to a stress which is atypical (Litman et al, 1974). The case of J.D. provides a good illustration of a time-limited crisis of this sort.

Case 10: J.D.

J.D. is a 34-year-old man with a long and stable employment history as a skilled electrician. His work has been a major source of his pride and self-esteem. Through the years he built a reputation for competent, rapid, and reliable work in the highly competitive construction industry. He gained the respect of fellow workers and was sought after by employers. At this point, after some years of free spending with his drinking buddies and the many different women in his life, he began to understand the need to save his money, with investments in mind. J.D. was married briefly during his early twenties. For the past year he had sustained a regular relationship with one woman but continued to live alone.

While working on a multistory building under construction, J.D. was struck on the head by a large wooden beam. The blow was severe, fracturing cranial bones and resulting in a loss of consciousness for about 15 minutes. Subsequently he experienced headaches, blurred vision, and inability to concentrate or to perform simple tasks. These were disabling symptoms that prevented him from returning to work. Following hospital treatment which involved reconstructive surgery, symptoms persisted, and J.D. was unable to resume employment. With the aid of Workman's Compensation insurance, he consulted an attorney and a neurologist. The neurologic findings did not identify specific damage, and there was an initial diagnosis of posttraumatic syndrome.

J.D. was eventually referred to a psychologist for psychodiagnostic evaluation. He told the psychologist about his depression. It was then five months after his accident, and J.D. felt frustrated and helpless. He feared that he would never be able to work again and that his plans for the future would never be realized. Sleeping was very difficult for him—he had trouble falling asleep, slept restlessly, and awoke early in the morning. Favorite foods no longer interested him, although he had not lost weight. He reported great irritability and gradually withdrew from contacts with people. He was unable to make love to his girlfriend, and they quarreled.

The medication prescribed for J.D. failed to alleviate his severe headaches, which were constant, and the tranquilizers prescribed did not help him to sleep. He admitted that, contrary to his neurologist's advice, he "forgot" to take his medication. The psychologist initiated antidepressive psychotherapy twice a week. After three weeks of treatment, J.D. told the psychologist that when he was alone at night he often began to cry and had to fight off a strong impulse to get a gun and "blow out my brains." The psychologist considered psychiatric hospitalization, depending upon the course of the crisis over the next 24 hours. As part of the procedure, he called J.D. that night and arranged for a special appointment the following day. The improvement in J.D.'s mood was such as to allow the continuation of outpatient treatment.

J.D. presented an acute suicidal crisis, with depression, in response to injuries which he experienced as a direct threat to his picture of himself and his self-esteem. It was possible that his disabilities would not be permanent and that he would eventually be able to return to work. Should his disabilities prove to be permanent, however, he needed time to understand that a satisfying life was possible within the limits of his newly restricted abilities. His stable character, along with his existing and future relationships, would enable him to leave his depression and suicidal state behind. His life is such that he has the resources to reconstitute it with relative speed and to reorganize it successfully.

About half of those recognized as potentially suicidal struggle with chronic suicide problems. They present a history of repeated suicidal episodes, recurrent depressions, and prior suicide attempts over a period of many years. For these people, crisis intervention may have some immediate antisuicide impact yet may fail to alter significantly the pattern of suicide. The case of C.T. is a typical illustration of a chronic suicide problem.

Case 11: C.T.

C.T. was 41 years old when he first called the Suicide Prevention Center. At that time his relationship with the man whom he had lived with and loved for 14 years had ended. Twenty years earlier, C.T. had made a suicide attempt with an overdose of sleeping medication following a broken love relationship. During the past 14 years, his life with his roommate had been stormy, with frequent fights and separations. He worked as a designer of women's clothing, but for the past few years had experienced difficulty in finding and holding a job.

A year and a half before his first call to the Center C.T. had sought outpatient therapy at a psychiatric hospital but discontinued treatment after a few months. When he first called the Center, he was experiencing suicidal impulses but had not yet formulated a suicide plan. He reported that he was depressed and had trouble sleeping despite the use of tranquilizers prescribed by his physician. Although the caregiver encouraged C.T. to reestablish his previous therapeutic relationship, he did not follow through.

During the next five years C.T. called the Suicide Prevention Center 48 times. He accepted a referral for psychiatric help and was hospitalized on two occasions. During this five-year period he experienced recurrent depressive and suicidal states. His love relationships were transient and of short duration. He was also unable to obtain employment. His drinking increased to the point where he consumed large quantities of wine each day. He considered himself "too proud at my age" to follow through with a referral for vocational rehabilitation. He had begun some training but discontinued it before getting very far. After one psychiatric interview, he was designated as emotionally disabled and began receiving welfare. He complained of a variety of physical ailments including stomach ulcers, a disintegrating spinal disc, rectal bleeding, and severe insomnia.

C.T. was found dead by his apartment manager, after his body remained undiscovered for four days. Postmortem decomposition thwarted the coroner's office in efforts to determine the cause of death. Empty prescription bottles for barbiturates and empty wine bottles were found in the apartment. During the month preceding his death, C.T. had been very depressed. He was facing eviction; his roommate had left him; he was out of money; and he was forced to sell his furniture.

C.T.'s fragile adjustment to adult life gradually disintegrated during the five years before his death. During this period the pattern of self-destructiveness became increasingly evident. His love and work relationships became progressively more unstable and more transient. In an effort to alleviate the pain of chronic "masked depression," (Litman and Wold, 1974) he used alcohol to excess. Both in- and outpatient therapy failed to break up this self-destructive pattern. He became increasingly alienated and isolated from others as his alcoholism contributed to hostile interactions with them.

Our experience at the Los Angeles Suicide Prevention Center with chronic suicide problems like those demonstrated by C.T. has revealed the need for intervention beyond the scope of a short-term crisis service. Yet through the crisis telephone service of the Center large numbers of people are identified who follow a "career of suicide." Most of these people are isolated and alone, confirming inversely the postulate of sociologic theorists that the greater the extent of a person's social relationships, the less his susceptibility to suicide, a proposition supported by clinical experience. Maris (1969) theorizes that interpersonal relationships act as external constraints with an antisuicide effect on the subject. For a suicidal individual, the fact of living by oneself is an indicator of high risk (Tuckman and Youngman, 1968).

An Experimental Outreach Program

On the basis of these observations, the Los Angeles Suicide Prevention Center set up an outreach service offering "continuing relationship" to suicidal individuals at high risk. Initially these clients were identified by their calls to the emergency telephone service at the Center. For an average time period of 18 months, clients were offered an outreach service conducted by a team of volunteers under the supervision of paraprofessional workers, themselves trained and supervised by the professional staff. Each client received at least one telephone call per week at a minimum, although most clients were contacted more frequently. These telephone exchanges were reinforced by occasional home visits, person-to-person interviews, and group meetings both at the Suicide Prevention Center and elsewhere. All contacts were made in the context of a befriending relationship, which was not considered therapy. All clients were encouraged to use existing community agencies and their own personal relationships as it seemed appropriate in the effort to minimize suicidal risk.

The outreach service conformed to a rehabilitation model of intervention, with emphasis on building the strengths of the client over time. This would have antisuicidal effects by decreasing the number of suicidal behaviors and committed suicides. Other program goals were to aid the client's development of a network of concerned and interested family and friends. Service workers were trained to keep their expectations for the client at a low level without indulging in hopes for a miraculous improvement.

The intensity and closeness of the relationships developed under the program tended to vary with the individual client's ability to tolerate involvement. Client's reactions fluctuated from an enthusiastically welcoming response to mistrust, withdrawal, and even overt hostility. The relationship with the outreach volunteer provided a number of clients a base from which to reach out for help to another community agency. This relationship also provided support for those clients whose histories of repeated failure had intensely sensitized them toward rejection. With this support many were helped to overcome their initial inhibitions toward taking a chance on help.

Results and Recommendations

Several goals of this program were realized. It was demonstrated that clients helped by the program felt less alone than before, improved their love relationships, made better use of professional help, suffered less depression, and enjoyed greater confidence in their use of community resources. However, there was no measurable reduction in suicidal ideation, or in the number of suicide attempts and committed suicides among program participants. Psychological autopsy of persons in the program who committed suicide revealed a significant constant—*all but one chronically abused alcohol.* This was an important finding, since somewhat less than half of all high-risk clients were involved in alcohol abuse. Nevertheless, it seemed to Center professionals that "continuing relationship" is a low-cost, postcrisis intervention technique which improves the quality of life for chronic, high-risk, suicidal persons who have had poor personal relationships but are not alcoholic. "Continuing relationship" as it was offered, however, proved to be too little and too late to effect a significant life change sufficient to prevent suicide and suicide attempts among high-risk suicidal persons who also abuse alcohol.

It was clear too, as a result of the program, that volunteer workers trained in crisis intervention techniques are inadequate to the task of maintaining a long-term relationship with the most severely suicidal alcoholics. Volunteers were unable to sustain their own enthusiasm and optimism when confronted by the pessimism, sharp mood changes, orientation to failure, and dissatisfied dependency of these suicidal alcoholics, for whom maintenance of a relationship on a "once a week, we call you" basis was insufficient.

Nonetheless, in the opinion of the evaluators, these severely suicidal alcoholics should be encouraged to use the Suicide Prevention Center at their own option, repeatedly, as they feel the need. Futhermore, they should be the target of an expanded and intensive crisis intervention effort aimed at transferring them to participant status in some ongoing alcoholism treatment program in the community.

The importance of the relationship between alcoholism and suicide has become the subject of considerable interest and concern. In this connection it has become apparent locally that the referral process for transferring Suicide Prevention Center crisis clients to alcoholism treatment facilities is comparatively ineffective, or else the efforts of the existing alcoholism treatment facilities are inadequate to meet the needs of suicidal alcoholics, or both. These issues need to be clarified. Chronic alcoholism frequently precedes suicide, and acute alcoholism often facilitates suicide. In fact, suicide is one of the most common causes of death among alcoholics. Unfortunately, a review of the literature by Center personnel failed to locate reports of programs that specifically confront the issue of improving treatment for suicidal alcoholics.

In view of the demonstrable need, the Los Angeles Suicide Prevention Center has plans for initiating a service specific to the requirements of suicidal alcoholics. Service will be provided by professionally trained paraprofessionals experienced in both alcoholism counseling and antisuicide work. Their intervention with high-risk suicidal, alcoholic callers to the Suicide Prevention Center will be immediate. The Center response will be an intensely focused outreach to the client by telephone and by personal visit at the Center, at the client's home or elsewhere—within ethical limits. The relationship will be focused on an extension of the original crisis telephone contact, with a strong push from the caregiver toward involving the client in an existing alcoholism treatment facility in the community such as Alcoholics Anonymous or one of the medical or social rehabilitation program available to alcoholics. This effort with the client on the part of the paraprofessional "alcoholism treatment facilitator" will last about one month. Once the client has accepted and has begun treatment for alcoholism, the treatment facilitator will remain in a relationship with the client to help insure continuation of treatment. The client will be offered support and reassurance in resisting the desire to discontinue the alcoholism treatment prematurely.

Summary

Although crisis intervention does provide some support to the chronically suicidal person, this is not enough to effect change. Research data show that we do not yet have a successful treatment plan which significantly alters personality patterns of the chronically suicidal person. Clinically, we have described this pattern as that of:

1. An individual who has eliminated his resources—he is isolated and withdrawn from significant others
2. Alcohol abuse, which is present in 50 percent of suicide attempters and present in almost all clients who later commit suicide
3. Recurrent depression
4. Many prior suicidal episodes (threats or ideation) or suicidal attempts over a span of several years
5. Numerous bids for help which have yielded little or no relief
6. A pattern of instability in job performance or personal relationships or both

Obviously, a long history of alcohol abuse in a chronically suicidal person poses a difficult management problem and presents a serious risk. Dependency upon other intoxicants or mood-altering drugs in addition to alcohol compounds the problem both in terms of the client's eventual ability to function and in terms of the emergency risk at any given time. Alcohol potentiates the effects of tranquilizers and sleeping preparations so that what might ordinarily be considered a moderate consumption of alcohol, when combined with ingestion of these drugs, can be quite dangerous or actually lethal.

Indications for further research are glaringly apparent. However, further clinical study and research will give more accurate indications for intervention with the chronically suicidal person.

WHAT TO DO IN AN EMERGENCY

Corrine Loing Hatton
Sharon McBride Valente
Alice Rink

When a suicide attempt is in progress, the client's state of alertness, orientation, and panic will give you the cue to the manner in which you must ask questions for the basic information you need and the cooperation you must have. If the client is in the same room with you, you may be able to do many helpful things, but if the interview is by telephone, you will have to direct the client to first-aid measures.

Emergency intervention may be divided into four main components: data collection, first aid, plan of action, and follow-up.

Data Collection

You must get certain basic information from the caller (usually the client) in order to help and to be able to callback should this prove necessary; as well as summon help to the correct address.

1. **"Tell me exactly where you are."** Check off the information as you go. This will include the street address and zip code, the apartment number, if any, the telephone number and area code. If the caller does not know the number or is confused, tell him to "read me the number from the center of the dial." This first step is essential, since the client may lose consciousness during the call.
2. **"Tell me what you did."** If the client is threatening suicide, ascertain the plan. If the client has ingested pills, however, that is another matter. Ask firmly, "What pills did you take?" Also, "Read the label to me. What is the name of the pill? What kind of pill is it? Describe it." If the client is confused, ask for the information on the pill bottle label: "When was the prescription filled? How many pills are still in the bottle? Is it empty, half full?" Ask, "Are these pills prescribed for you?" If so, "How many do you usually take a day? How many did you take today? When did you take them?" The caregiver may be able to determine the lethality of the drug by having someone else call the pharmacy to inquire but do not leave the client alone in order to do this. Where lethality cannot be ascertained, assume that the ingestion was lethal. Always check alcohol intake: "Have you been drinking?" If the client has been drinking, ask him "How much? When?" Any drug taken along with alcohol is considered potentially lethal, so this must be checked out in every case.
3. **"Is there anyone with you?"** If not, "Is there anyone nearby whom you can call (friend, neighbor, manager, bystander, housekeeper, etc)?" If that person can be summoned for aid, tell the client "I want to talk with him (or her) NOW!" Be firm: "I want someone to be with you and take you to the hospital if you need to go."

First Aid

First aid may be necessary at once where a client has swallowed some noxious substance including pills.

1. **Induce vomiting** unless the client has ingested a caustic substance such as lye, a petroleum product, or some household cleaning product. Try different methods to induce vomiting only if the client is fully conscious:
   a. Tell the client to stick a finger down his throat.
   b. Have the client drink syrup of ipecac, if available, according to label directions, followed by several glassfuls of water until vomiting starts.
2. **Stop any bleeding.** Where a client has cut or slashed his wrists or other part of the body, apply a clean bandage and press on the wound until bleeding stops, then proceed to the hospital as rapidly as possible, or direct any caller to do so, where someone else has made the call.
3. **For inhalation poisoning** there are three things you should do, or direct the person to do:
   a. Provide a supply of clean fresh air at once.
   b. Loosen tight clothing.
   c. Administer mouth-to-mouth resuscitation if necessary.
4. **Treat the unconscious client.** There is a lot you can do for an unconscious client or can ask the person who has called you to do:
   a. Keep the client warm.
   b. See that the client is lying on one side to prevent choking.
   c. Watch the client's breathing—if breathing stops or lips and fingertips turn blue, mouth-to-mouth resuscitation is needed at once. Make sure, however, that the client's mouth is free of debris first (unconsumed pills, mucus, vomitus, etc).
   d. Summon the fire department rescue squad or ambulance
   e. *Caution:* DO NOT induce vomiting or attempt to give liquids or solids to an unconscious person!
   f. Get the client to a hospital where other, more rapid emergency treatment is available.
   g. Take along with the client to the hospital any open pill bottle or other possible clue to what caused the unconsciousness.

Plan of Action

If you are talking by phone to a conscious client, you should give firm directions how to handle the situation and in what order:

1. Tell the client to **unlock the door** and leave it open for the ambulance.
2. **Arrange transportation** to the hospital or emergency room:
   a. Call an ambulance or the fire department rescue unit or the police.
   b. If someone is with the client, ask whether that person can drive the client to the nearest emergency facility.
   c. If so, give exact directions for getting there from the location given you.

    d. *Note.* This is the fastest way of getting the client to professional emergency care, but it does not insure possibly needed first aid or medical care during transport.

    e. A client whose medical condition seems stable and who will probably remain conscious and alert may call a taxi or drive to the hospital when other transportation is unavailable. However, a client should not drive after taking **any** amount of alcohol or drugs.

3. **Keep the telephone line open.** Talk to the client or the client's companion and to the help that arrives in response to the call for assistance (ambulance personnel, fire rescue volunteer, police officer, etc).

    a. Find out what emergency facility was called.

    b. Ask approximately when the client will be served and where (a fire department rescue squad may act at once, or an ambulance may bring along medical assistance for interim measures on the way to the hospital).

    c. Ask the person you speak to to have the hospital call you when the client gets there. You may, of course, have to get in touch with the hospital yourself.

4. **Tell the client what will happen.** Be clear and brief:

    a. "The ambulance will arrive. You will lie down on the stretcher. They will drive you to the hospital."

    b. "In the hospital the doctors and nurses will help you, but they will also have to ask you questions. You need to take with you any leftover pills or liquid you took, or at least the empty bottle."

    c. "I will call you in the emergency room. They may move you to another part of the hospital for rest or observation after treating you."

Follow-up

Sometimes follow-up is not possible after an emergency of this kind. And of course sometimes it is not necessary.

1. If the client wants you to notify anyone of what happened, or to forward some message to anyone, follow up on this request promptly, calling the client back either at the emergency room or at home once you have done so.

2. In any case, you will want to make at least one follow-up contact with the emergency service or the client, if that is possible, as a bridge toward a future for the client in which some caring relationship may pave the way for restored function.

REFERENCES

Adam KS: Childhood parental loss, suicidal ideation and suicidal behavior. In Anthony EJ, Koupernick C (eds): The Child in His Family. New York, Wiley, 1973

Anthony EJ, Koupernick C (eds): The Child in His Family. New York, Wiley, 1973

Bowlby J: Attachment and Loss, vol 2. New York, Basic Books, 1973

Farberow NL, Heilig SM, Litman RE: Techniques in Crisis Intervention: A Training Manual. Los Angeles, Calif, Suicide Prevention Center, December 1968

Gullo SV: Games children play when they're dying. Med Dimensions 2:22, October 1973

Haider I: Suicidal attempts in children and adolescence. Brit J Psychiatry 114:514, September 1968

Ilan E: The impact of a father's suicide on his latency son. In Anthony EJ, Koupernick C (eds): The Child in His Family. New York, Wiley, 1973

Jacobziner H: Attempted suicide in adolescents. JAMA 191:7, 1965

Lebovici S: Children who torture and kill. In Anthony EJ, Koupernick C (eds): The Child in His Family. New York, Wiley, 1973

Litman RE, Farberow NL, Wold CI, Brown T: Prediction models of suicidal behaviors. In Beck A, Resnick H, Lettieri D (eds): The Prediction of Suicide. Bowie, Md, Charles Press, 1974

Litman RE, Wold CI: Masked depression and suicide. In Lesse S (ed): Masked Depression. New York, Jason Aronson, 1974

Lyman JL: Student suicide at Oxford University. Student Med 10:218, 1961

Maris RE: Social Forces in Urban Suicide. Homewood, Dorsey Press, 1969

McIntyre MS, Angle CA: The Child's Concept of Death. Presented at the Workshop in Methodology, Atlantic City, Ambulatory Pediatric Society, April 1970

Peck ML:Research and training in prevention of suicide in adolescents and youth. Bull Suicidol 6:35, Spring 1970

———, Litman RE: Current trends in youthful suicide. Sociol Muerte (Madrid), Trubuna Medica, Spring 1974

———, Schrut A: Suicidal behavior among college students. HSMHA Health Reports 86:149, February 1971

Petrillo M, Sanger S: Emotional Care of the Hospitalized Child. Philadelphia, Lippincott, 1972, pp 244-48

Schrut A: Suicidal adolescents and children. JAMA 188:1103, 1964

———: Some typical patterns in the behavior and background of adolescent girls who attempt suicide. Am J Psychiatry 125:69, July 1968

Seiden RH: Suicide Among Youth: A Review of the Literature, 1900/—1967, Bull Suicidol Suppl, Washington, DC, USGPO, December 1969

Shaffer D: Suicide in childhood and early adolescence. J Child Psychol/Psychiatry 25:275, October 1974

Treffert D: Why didn't Amy live happily ever after? Prism 2:63, November 1974

Tuckman J, Youngman W: A scale for assessing suicide risk of attempted suicide. J Clinical Psychol 24:17, January 1968

CHAPTER 8
Eight
Clinical Examples

Corrine Loing Hatton
Sharon McBride Valente
Alice Rink

In suicide prevention, it would be impossible not to fail in the helping mission on some occasion or other. However by carefully assessing each failure, the caregiver may prevent future failures in comparable cases.

We have all made the observation over the years that most case studies presented in the professional literature have a happy ending. The caregiver makes the appropriate assessment, the intervention is effective, and the client improves or the problem, whatever it may be, is solved. Although it is useful to the learner to be able to identify with an expert, we believe it is equally useful to be exposed to the real world. And the real world of mental health is often not captured by the clichè, "They lived happily ever after." Often this world is confused and distorted, and solutions to the problems are not easily identifiable.

This state of affairs does not necessarily prevail because of carelessness or negligence on the part of the caregiver. It may be due to the peculiarities of the individual client or to the particular problem. Or it may be due to the complexities of a problem for which the mental health field does not yet have satisfactory solutions. Although needed clinical study and research in suicidology have been accomplished in the past several decades, much more remains to be done. Even though assessment and intervention techniques have been improved markedly, many questions have yet to be answered.

Following are examples that vary from the more easily identified problems yielding to classic assessment and intervention techniques to complex problems for which solutions are not often obvious or readily available, and at least one case where a major concern of the caregiver may be a consistent effort to avoid his or her own prejudicial reactions.

Cases 12 and 13 follow a particular design fairly well documented by research and clinical theory.

Case 12: Gerald B.

Assessment.   Gerald B. was 23 years old when he sought professional help because he was upset over the loss of his girlfriend, who was leaving him after a relationship of two and a half years. The relationship had become more distant and less involved during the past three months. Two days before his appointment, Gerald's girlfriend told him she did not want to see him except for occasional visits and furthermore did not want a more permanent relationship with him.

It was at this point that Gerald "just fell apart." He became very upset and anxious, cried, and experienced some suicidal ideation. He felt he couldn't live without her, that his world was tumbling down. He had wild urges to run his car off the freeway, or slash his wrists with a razor blade, or shoot himself with a pistol to which he had access. However, these thoughts were fleeting, they were not very strong, and they were not directed or planned. Gerald was eating and sleeping fairly well and was maintaining his daily work schedule. He was most desirous of some form of therapy that would help him cope with this crisis. He was identified by his interviewer as moderately depressed and moderately suicidal.

Gerald was a graduate student who worked part time in a department store. He described his college years as being active and happy. He dated occasionally but no one steadily until he met his girlfriend, with whom he had been living for the past two and a half years. Gerald described himself as "terribly, terribly shy" and reticent in meeting people. He said he had very few friends because his work and school schedule did not allow for many interpersonal pursuits or extracurricular activities.

Gerald had not suffered any loss in the past that could be compared with the loss of his girlfriend, and he felt threatened and fearful in coping with it. His usual way of handling other problems had been to isolate himself, take long walks, or study harder. He had never sought professional help before, nor had he ever felt so depressed.

Gerald described his parents as being "typical middle-class types." Along with him and his two sisters, they had lived a seemingly stable and satisfactory family life. His parents lived near Gerald and offered him their support and reassurance during his crisis. His older sister, away at college, had been in contact with him by telephone and was concerned about him.

Intervention.   Gerald was seen in therapy using a crisis intervention modality, and after six weeks was feeling much better. Although he was still sad at the loss of his girlfriend, he had accepted it as a fact and was readjusting his life into other avenues of gratification. He had one stormy period after he saw his former girlfriend with another man, but he handled this by calling the therapist, who immediately offered reassurance and support. Gerald was cutting down on his study hours to allow more time for social activities even though it was a painful effort for him. He had no more suicidal ideation, however, and although feeling sad and lonely, he believed he would be able to find and enjoy other female companions.

Discussion.   This is an example of someone who sought help for an identifiable hazard and crisis, had significant others in his life available for support, and with reassurance and insight could cope with the current upsetting situation. This kind of crisis is amenable to the crisis intervention modality, and clients usually do well after the period of crisis is over.

Case 13: Barbara Dunn

Assessment.   Mrs. Dunn called a crisis center one evening in reference to her daughter, Barbara, a successful 17-year-old high school student. Barbara was a bright, active, happy young lady who enjoyed school, family, and a small circle of close friends. However, her mother remarked that within the past three weeks Barbara had shown a noticeable change in behavior. On this particular evening she had locked herself in the bathroom and was threatening to slash her wrists. Barbara had never been suicidal in the past. Normally, she shared her feelings, thoughts, and problems with her mother, but lately she had been sullen, quiet, and uncommunicative.

This particular evening she had come home more quiet than ever before. She seemed tearful, and had locked herself in the bathroom about an hour before Mrs. Dunn called the Center.

The caregiver ascertained from Mrs. Dunn that Barbara had not had any dramatic change to cope with in recent events—her grades had remained stable, no family or peer relationship had been disrupted, and no new decision making had been required of her. Mrs. Dunn further stated that Barbara had no steady boyfriend but she did see one young man more frequently than anyone else.

At this point, the caregiver felt she had to talk to the daughter. She told Mrs. Dunn to do anything necessary to open the bathroom door. If Barbara hadn't already slashed her wrists then the caregiver wanted to speak to her. However, if Barbara *had* slashed her wrists amd the injury was severe, she should be taken to an emergency facility at once for treatment. The caregiver told Mrs. Dunn to call her back after carrying out these instructions.

Twenty minutes later Mrs. Dunn called back. She said that her daughter had made some superficial to moderate slashes on her wrists, but that the bleeding had stopped, although stitches would possibly be required. The distraught girl was crying and would not tell her mother what was troubling her. However, she did agree to talk with the caregiver on the telephone.

Intervention.   When talking to Barbara, the first thing the caregiver did was to determine whether the girl had suffered some recent change in her life that she was fearful of telling her mother about. Ordinarily, the most fearful thing a girl at this age could talk to her mother about is sex. Barbara denied any problems about school or family. The caregiver then inquired about problems with boyfriends, to which Barbara replied,"No." The caregiver asked whether Barbara had thoughts or fears about sex, menstruation, or in fact anything about sex, to which Barbara replied,"Yes." She added that she did not want to talk about it because her mother might overhear, so the caregiver then continued asking questions that Barbara could answer yes or no. Finally, she asked whether Barbara had been engaging in sexual play with her boyfriend and had become fearful that she might be pregnant. Barbara's reply was "yes".

The caregiver discovered that Barbara was four or five days late in menstruating, and although she hadn't been involved in sexual relations, she had participated in some sexual play. This self-disclosure seemed to allay Barbara's anxiety. She spoke more slowly, had stopped crying, and had established some rapport with the caregiver. Barbara was advised that her wrists should be attended to by some medical person and that she should perhaps be seen for an evaluation of her emotional state. The caregiver showed empathy with Barbara's fears and reassured her that she might very well not be pregnant.

Barbara agreed to go to an emergency room for treatment and further evaluation.

The caregiver now spoke to Mrs. Dunn, merely advising her where to take her daughter. She reassured Mrs. Dunn with the information that Barbara was having some difficulties relating to a boyfriend and would agree to a further evaluation of her condition. She asked Mrs. Dunn to call back in a couple of days to report how matters were progressing.

Three days later Mrs. Dunn phoned the caregiver. She said that her daughter had been hospitalized for three days in a psychiatric unit. Barbara had been discharged, was now feeling much better, and had revealed her fears and feelings to her mother and other members of the family. The situation seemed to be ironing out. Barbara was not pregnant but she did, indeed, have a fear of pregnancy and was helped to understand this better. Mrs. Dunn was grateful for the help the caregiver had given. She felt that this situation had opened up new avenues of communication with her daughter and that they would call again if the need arose.

Discussion. In this case, the threat of pregnancy was so anxiety-provoking for a 17-year-old that she could not reveal it to her mother. However, the caregiver was able to make an accurate assessment of the real problem based on her knowledge about adolescent fears and anxieties, and the reluctance of adolescents to discuss their sexual concerns with adults. The caregiver could then empathetically offer the support necessary to help the girl through this crisis. Barbara was amenable to further evaluation, knowing that the problem probably was not as serious as she had first thought, and that the adults around her understood her.

* * * * *

In some cases of intervention a block occurs in the intrapersonal process, when stereotyping or some prejudice held by the caregiver complicates the assessment, so that the intervention cannot be completed or perhaps not even started.

Case 14: Mrs. Sawyer

Assessment. Mrs. Sawyer called a crisis center, saying that she wanted to talk to someone about "my depression." She said she had felt miserable for years and had sought help from various kinds of therapists, but found relief from none of them. The caregiver could identify no recent changes or problems in Mrs. Sawyer's life and felt that her depressed feelings were probably of a longstanding nature. She did not seem to be particularly upset at the time of her call, saying that she was bored and decided to try the Center phone number.

During the telephone interview, the caregiver obtained information about Mrs. Sawyer's background and current living situation. She was a 45-year-old housewife who lived in luxury and had nothing tangible to complain about. "We are financially well off. My husband works hard in his business, my kids are growing up O.K., and we are all physically well. Why should I be so depressed all the time? Life is a bore, nothing interests me, so what?"

Intervention. The caregiver found herself annoyed by Mrs. Sawyer, her boredom, her depression, and the casual way in which she related to the caregiver, who couldn't imagine why anyone with money, a family, and good physical health would feel bored and depressed. She was annoyed at Mrs. Sawyer for taking up her time when other people who have real troubles were waiting to be heard.

The caregiver began to identify for Mrs. Sawyer a lot of positive things to be grateful for and pointed out she should be looking on the brighter side of her situation. These comments caused Mrs. Sawyer also to become annoyed. She told the caregiver this wasn't what she expected to hear, because everyone told her that and it bored her. The caregiver became even more disgusted at another mention of boredom and suggested that Mrs. Sawyer accept a referral for further evaluation the next day. Mrs. Sawyer replied that the caregiver was rejecting her and then hung up the telephone.

Discussion. In this case, the caregiver's stereotype about what people should and should not be feeling based on money, family, etc probably broke communication with the client. Because the depressed feelings seemed to be of a longstanding nature, a more thorough assessment was not possible due to the annoyance of the caregiver. The word "boredom" and the seemingly casual way Mrs. Sawyer approached the call to the caregiver further added to the annoyance. The caregiver expected Mrs. Sawyer to behave in a certain way and when she didn't, this elicited a negative reaction from the caregiver followed by a defensive reaction on the part of Mrs. Sawyer, who hung up on the caregiver, thus cutting off further communication.

Case 15: Mr. Peck

Assessment. Mr. Peck called a crisis center at 1:45 A.M. from a bar where he had been drinking most of the evening. The bar was closing in 15 minutes. The caller's speech was slurred and although he said he was not drunk, he admitted he was very close to it. Mr. Peck had been drinking heavily lately and it had become usual for him to drink to relieve the tension created by his problems. He felt like "drinking until I don't wake up." Another idea he had was to drive recklessly on the freeway and crash into a cement wall and kill himself. He had made a suicide attempt twice in the past, in each case when a marriage had ended in divorce.

Mr. Peck had been having a great many problems with his two teenage daughters and felt he did not have the support or the help he needed from his ex-wife or his girlfriend. He said the crowning blow was an ultimatum from his boss that he would have to improve his sales volume or face the prospect of being terminated at the end of the following month. Although he tried to conceal his drinking, he believed his boss was becoming suspicious.

Mr. Peck threatened to kill himself unless the caregiver came down to the bar and drove him home. He would not disclose the address or phone number of the bar unless the caregiver promised to do as he asked.

Intervention.   The caregiver explained to Mr. Peck that this service was not rendered by the Center. He suggested that instead he would be glad to call a friend of Mr. Peck's who might help him. Mr. Peck replied that he had no friends. Nor could he understand why the service he was requesting was not available from the Center. "After all," he said, "I am a taxpayer, too." This remark annoyed the caregiver who pointed out that being a taxpayer had nothing to do with it. In fact, he found himself suspicious of "this drunk," silently wondering whether Mr. Peck was really suicidal at all. He believed it far more likely that the man only wanted some attention and someone to talk to.

When the caregiver repeated his offer to call a friend for Mr. Peck, the latter began cursing at the caregiver, reproaching him for being "just like all the rest of them." At this, the caregiver, his irritation mounting, replied that Mr. Peck was being unreasonable and was not listening, Mr. Peck replied with the threat, "That's it, you'll be sorry," and hung up the telephone.

Discussion.   The hostile and accusatory remarks made by the client eventually outraged the caregiver. When he retaliated with clear annoyance, this created more anger in the client. The mistake of the caregiver was in repeating his offer to call a friend rather than considering at once other alternate means of getting help for Mr. Peck at the bar.

Inwardly the caregiver questioned the validity of Mr. Peck's suicidal feelings, viewing him negatively as "a drunk." This attitude perhaps prevented him from searching for another acceptable alternative solution when Mr. Peck excluded the first alternative. When the caregiver repeated the unacceptable proposal, Mr. Peck felt he was being rejected and retaliated by rejecting the caregiver. The question remains unanswered whether or not Mr. Peck did indeed kill himself that early morning.

* * * * *

In the following examples (Cases 16 and 17) the client frustrates the caregiver by asking for help but refusing it. This is referred to as the "Why Don't You—Yes, But" game. For further explanation the reader is referred to Eric Berne's formulation of this game concept in Eric Berne, *Games People Play* (New York: Grove Press, 1964), pp. 116–22.

Case 16: Mr. Litton

Assessment.   Mr. Litton called a crisis center one afternoon and told a story of lost youth, wasted talent, no money, no food or lodging, and no support system. He was 55 years old and unable to find a job due to his numerous bouts with alcohol. Currently he was being evicted from a "closet" he shared with another man. He had no place to go and had panhandled a dime to call the Center. He did not feel suicidal—he just wanted to talk to someone "who might be able to come up with an answer for him." He said he was a complete failure in everything.

Intervention.   The caregiver diligently offered alternatives for Mr. Litton's consideration. At each suggestion Mr. Litton would counter with a "Yes but"—and pose reasons why it wouldn't work out, or say he'd tried that already and it had failed. The caregiver exhausted all the possibilities she felt were appropriate for Mr. Litton, all of which were disposed of by the "Yes, but" response. Nevertheless, she was able to convince Mr. Litton to panhandle a quarter and come by bus to attend an open group session being held that afternoon at the Center, but when the session started that afternoon, Mr. Litton was not present.

Discussion.   The caregiver was conscientious in her efforts to help Mr. Litton who used the "Yes, but" response to defeat all her suggestions. Mr. Litton felt he was a failure and that he had exhausted all the resources available or that any still available would also result in failure.

The question underlying the "Yes, but" game is whether the client *will not* or *cannot* utilize the alternatives offered. The conscientious caregiver often ends one of these sessions feeling herself a failure much like the failure the client claims to be.

Case 17: Miss Morgan

Assessment. Miss Morgan sought professional help at the age of 33 because she hated her job as a telephone operator, had few friends, few social activities, no family in the area, and felt totally incapable of changing or doing anything about what was bothering her. She said she felt mildly depressed and very lonely. She had never felt suicidal but could see no more future in her life.

Intervention. The caregiver was empathetic and understanding in offering support but Miss Morgan replied, "That's all very well but how would *you* know—you've probably never felt this way." When the caregiver attempted to find out what recent events may have been upsetting to Miss Morgan by pinpointing possibilities, she said, "Yes, but that is nothing." At any possible suggestion for solving her problem, Miss Morgan replied, "Yes, but I can't see that." On the one hand she sought help, and on the other she seemed to be saying, "Yes, but I can't be helped." When leaving, she said she might return for another appointment.

Discussion. The difficulty with the "Yes, but" game is to identify what seem to be the *most recent* events distressing the client, help the client to agree that these are the chief culprits in the culminating situation, and offer the reassurance that she deserves to be helped. If Miss Morgan is *not willing* to be helped or *cannot* accept help, then the risk is that she won't return to the Center for appointments. Instead she may "Yes, but" herself into greater loneliness, further isolation, deeper depression, and eventually harbor thoughts of suicide, attempt suicide, and finally, perhaps, even kill herself.

* * * **

In some cases there would *seem* to be very little hope for the client, no matter how earnest the endeavors of the caregiver.

Case 18: Mr. Avery

Assessment. Mr. Avery sought professional help because in his words, "At 69 years of age, my life is over and there is no use going on like this. I hate struggling every day." He told a sad story about his loneliness since widowhood five years before, his loss of close family ties, and his current inability to travel by bus in order to take care of his needs and maintain his few social activities. Mr. Avery's financial resources were at the bare minimum, and he considered the struggle to go on every day a waste of time. He felt he'd be better off dead and there was no one to grieve over his passing.

Intervention. The caregiver, too, began to feel the loneliness and isolation plaguing Mr. Avery and it was difficult for her to reach out of their mutual frame of reference box and offer him any hope for the future. It appeared to the caregiver that Mr. Avery did indeed have such a daily struggle to live for the basic necessities that she too was inclined to question whether it was worth the effort.

Discussion. Finding or giving hope to Mr. Avery is extremely difficult. The reality is that for many older people in our culture with lowered incomes and isolation from others, there is very little for them to look forward to. Every day becomes a struggle and future prospects seem dim. It is a challenge to the caregiver (and to all of society as well, perhaps) to face the dilemma confronting so many older people in our society. It is an even greater challenge to search out and find some avenues of improvement, some cause for hope.

Case 19: Mrs. Burton

Assessment. Mrs. Burton sought professional help when her minister suggested that she talk to "someone with your background." She was 43 years old and felt that life was no longer worth the struggle. Due to a series of back problems, she had been confined to a wheelchair for the past three years. She was also diabetic, and it was difficult for her to control this condition because her eating habits were irregular. She could not manage shopping, cooking, and her own daily care without assistance, and such assistance would have strained her meager budget. Had it not been for the minister of her church and a neighbor, Mrs. Burton said she would have killed herself long ago.

Mrs. Burton gave a chaotic history marked by severed relationships, numerous geographical shifts, and much physical pain and emotional suffering. She now felt that she had struggled and suffered long enough—"It's time to turn the gas on and be done with it." Her minister was concerned that she might carry out this threat and so he brought Mrs. Burton to the Center for help.

Intervention. The caregiver found it very difficult to see a ray of hope for Mrs. Burton upon which to project a future. He was overwhelmed at the enormity of her problems and by the long ordeal required before both he and the client could find some solution. In addition to her physical problems, Mrs. Burton lacked any support systems and felt depressed and suicidal. The caregiver, too, questioned the value of struggling just to stay alive, and the effort required to solve all these problems seemed prohibitively exhausting.

Discussion. Finding solutions and offering hope to the client seemed an overwhelming task to the caregiver. To be realistic, he could not visualize any plan of assistance which did not entail an enormous amount of contact and work with other agencies, professional personnel, and the client as well. Would a mental health center be prepared or willing to handle all these difficulties? Or would it exclude Mrs. Burton as beyond the scope of its responsibility? Again, the challenge is before us: There are many people like Mrs. Burton who have good reason to question the struggle, and some of them do indeed give up when their multiple problems accumulate beyond the provisions of the larger society to care for them.

CHAPTER 9
Suicide Prevention:
Two Personal Statements

Every caregiver must take the lonely journey through a confusing jungle of options in order to find the personal values, personal positions, and personal ethics by which to live and work. In this soul-searching struggle for realization each individual considers the right to die, the right to prevent suicide, and the right to help or interfere in any way in the lives of others. In this chapter, two suicidologists share their efforts to grapple with these issues.

A PERSONAL STATEMENT

Paul W. Pretzel

I entered the field of suicide prevention nearly 15 years ago as a graduate student in psychology. At that time the ethical issue of whether or not all suicides ought to be prevented, had either not been raised or at best had been dealt with very simply. The task we accepted was that of preventing suicide regardless of the circumstances. The only problem we acknowleged was that of learning enough about suicide and its causes so that we could develop effective techniques to prevent its occurrence. Once having developed these techniques, we were to train other professionals and paraprofessionals around the world in their use, and to inform the public that suicide is preventable and reflects a state of mind that can be diagnosed and treated.

The model we adopted for our thinking was the medical model.

The use of terms like "diagnosis" and "treatment" supported the basic value assumptions that suicide like any other disease represents a needless loss of life and that suicide prevention is therefore good, providing as it does that second chance at life so many people are grateful for having.

Writers who at that time expressed other points of view were not taken very seriously. Men like James Hillman, who expressed the then heretical viewpoint that everyone is responsible for his own life and should be able to retain the freedom to end his life when he wishes if only in order that he may then choose to continue living, were considered hopelessly naïve or theoretical. Nor was Thomas Szasz taken very seriously when he wrote of his concern about the power of the state to impose its will in such an intensely private matter as the personal decision to live or die.

As a graduate student in psychology during this period, I was trying to learn how to function effectively in the field of mental health. Along with my colleagues, I did not want to hear that what was formerly seen as mental illness might more accurately be construed as a human right and not an illness at all. I did not want to have to consider the possibility that suicide might be an innate individual right which had nothing to do with my new-found profession and that all my newly developed techniques might in fact be irrelevant or even harmful to the integrity of the individual I sought to assist.

Still, our position that suicide was a phenomenon to be prevented and that it invariably represents a failure was not based on simple prejudice. A wealth of experience and recorded data lay behind this position, to justify and support it. For example, most of the suicidal persons with whom I had had contact were chronically depressed. They exhibited the classic symptoms of depression and labored under the natural limitations of one depressed—their energy level was low and they were neither living productive lives nor were they deriving much satisfaction from their lives. Their depression also limited their problem-solving capabilities and so trapped them within their problems, which made them feel ineffectual and helpless. Their ability to perceive the future was also impaired. They could not imagine that life might change for the better. In fact, their feelings of hopelessness and helplessness weighed so heavily that for most of them suicide seemed the only possible course of action. When life is intolerably painful and the sufferer feels unable to handle the issues confronting him at the same time that there is no possibility of change, it is understandable when a prompt exit from life is perceived as the only way out.

What these depressed persons didn't realize was the very fact that they were depressed, and that it was the *depression* which was painful and limiting. What we knew as professional mental health workers, and what the patients had lost sight of, was that depression can usually be treated so that the patient's view of the life situation can improve dramatically. Moreover, his ability to function in life can be so improved that his unfavorable situation will change radically for the better.

We saw this happen often enough to realize that the will to suicide as expressed by most people is really the expression of a depression and not a genuine desire of the individual himself. Even when the depression was untreated it would often lift of its own accord within a matter of weeks, and the suicidal individual no longer wished to die. From these repeated experiences we learned that the will to commit suicide is usually temporary in nature. What a waste, then, for a person to throw away a whole life on a momentary impulse to suicide arising out of a single crisis when, if that same person could perservere a few days longer, a resolution for his problems could almost surely be found.

Still another fact supporting the view that suicide is bad was the observation of many that suicidal persons have mixed emotions about their own death. We called this mixed attitude "ambivalence." In even the most seriously suicidal person there appears to be some element of self that wants to survive. A part of self—although often weak and obscure—wished that circumstances would change so that one might live out the full course of one's life. Ignoring this side of the suicide's ambivalence, leaving it unsupported and unaided, is tantamount to abandoning a person when that person most needs help, and this in good conscience we could not do.

It is on the basis of these factors that a rationale of suicide prevention was based: briefly, (1) the nature of depression, which is, such that no major decisions should be made by the subject during a period of depression; (2) the temporary nature of the decision to commit suicide; and (3) the ever-present ambivalence of the victim toward the life-death decision. To stand by and watch a depressed, temporarily suicidal person override the will to survive and kill the self seemed at best irresponsible, and at worst openly hostile.

Side by side with our concern for the suicidal persons, there existed a concern for the lives of those close to them. The pain and suffering, and frequently the lasting emotional damage inflicted on friends and family members, especially the children, could not be ignored. Research has adequately documented the aggravated process of mourning experienced by the survivors of a suicidal family member. When some other solution for the problems of a suicidal person can possibly be found, it should be used, if only for the sake of the survivors. It is not surprising, then, that we were almost militant in our efforts during this period to prevent what we saw as a tragic, premature, needless loss of life.

This unquestioning, uncompromising attitude toward suicide had pragmatic value for the task of prevention. Depression is contagious, and when a therapist regularly works with a seriously depressed, hopeless, suicidal person, fatigue and one's own depression are then never far away. For his own effectiveness, the therapist needs both the continual support of colleagues and a deeply held conviction of his own that he is acting in accordance with the highest ethical standards. For the therapist to begin to question whether this patient's suicide may not actually be justified is to open oneself up to the same feelings of hopelessness, helplessness, and despair that have trapped the patient. The result could be that both therapist and patient become immobilized, and the energy and objectivity the therapist originally brought to the relationship is lost. At least, so we thought. If our style of crisis intervention was such that we "took over" the patient's responsibility for his own life, we justified our action by pointing to the nature of the work in which we were engaged, which is to intervene in a crisis.

But the nagging question of a rational suicide was never really resolved for me, and it never went away. What about the terminally ill, suffering cancer victim, draining a loving family emotionally and financially, who wishes to end it all as a final act of love? What about the ruined derelict, friendless and even dangerous who wants to die? What about the old and lonely, who feel tormented by life which they once enjoyed and who pray nightly that death may come to end their ordeal? When some of them finally carry out the agonizing decision to take matters into their own hands, are we really justified in pumping their stomachs, placing them in mental hospitals imploring them to continue the daily struggle when we know that the goal of that striving can only insure the continuation of their suffering?

We do all these things—but why? What motivates us to do them? What should our response be to the man in Southern California who recently unplugged himself from his kidney dialysis machine because the lifesaving treatment was, in his words, "sheer agony for me"? In public newspapers this man went on to say, "A person has the right to choose between life and death. I respect my family and friends very deeply and I'd rather die and be remembered in a cheerful state." On what basis, then, should any of us interfere with this man's decision? Afterwards, his family members talked freely of the dignity of his death and of the deep, warm, unashamed respect they had for the courage of his decision.

When I entered full-time private practice, the framework of my functioning and therefore of my thinking began to change. I was no longer working within the structure of a suicide prevention center, functioning on the basis of a crisis model. The suicidal patients with whom I now worked were long-term patients. I had greater access to the fullness of their lives, not just the fact that they wanted to end those lives. I found I was more concerned for them, I trusted them more—and ironically, I felt less urgent about wanting to prevent their suicide.

I have also become more thoughtful about the arguments of those who attack the concept of suicide prevention. Hillman (1964) said, "We are not responsible for one another's lives or death, each man's life and death is his own, but we are responsible to our involvements in those lives." That made me wonder: What is my responsibility to those who say they want to die? If I participate in taking away the freedom of that choice from suicidal patients—whether by locking them up in the hospital; or, more subtly, by contributing to their guilt feelings about doing what they want to do; or by forcing them to delay the suicidal act; or by fostering false or remote hopes—whose peace of mind am I really concerned with?

Some defenders say we try to prevent suicide because our Christian heritage values all human life. In answer, Thomas Szasz (1971) has observed that in light of our own involvement in slavery and Indian genocide, "this assertion flies in the face of the most obvious and brutal facts of history." If, then, our respect for life is not our motivation for preventing suicide, what is? Szasz offers several possibilities. One is that since physicians are committed to saving lives, a suicidal person

. . . is more than most physicians can take. Feeling insulted in the center of their spiritual identity, some take to flight while others fight back. They seem to perceive suicide as a threat not just to the suicidal person's physical survival, but to their own value system. They strike back and strike back hard. This explains why psychiatrists and suicidologists resort apparently with clean conscience to violent methods. They must believe that their lofty ends justify the basic means. Hence, the use of force and fraud in suicide prevention. The consequence of this kind of interaction between psychiatrist and patient is a struggle for power. The psychiatrist wants to gain control over the patient's life in order to save himself from having to confront his doubts about the value of his own life. [Szasz, 1971]

In recent years, I have been probing again my own feelings and attitudes about life and death, responsibility and freedom. I have been looking more carefully at the lives of my patients, not from the viewpoint of preventing an action, but from the viewpoint of understanding and affirming their wishes. I have been re-reading authors like Szasz and Hillman, and I have also been watching more closely some of the people who have chosen to die.

Dr. Henry P. VanDeusen was the former head of Union Theological Seminary, one of the nation's most prestigious seminaries. In February of 1975 he and his wife entered into and completed a suicide pact. Elderly and ill, they viewed their action as a positive, responsible one and left a note expressing the belief that old people should have the right to determine when to die.

Traditionally, the Christian Church has viewed suicide as a sin. Its response to suicide has varied from one of vengeful outrage to the more contemporary reaction of sad regret, one usually qualified by the rationalization that the suicide was insane at time of the act, hence not responsible for it. Hillman would probably endorse the action taken by the VanDeusens as a fulfillment of their lives. Szasz might rejoice that they had not fallen into the hands of professional suicide preventers and suffered the humiliation that he feels was meted out to James Forrestal, Marilyn Monroe, and Ernest Hemingway.

Should any of these suicides have been prevented? How far should a therapist go in attempting to dissuade the subject from such action, or should he make any attempt at all? Is his proper role one of respecting the wishes of such a patient, or one of attempting to persuade or even coerce a patient to accept the frustration of continued existence.

Some would go even further than merely accepting another's suicidal wish. Max Delbrück, Ph.D., Nobel Prize winner in biology believes that our culture should provide suicide education as it now provides birth control information: "The taking of one's life should be a matter of maturity as it was during the last hours of Socrates." He cites the case of the 1946 Nobel Laureate, Percy W. Bridgeman, who, upon becoming seriously ill with cancer at the age of 80, killed himself:

He left a note that said, "It isn't decent for society to make a man do this last thing himself. Probably this is the last day that I will be able to do it myself." He then shot himself. Both his family and his physician should have given him the opportunity of taking his life in a dignified way, but because of society's emphasis on the longevity of life at all costs, he had to end his life in a lonely and agonizing way. [Delbrück, 1974]

As might be expected, such a view raises some controversy. Robert Kastenbaum, Ph.D., past president of the American Association of Suicidology, considers such views to be ill thought out and dangerous. Kastenbaum is particularly upset at "the selective attention and premature judgment" of which he feels Delbrück guilty. Kastenbaum is also upset that someone other than a professional suicidologist would dare offer opinions on such matters. He assures us that "we don't have to buy his [Delbrück's] current proposals' any more than we must feel compelled to drink the beer or purchase the clothes touted by a famous athlete" (Kastenbaum, 1975).

I can't say that I would subscribe to Delbrück's views literally, but I find myself as much put off by the reaction of the former president of the American Association of Suicidology.

Suicide is a highly personal act and although it does affect the culture in general and certain specific related individuals in a special way, I think we have often gone too far in trying to protect individuals from their own wishes about their own death. I know that my own thinking is still in process, so that I cannot at the moment formulate a statement on what I think other therapists should do about their suicidal patients.

I also know that I am a far less committed suicide preventer than I was ten years ago, and I am far more likely to watch one of my patients kill himself than I was ten years ago, just as I am far less likely to go out of my way to prevent the suicide of someone who is not my patient. Am I getting colder, less caring? It doesn't feel that way. It feels to me that just as I would not want to be trapped into life, so I would not want to trap another. Just as I would not want my humanity reduced to a simple diagnostic statement, so I would not want to label anyone suicidal and respond as though this were the only significant truth about that person. As I would not want doctors deciding on the basis of their own value system what's good for me and then enforcing it, so I would not want to impose on another.

What I do feel I owe all my patients and all my friends is the benefit of my experience, knowledge, and whatever caring I can offer.

Specifically, I want time to explore his depression with that person so as to be sure it is the person and not the depression that is making the decision. I want that person to know the effects of depression, the distortions in thinking, the energy drain, and the impulsivity sometimes associated with depression. I want to explore with that person the ambivalence I know is there either consciously or unconsciously. I want to delay suicidal action, if I can—to gain time that will permit the crisis to pass and true judgment to emerge.

I want that person to feel my concern, if possible, so that he knows he is capable of feeling cared for. I want that person to feel that he is heard by me, understood by me, and accepted by me to the extent that I can hear, understand, and accept. I want that person to listen to me—listen to my reactions to his situation, my suggestions if any, and my thoughts about the possible influence his suicide may have on his family. And I want that person to explore seriously whatever other possible alternatives may be open to him.

Theoretically, I know that this process will work in one of two directions: It may help my patient move back from the edge of death and give him the courage for life, or it may harden the resolve to suicide and provide the courage to embrace death. The latter would be hard for me.

In conclusion, I must say that no patient whom I have seen privately has died by suicide, so I do not know how fully I would live up to these self-imposed standards for respecting the person's right to decide. But at this point I find myself comfortable with this standard of ethics and I can only hope, as justification for the writing of this statement, that others may find some value in it, too.

REFERENCES

Delbrück M: Education for suicide. Prism 2:16, November 1974

Hillman J: Suicide and the Soul. New York, Harper & Row, 1964

Kastenbaum R: Suicide, the coming way to go? Newslink (Newsletter of the American Association of Suicidology) 1:4, April 1975

Pretzel PW: Understanding and Counseling the Suicidal Person. Nashville, Tenn, Abingdon Press, 1972

Szasz T: The ethics of suicide. Antioch Rev 1:7, Spring 1971

A PERSONAL STATEMENT

Sam M. Heilig

This whole question—Is suicide prevention ethical?—has always disturbed me and left me feeling that there was something grossly inappropriate about it. My day-to-day experience simply proves to me that there are many people in the Los Angeles community as there must be in every community, who are desperately seeking help. They come to me and they ask for help. I'm not running about, trying to

206 SUICIDE PREVENTION: TWO PERSONAL STATEMENTS

capture people and lock them up in hospitals. As a matter of fact, I never come into any situation calling for my services unless I'm invited.

The questions about the morality of suicide prevention may possibly be prompted by an attitude, observed increasingly in our society, that we do not wish to involve ourselves in other people's troubles. The most dramatic illustration of this wish to be uninvolved with others who are in trouble is best illustrated by the celebrated case of Kitty Genovese, who was observed by many people while she was being murdered on a New York street and not one of them offered to help or even so much as called the police in response to her cries.

Many people, of course, do not want to be engaged in the work of suicide prevention. They have every right in the world to do as they wish. However, why question the humanity of those who want to help prevent suicide? Why challenge those who need help? In my mind, such questions have always sounded specious and unreal. After 20 years of professional involvement in suicide prevention research and practice at the Los Angeles Suicide Prevention Center, I have yet to see the question of infringing the person's individual freedom during suicidal crisis emerge as a real, substantive human problem. I have been involved with literally thousands of individuals in helping them through a suicidal episode in their lives and cannot recall an instance where anyone complained or objected to my having intervened to save his life.

Of the hundreds of people I have known over the years who have worked in the field of suicide prevention, my clear impression is that they are more often than not civil libertarians who would defend individual rights and freedom. It is possible, of course, to conduct a discussion on theoretical terms but, personally, I find it very difficult to confront the issue in other than human terms. The basis of my opposition rests on two obvious realities: (1) The more important is the fact that the suicidal person is rarely if ever concerned with individual freedom, but rather desperately searching for some means of relieving personal anguish and suffering; (2) I know full well that despite our best efforts, even in those instances where the would-be suicide is incarcerated, that person is free to end his or her life if determined to do so.

Any discussion of the ethics of suicide prevention usually raises the question: What shall we do about the person with a terminal illness, suffering unbearable pain in the last few weeks of life? Most well-meaning, reasonable people would probably agree that there are serious reservations about unnecessarily extending the life of a dying person for a short period when that means enduring so much more dreadful physical pain and suffering. Very often people involved in the medical care of a dying person may have the same question the patient articulates about the purpose of extending or prolonging life. Most humane and reasonable people would agree that if that person wished to die and put an end to suffering, he or she should be allowed to do so.

This is really not a question of suicide prevention but rather one of allowing people to die with dignity. The difference here is that the person is in the process of dying and none of us is going to prevent that death. This is a situation very different from that, let us say, of a 25-year-old woman, reacting to the loss of a lover, who wants to end her life because she is temporarily distraught. When people are in the terminal phase of an illness, the question usually revolves around what medical intervention we should provide in an effort to extend life. Frequently, in a terminal illness, it is not a matter of preventing suicide, but rather one of allowing death to come. As it so happens, many people who have been leaders in the field of suicide prevention have also engaged in the study and the work involved in understanding the dying process, with the objective of helping people to die more comfortably.

Everyone who has worked with people who are suicidal and has tried to understand something about that particularly poignant paradox in man has commented on the factor of ambivalence. This has been discussed elsewhere in this book and does not bear any elaborate discussion here. For clarity, however, I repeat that we have all observed that suicidal people are pulled in contrary directions, wishing to die and to live at the same time. This ambivalence is really what plagues us and what answers the first question, for if people clearly and unequivocally wanted to kill themselves, we would not have an ethical problem to consider. However, I have never seen such certainty even in people who have gone on to die by suicide.

Let me present two examples which illustrate the dilemma and presents the question.

John was a 32-year-old machinist. He was married and had one child. On one occasion his wife called the Suicide Prevention Center in a state of alarm about John's threats to kill himself. He continued to be a client of the Suicide Prevention Center for a year and a half.

John was of average intelligence, in good health, an excellent worker, and cared about his wife and child. He came in regularly for his appointments. Periodically, however, he would become unpredictably agitated and disturbed and would go on a drinking spree, running away from job and home for a few days. On one occasion, he drove nonstop from Los Angeles to Boston and back. Frequently these episodes would end in a suicide attempt, the usual mode being the ingestion of pills.

During one of these bouts John returned home and knocked on the door. When his wife answered, he swallowed a pint of carbon tetrachloride on the spot and was immediately rushed to the hospital. He was given medical care to keep him alive. I visited him every day while he was in the hospital for the following six days. His doctors gave him no chance to survive. He knew this and became extremely disturbed about dying. The fact of the matter was that he had changed his mind and now struggled mightily to survive. He died of kidney failure after six days.

Another example concerns a young man who shot himself but did not die from his wound. During the course of his hospital stay, he developed a brain infection as a result of the gunshot. During the three weeks before he died, he changed his mind about death and he, too, was very distraught about the fact that he would die.

What can we learn from examples such as these? Obviously, these men both died by suicide, but, given some additional time to consider whether or not they really wanted to die, both changed their minds and decided they wanted to live. The prolem is that once someone commits suicide, it is all over. Suicide prevention services at least allow that person the right to extend the consideration of what may be a final decision long enough to make it as a considered choice rather than an irreversible impulse.

The suicidal person, as illustrated by these two cases, faces a dilemma. On the one hand, does he know that this is really what he wants? On the other, is he sure he is not simply making a mistake that may cost him his life? If there were no other question about the morality of suicide prevention, I would propose that at the least we do whatever we can to extend everyone who considers suicide as much time as he needs to think it over.

What one observes with people who are suicidal is that the problem is not one of individual freedom—whether a person has the right to dispose of his life as he wishes—but rather how to reduce the suffering of that person. People who are suicidal are obviously in a state of physical or psychic pain and anguish. It is really the task of suicide prevention to relieve it. When people exhaust their own capacities to reduce their suffering and see no hope that their situation will ever improve, many will arrive at the idea of suicide as a way out. It is not really death which is wanted but rather an end to suffering and pain.

One has only to spend a day in any suicide prevention center, or talk to any suicidal person and this becomes eminently clear.

I know that I, personally, am unable to prevent suicide, but I can certainly help people who are suicidal to find other ways out of their problems when they seek my help. I am currently working with a woman who is chronically and severely depressed, who always has the idea of suicide in her mind. She keeps a lethal dose of pills on hand in case she should decide to kill herself. Some years ago, she made a serious suicidal attempt with pills and was saved by prompt medical intervention. She has not made a suicide attempt in more than five years. She and I both know that I am unable to prevent her suicide should she decide to take the pills in her possession. She knows she can do this any time and I know that, too.

I have a question to ask those who think that to prevent a person's suicide might be an infringement of his personal liberty: Why does this woman continue to come to me? She and I both hope that her depression will pass or that we will find a way to relieve it. We both know that in many people, depressions simply go away, and we also know that frequently, with a proper medication, the intensity of depressed feelings can be considerably reduced.

One of the real issues in the discussion of the ethics of suicide prevention revolves around the question of intervention, voluntary or involuntary. Does society have a right to detain someone in the hospital against his will? The law in most states says that a person who is a danger to himself may be detained against his will. However, most suicidal people will seek help somewhere, and many will take precautions to protect themselves from their own self-destructive impulses. If the person agrees to hospitalization, of course, we do not have an ethical conflict—he is acting of his own free will. However, what about the person whom we hospitalize despite his own unwillingness?

On what basis do people find themselves in a hospital against their will? Usually it is a matter of disordered thinking and behavior, where the person hospitalized is unable to use reasonable judgment. These are states of psychosis, severe intoxication, acute agitation, panic states, and severe depressive disorders. Another way that people get admitted into hospitals against their will is by engaging in self-destructive or life-threatening behavior in the presence of someone else. If this someone else happens to be a health worker, a police officer, or any helping person, the attempter may be taken to a hospital. The question then could be raised, why did that person behave in this destructive way in the presence of someone he might reasonably expect would hospitalize him? People with these associated conditions who are suicidal deserve at least an interim of time and help to clear their thinking before taking an action that may end their lives.

For me, the question is really posed from the other side. Some years ago I investigated the death of a woman after she had committed suicide. I learned that she had tried on the day of her death to commit herself into three large hospitals so that she might be protected from her suicidal impulses. She had presented herself at the admissions area of these hospitals, each of which has a psychiatric unit. She was turned away by all three and later on that same day did commit suicide. Thus, the problem may be not one of involuntarily hospitalized people but, rather, where a person desperately seeking help in a hospital setting can find it. Even though this is an isolated example, it is a serious omission of adequate treatment.

Then, there is an overwhelming reality to consider: the past 15 years of the development of suicide prevention programs in this country. Why have suicide prevention programs been initiated during this period in more than 200 cities throughout the United States? And what about the tens of thousands of people who come to these suicide prevention centers asking for help? This may be the real ethical question in the area of suicide prevention: Are we providing sufficient resources to assist these thousands of people who are so desperate and whose lives are in such danger? Those of us who work daily in suicide prevention know the terrible straits and the dreadful suffering of the people who ask us for help. We also know our own inadequacies, our insufficient resources, and our many other weaknesses. And finally we know that because of our inadequacies many of these people who are seeking our help will go on to commit suicide, in spite of all our efforts.

While it is essential that we consider ethical questions, it is also essential that we do not neglect humane considerations. At issue in this discussion are two values that are most highly prized by most of mankind—life and liberty. Dr. Jerome Motto, speaking on the ethics of suicide prevention at the American Association of Suicidology 1976 Conference in Los Angeles, epitomized the problem:

> The dilemma of suicide prevention is posed by the fact that too vigorous protection of either of these values [life and liberty] leads to sacrifice of the other. The ethical problem can therefore be simply stated. In a given situation, does life or liberty have precedence, and in the practice of suicide prevention is this order violated?
>
> Those who, regardless of circumstances, consider suicide only as a legitimate expression of personal liberty, may turn to history to echo an impassioned "Give

me liberty or give me death!" while those of us who see suicide as a social as well as a personal act, and so subject to social and humanistic consideration, may likewise invoke history to support our position by crying out with equal passion, "Oh, liberty! liberty! what crimes have been committed in thy name!"

Index